Executive Politics and Governance

Series Editors
Martin Lodge
London School of Economics
and Political Science
London, UK

Kai Wegrich
Hertie School of Governance
Berlin, Germany

The Executive Politics and Governance series focuses on central government, its organisation and its instruments. It is particularly concerned with how the changing conditions of contemporary governing affect perennial questions in political science and public administration. Executive Politics and Governance is therefore centrally interested in questions such as how politics interacts with bureaucracies, how issues rise and fall on political agendas, and how public organisations and services are designed and operated. This book series encourages a closer engagement with the role of politics in shaping executive structures, and how administration shapes politics and policy-making. In addition, this series also wishes to engage with the scholarship that focuses on the organisational aspects of politics, such as government formation and legislative institutions. The series welcomes high quality research-led monographs with comparative appeal. Edited volumes that provide in-depth analysis and critical insights into the field of Executive Politics and Governance are also encouraged.

More information about this series at
http://www.palgrave.com/gp/series/14980

Peter Volberding

Leveraging Financial Markets for Development

How KfW Revolutionized Development Finance

palgrave
macmillan

Peter Volberding
New York, NY, USA

Executive Politics and Governance
ISBN 978-3-030-55007-3 ISBN 978-3-030-55008-0 (eBook)
https://doi.org/10.1007/978-3-030-55008-0

This Palgrave Macmillan imprint is published by the registered company Springer Nature Switzerland AG
The registered company address is: Gewerbestrasse 11, 6330 Cham, Switzerland

To François, my family, and Toby

Preface

In the nearly two years since the first draft of the book was completed, marketized development financial instruments have only grown in size and stature. Global development institutions have continued to create structured funds across new and existing markets, waded more boldly into securitization schemes, and have double-downed on innovative climate financing programs.

With the near-limitless demand for development finance, development institutions have reemphasized that private investors are critical partners. In fact, development institutions have ambitiously committed to increasing private finance mobilization between 25% and 35% in only three years. As part of that objective, the World Bank announced in 2017 its Maximizing Financing for Development (MFD) initiative. This strategy seeks to systematically leverage all sources of financing to achieve the SDGs through increased support for recipient governments to identify bottlenecks, the development of legal and regulatory frameworks, and the expansion of coordination with other private and public financing sources. As one World Bank document notes, this is meant to make private sector solutions the norm for how the World Bank does business. KfW has followed a similar trajectory. Over the past two years, KfW has increased its development financing offerings, ranging from agricultural finance to digital finance. One noteworthy addition has been its AfricaGrow initiative, a new "fund of funds" that provides equity capital for SMEs and start-ups in Africa. KfW co-founded the fund with BMZ and Allianz

Global Investors and the fund has an initial working capital of EUR 170 million.

Despite exponential growth, marketized development financial instruments may now be facing their greatest existential challenge. The onset of COVID-19 and the ensuing economic downturn has revealed the potential shortcomings. Private investors have reoriented their investment portfolios towards lower-risk profiles, a trend that generally disadvantages developing countries; in fact, developing countries have registered record capital outflows that have vastly outpaced those during the 2008 Global Financial Crisis. The sudden collapse of export markets for developing country industries and SMEs has also financially strained development finance recipients and limited new opportunities. For the development banks themselves, while well-capitalized banks like KfW will be able to ride out the market turmoil, increased political pressure to focus domestically may restrict appetite for accumulating additional developing country financial risk. All of these trends potentially undermine marketized development financial instruments. While no financial instrument has yet been terminated because of COVID-19, uncertainty over their future is undoubtedly at its highest level in decades.

Within this fluid context, I believe this book provides an important window into understanding the political economy of marketized development financial instruments. It may additionally provide insights into what the future might hold for development finance, particularly as global markets are reshuffled. Yet given the complexity and breadth of development finance, this work is only one small, first step. It is my hope that this book inspires and provokes both scholars and practitioners to continue investigating these marketized development financial instruments, as well as their evolving relationship with donors, recipients, development institutions, and private investors.

New York, NY, USA
May 2020

Peter Volberding

Acknowledgments

I never anticipated to write a book about KfW, Germany, or development finance. I began my Ph.D. as a scholar of China, and my original dissertation focused on the intersection of Chinese foreign investment and the emerging China Development Bank (CDB). Thwarted by geopolitics and archival inaccessibility, I searched for months for a new topic, and stumbled upon KfW by accident. Through these twists and turns, I leaned heavily on my advisors, each of whom steered me in fruitful directions. The co-chairs of my committee—Jeff Frieden and Beth Simmons—both provided invaluable support throughout the process. Jeff was a great mentor and always pushed me to think broader and bolder. Beth was meticulous in her feedback and supportive of my vision, and I appreciated her endless dedication to ensuring my success. Rawi Abdelal brought his expertise in finance and constructivism to our conversations, and I was grateful to have his support as I embarked on an unfamiliar topic. And Iain Johnston always remained engaged with my work and provided thoughtful comments, even as it drifted further and further away from my original China focus. I could not have asked for a more supportive or inspiring committee.

The majority of the research for this book was conducted in Frankfurt, Germany. During this multiyear period, I am particularly grateful to Andreas Nölke and his team for hosting me at the Institut für Politikwissenschaft at Goethe Universität. His generosity in providing me an academic home, in addition to his expertise in European political economy, were both critical factors in the completion of this book. While based at Goethe Universität, I also met two colleagues—Matthias Thiemann and Daniel Mertens—who have not only become great friends, but reliable co-authors as well. Ideas for subsequent projects on development banks were conceived over *Kaffee und Kuchen* breaks during this period. Moreover, both have motivated me with their deep theoretical and substantive knowledge, as well as their passion for academic inquiry.

Additionally, I am thankful for the inspiring and thoughtful comments from colleagues and friends. Tess Wise has been particularly generous with her time, and I am appreciative for her near endless willingness to read chapter iterations. Alex Hertel-Fernandez and Glory Liu also provided invaluable feedback throughout the process. Chase Foster was instrumental in encouraging me to publish my dissertation as this book, in addition to sharing his expertise on European politics. Elisabeth Köll and Tamara Kay provided methodological advice and crucial moral support during the most challenging times. I am also grateful for the thought-provoking comments from numerous other colleagues and friends, which includes (but is certainly not limited to) Jeffrey Javed, Jason Warner, Stephen Pettigrew, Gabrielle Ramaiah, Simone Claar, Sebastian Möller, Michael Schedelik, Johannes Petry, Marcel Zeitinger, Tobias ten Brink, Christian May, as well as members of the Government 3005 International Relations Seminar at Harvard University and the monthly politics seminar at Goethe Universität.

In order to deepen my knowledge about development finance, I am thankful for the dozens of discussions with experts and practitioners. Armin Grünbacher, a rare scholar on KfW, was the first expert I talked with, and he pointed me in the right direction. From there, I was able to engage with a variety of scholars familiar with KfW and German development finance, including Reinhardt Schmidt, Adalbert Winkler, Jan-Pieter Krahnen, Manfred Nitsch, Ulf Moslener, and Hans Siebel. Their commitment to my project was extraordinary.

I am also indebted to the dozens of librarians, archivists, and researchers at institutions across the world that have helped assemble the countless documents for this book. This has included the staff of the Harvard University Library System (Cambridge, MA), the KfW Historisches Konzernarchiv (Berlin, Germany), the World Bank Archives (Washington, DC), the Goethe Universität Library (Frankfurt, Germany), the Deutsche Nationalbibliothek (Frankfurt, Germany), the Deutsche Zentralbibliothek für Wirtschaftswissenschaften (ZBW; Kiel, Germany), the Ibero-Amerikanisches Institut (Berlin, Germany), the Koninklijke Bibliotheek (The Hague, The Netherlands), the British Library (London, UK), the National Library of China (Beijing, China), and the National Archives of Singapore (Singapore).

For financial support, I am grateful for the numerous grants from Harvard GSAS, the Asia Center, the Weatherhead Center, and the Center for European Studies. This book would not have been possible without their generosity.

At Palgrave, I am thankful to have an enthusiastic team of editors who have facilitated the process, as well as the anonymous reviewers for the manuscript. Their thorough feedback was incredibly helpful in revising and strengthening the book.

Finally, I am eternally grateful for my wonderful family. They have stood behind me for more than three decades, encouraging me to pursue my passions and facilitating my growth. Their endless support and patience for me have always served as an inspiration. Also, thank you to my amazing partner François for his steadfast support through the weekly (and sometimes daily) ups and downs. He constantly challenged me to think and communicate more clearly and always distracted me with much-needed breaks and unconventional vacation proposals, many of which were brought to fruition. This book is dedicated to them.

New York, NY Peter Volberding
May 2020

Praise for *Leveraging Financial Markets for Development*

"This is an excellent book on an increasingly important topic. Peter Volberding carefully analyzes how development institutions spearheaded the creation, development, and expansion of marketized development financial instruments to attract private funds, and how German KfW was central in this evolution. He studies how development banks did this task, and evaluates rigorously the advantages, but also the many limitations and challenges of these marketized development financial instruments. A very valuable book for academics, students, and policy-makers."

—Stephany Griffith-Jones, *Professor, Columbia University, USA*

"Peter Volberding addresses a long-standing issue of delivering effective financing for sustainable economic development. He does not simply provide the origin, evolution and challenges of marketized development financial instruments, he goes beyond! He has a vision of the kind of development finance many institutions should follow and gratefully acknowledges that the maturation of marketized development financial instruments follow a learning process in which some interventions failed while others succeeded."

—Désiré Kanga, *Centre for Global Finance, SOAS University of London, UK*

"Peter Volberding's Leveraging Financial Markets for Development explains how development finance shifted from and aid approach to the discipline of the market. His engaging account documents the actors and institutions—notably, the German state-owned KfW—that made this revolutionary change possible."

—Beth Simmons, *Professor, University of Pennsylvania, USA*

"In this book, Dr. Volberding provides a historical genealogy of the spread of developmental financial instruments, focusing on a surprising key actor: the German KfW and its first successful engagements with these funds. Rather than private actors or the World Bank, he shows based on extensive interviews and careful archival research that this national development bank and its financing department was one of the crucial actors in the rise and diffusion of these instruments, complicating simple stories of capture."

—Matthias Thiemann, *Sciences Po-Paris, France*

Contents

Acronyms

AAAA	Addis Ababa Action Agenda
AADFI	Association of African Development Finance Institutions
ADB	Asian Development Bank
AIDB	Ethiopian Agricultural and Industrial Development Bank
AIFMD	Alternative Investment Fund Managers Directive
AIIB	Asian Infrastructure Investment Bank
ARC	African Risk Capacity Insurance Company
AU	African Union
BAF	Blue Action Fund
BCF	Blended Climate Finance
BGK	Bank Gospodarstwa Krajowego (Poland)
BIO	Belgian Investment Company for Developing Countries
BMZ	Bundesministerium für wirtschaftliche Zusammenarbeit und Entwicklung
BNDE	Banque Nationale de Developpement Economique (Morocco)
BNDES	Banco Nacional de Desenvolvimento Econômico e Social (Brazil)
BRI	Bank Rakyat Indonesia
CAF	Corporacion Andina de Fomento
CCRIF	Caribbean and Central American Catastrophe Risk Insurance Facility
CDB	China Development Bank
CDC	Commonwealth Development Corporation (UK)
CDP	Cassa Depositi e Prestiti (Italy)
CDU	Christian Democratic Union
CFG	Credit Guarantee Facility
CIF	Climate Insurance Fund

CIS	Commonwealth of Independent States
CMAC	Caja Municipal de Ahorro y Crédito
COMECON	Council for Mutual Economic Assistance
CORFO	Corporación de Fomento de la Producción de Chile
CTF	Clean Technology Fund
DAC	Development Assistance Committee
DBE	Development Bank of Ethiopia
DBJ	Development Bank of Japan
DBN	Development Bank of Nigeria
DBS	Development Bank of Singapore
DBSA	Development Bank of South Africa
DEG	Deutsche Investitions- und Entwicklungsgesellschaft
DFC	Development Finance Company
DFCC	Development Finance Corporation of Ceylon
DM	Deutsche Mark
DSE	Deutsche Stiftung für internationale Entwicklung
DSGV	Deutsche Sparkassen- und Giroverband
EBF	Eco Business Fund
EBRD	European Bank for Reconstruction and Development
EC	European Commission
EDI	Economic Development Institute
EFBH	European Fund for Bosnia and Herzegovina
EFK	European Fund for Kosovo
EFM	European Fund for Montenegro
EFS	European Fund for Serbia
EFSE	European Fund for Southeast Europe
EFSI	European Fund for Strategic Investment
EIB	European Investment Bank
EIF	European Investment Fund
ENR	European Neighbourhood Region
ENSI	EIF-NPI Securitisation Initiative
ERP	European Recovery Program
ESAF	Enhanced Structural Adjustment Facility
ESG	Environmental, Social, and Governance Objectives
EU	European Union
EUR	Euro
EXIM	Export-Import Bank of China
FAFIN	Fund for Agri-Finance in Nigeria
FASA	Financing the Agricultural Sector in Armenia
FDI	Foreign Direct Investment
FEFAD	Foundation for Enterprise Finance and Development
FfD	Financing for Development
FiM	Finance in Motion

FMH	FINCA Microfinance Holding Company
FMO	Nederlandse Financierings-Maatschappij voor Ontwikkelingslanden
FPAS	Forecasting and Policy Analysis System
GAFSP	Global Agriculture and Food Security Program
GCF	Green Climate Fund
GCPF	Global Climate Partnership Fund
GDP	Gross Domestic Product
GDR	German Democratic Republic
GGF	Green for Growth Fund
GIB	Green Investment Bank (UK)
GIZ	Deutsche Gesellschaft für Internationale Zusammenarbeit
GTZ	Deutsche Gesellschaft für Technische Zusammenarbeit
HBOR	Croatian Bank for Reconstruction and Development
IBRD	International Bank for Reconstruction and Development
ICICI	Industrial Credit and Investment Corporation of India
ICO	Instituto de Credito Oficial (Spain)
ICSID	International Centre for Settlement of Investment Disputes
IDA	International Development Association
IDB	Inter-American Development Bank
IDFC	International Development Finance Club
IFC	International Finance Corporation
IFG	International Foundation for Greece
IICY	International Investment Corporation of Yugoslavia
IMDBI	Industrial and Mining Development Bank of Iran
IMF	International Monetary Fund
IMI	Internationale Micro Investitionen
IPC	Interdisziplinäre Projekt Consult
IsDB	Islamic Development Bank
ISF	InsuResilience Solutions Fund
KDFC	Korea Development Finance Corporation
KWG	Krediwesengestz
LBDI	Liberian Bank for Development and Investment
LIP	Local Initiatives Project
MDB	Multilateral Development Bank
MDG	Millennium Development Goals
MEB	Micro Enterprise Bank of Kosovo
MEF	Microfinance Enhancement Facility
MENA	Middle East and North Africa
MIDF	Malaysian Industrial Development Finance
MIF	Microfinance Investment Fund
MIF	Multilateral Investment Fund
MIFA	Microfinance Initiative for Asia

MIGA	Multilateral Investment Guarantee Agency
MSME	Micro-, Small-, and Medium-sized Enterprise
NDB	National Development Bank
NDB	New Development Bank (formerly BRICS Development Bank)
NGO	Non-Governmental Organization
NHIF	National Health Insurance Fund
NIDB	Nigerian Industrial Development Bank
NIF	Nordic Investment Fund
NORAD	Norwegian Agency for Development Cooperation
ODA	Official Development Assistance
OECD	Organisation for Economic Co-operation and Development
OED	Operations Evaluation Department
OeEB	Oesterreichische Entwicklungsbank
OOF	Other Official Flows
OPEC	Organization of the Petroleum Exporting Countries
PDCP	Private Development Corporation of the Philippines
PICIC	Pakistan Industrial Credit and Investment Corporation
PPP	Public-Private Partnership
RDFI	ReDesigning Development Finance Initiative
RMB	Renminbi
RSBF	Russia Small Business Fund
SBCI	Strategic Banking Corporation of Ireland
SDG	Sustainable Development Goals
SDIP	Sustainable Development Investment Partnership
SEC	Securities and Exchange Commission
SEP	Special Energy Programme
SIDA	Swedish International Development Cooperation Agency
SIFIDA	Société internationale financière pour les investissements et le développement en Afrique
SME	Small- and Medium-Sized Enterprises
SNI	Societe Nationale d'Investissement (Tunisia)
SOCOFIDE	Société Congolaise de Financement du Développement
SOE	State-Owned Enterprise
SWF	Sovereign Wealth Fund
TCX	The Currency Exchange Fund
TOSSD	Total Official Support for Sustainable Development
TSKB	Türkiye Sinai Kalkinma Bankasi
UN	United Nations
UNCTAD	United Nations Conference on Trade and Development
UNDP	United Nations Development Programme
UNIDO	United Nations Industrial Development Organization
USAID	United States Agency for International Development
USD	US Dollar
VEB	Volkseigene Betriebe
WEF	World Economic Forum
WFP	World Food Programme

List of Tables

CHAPTER 1

The Marketization of Development Finance

On 10 October 2016, a diverse group of high-level government officials, civil society representatives, and private sector businessmen convened at the United Nations headquarters in New York City. At hand was a discussion over how to best implement the recently adopted 2030 Agenda for Sustainable Development and its attendant Sustainable Development Goals (SDGs), a comprehensive 17-point agenda that, if achieved, aimed to improve the living conditions of hundreds of millions of people through transformational investments in infrastructure, industry, entrepreneurship, and environmental protection. The SDGs were lauded for their ambitions. At the meeting, then UN Secretary-General Ban Ki-moon hailed the goals as "the people's agenda, a plan of action for ending poverty in all its dimensions, irreversibly, everywhere, and leaving no one behind" (UN 2015b).

However, it was ubiquitously acknowledged that implementing the SDGs would be extraordinarily expensive. One study estimated that developing countries would collectively need more than USD 4.5 trillion in investment annually, a sum that eclipsed the combined financial power of the world's development agencies by more than 30 times (WEF and OECD 2015a, 4). With development assistance (as a percentage of donor country GDP) waning, donor government funds alone would be insufficient; development institutions would need to mobilize funding from the private sector. With global private capital markets worth more than

P. Volberding, *Leveraging Financial Markets for Development*, Executive Politics and Governance,
https://doi.org/10.1007/978-3-030-55008-0_1

USD 200 trillion, private enterprises, commercial banks, and institutional investors would be critical to marshalling these resources. As H. E. Peter Thomson, President of the UN General Assembly, remarked, "the private sector serves as the custodian of the largest pools of the world's resources, and the main engine driving entrepreneurship and innovation around the world. It is therefore vital that the private sector is brought in as a key partner in our discussions on how to mobilize the investments that are needed to achieve the SDGs" (UN 2017b). Development institutions had fully embraced private capital as a key to achieving outcomes; development policy had become focused on its mobilization.

To be certain, the desire to use private capital to finance economic development had been a long-standing conviction. In the 1950s, development institutions like the World Bank prioritized funding for privately-led projects and avoided supporting state-owned enterprises as a matter of policy. In 1956, the International Finance Corporation (IFC) was established with the express objective to promote private entrepreneurship. This strategy reflected a deep-seated belief that developing country public institutions lacked the dexterity and capabilities to ignite economic growth. Three decades later, the landmark 1989 World Development Report emphasized that a vibrant domestic financial sector was critical to a developing country's growth potential and reemphasized private initiative as the central driving force. However, throughout this period, development institutions struggled to mobilize private investment. Foremost among the reasons was that development projects were often not financially viable for private capital. They were the projects that required large capital investment, had long—and uncertain—repayment horizons, and were located in countries with higher political and economic risk. These were—and still are—all factors that private investors eschew.

In order to attract private investment, development institutions began to align economic development policy with the logic of financial markets. This required two components. First, development projects hewed closer to commercial investment principles. Development institutions prioritized financing over grants in order to create projects with a revenue stream to pay back investors. To match projects to investors and avoid creating moral hazards, interest rates on those financing programs reflected, at least partially, the riskiness of the project. Second, in order to attract more private investors to these new and riskier investment opportunities, development institutions redeployed donor government funds to absorb risk within the newly-created financial instruments. Crucially, this risk assumption altered the risk-reward calculation for private investors and turned previously unbankable development projects into investment opportunities. As a result, these financial instruments grew in number and complexity over time, and attracted substantial private investment. Throughout this process, development institutions drove innovation for new instruments and their application to new sectors. These financial instruments, which relied on a mix of commercial logic and public risk assumption, constitute what I term ***marketized development financial instruments***.

Marketized development financial instruments are now so pervasive that their advantages are axiomatic. Development institutions and private investors alike have embraced them as way to bring private investment to, and catalyze growth within, development countries. Over the past decade, the World Bank has redoubled its efforts to create new financial instruments backed with donor government funds, ranging from future-flow securitizations to diaspora bonds (cf. Ketkar and Ratha 2009). The World Bank's president, Jim Yong Kim, has also publicly embraced private investors in development projects via World Bank risk-sharing schemes (Thomas 2018). KfW, the German development bank, has created more than a dozen investment funds, and participated in at least 30 additional investment vehicles with more than EUR 1.4 billion in funding since 2008. From the SDGs to smaller, targeted funds, marketized development financial instruments are now central to international development policy.

The Creation of Marketized Development Financial Instruments

While the evolution to marketized development financial instruments mirrored the global growth of financial markets, their creation was far from preordained. Given the unprofitable and riskier nature of development projects, marketized development financial instruments were dependent on one crucial factor: donor government risk assumption of developing country investments. Traditional development policy, which distributed assistance primarily as grants or project loans, provided few opportunities for financial instruments, and even fewer risk guarantees. Yet by the early 1980s, and accelerating through the 2000s, donor governments had come to embrace these new financial instruments as critical to development policy. Therefore, this book asks *why* donor governments, which were reluctant to add financial burdens from development assistance, supported these new marketized development financial instruments abroad in which they assumed investment risk? In addition, development institutions played a central role not only as the primary creator of these financial instruments, but also their greatest proponents. Why did development institutions—rather than the private financial sector—champion marketized development financial instruments? Finally, which institutions were critical in facilitating this evolution?

I argue that development institutions played a critical role in creating, managing, and promoting these new marketized development financial instruments as a way to solve two problems. First, beginning in the late 1970s, donor countries wanted to increase the speed and scope of development assistance in ways that served broader political interests but simultaneously preserved financial sustainability. Second, development institutions themselves had long desired to provide assistance in ways that maintained economic incentives and were financially sustainable. Marketized development financial instruments enabled development institutions to respond to these pressures. Development institutions—particularly the German development bank KfW—experimented by convincing politicians to redirect funds away from grants and loans and toward more complex financial instruments. This promotion of risk-sharing mechanisms through marketized development financial instruments allowed assistance to be faster, more flexible, and more attractive to private capital. Moreover, by using donor government assistance as risk buffers within financial instruments, development institutions were able to decrease investment risk to private investors while also reducing the annual outlays on the part of donor governments. Critically, in order to ensure that these new instruments pursued development objectives and avoided creating moral hazards, development institutions not only strictly adhered to market operating principles, but also created new financial instruments and maintained managerial control over them. This ensured that both financial intermediaries and end-users had incentives to pursue the development projects envisioned by donor governments.

Development institutions were the actors best suited to catalyze these new financial instruments. Since they already existed at the nexus of private markets and public ownership, development institutions had the familiarity with financial markets as well as a political mandate to pursue economic development abroad. Their access to government resources enabled innovations of new risk-sharing financial instruments that the private sector could not develop. Moreover, development institutions also had the institutional ability to maintain equity stakes and managerial control over investment decisions. This was a crucial factor in ensuring that these financial instruments balanced between pursuing development objectives while simultaneously maintaining proper incentives for recipients. In short, development institutions did what private financial institutions could not do—they leveraged donor government development assistance as a risk buffer in new financial instruments that made development projects attractive to private investors. Interestingly, private investors remained on the sidelines for much of this process. While they were beneficiaries of a government risk-subsidized investment vehicle, private investors remained skittish. In the end, development institutions not only strongly supported marketized development financial instruments, but also spearheaded their creation.

In order to examine the evolution of marketized development financial instruments, I focus on the understudied experience of Germany's KfW. Using archival research and over 70 interviews with development practitioners, I argue that KfW played a particularly important role beginning in the late 1980s in innovating new marketized development financial instruments. Three key institutional characteristics enabled KfW to become a pioneering development institution. First, KfW had the strong political and economic backing of the German government and was close to policymakers in developing new policies. Second, KfW's institutional flexibility to create, manage, and hold equity stakes in new marketized development financial instruments meant that it could ensure incentives were maintained. Third, KfW had extensive experience with private financial markets through its own domestic promotional business, meaning that it was institutionally experienced in mixing public institutions with private initiatives. These three characteristics became particularly important for KfW during critical junctures of political urgency for the German government. Reunification, the fall of the USSR, and the Balkan crisis provided the necessary political impetus to allow KfW to leverage its unique institutional characteristics and innovate with marketized development financial instruments. Moreover, as these instruments proved to be financially sustainable and developmentally impactful, KfW helped propagate their use to other sectors and countries and worked in conjunction with other development agencies to encourage their proliferation.

KfW was certainly not the only development institution to promote these financial instruments; however, I contend that it was a key institution in their evolution. While existing scholarship has focused on the contributions of the United States and the World Bank in establishing and guiding an international development paradigm, I argue that KfW—and more broadly the German government—provided crucial support in the creation and propagation of marketized development financial instruments. This book therefore aims to uncover both KfW's and the German government's contribution to the development paradigm and, critically, provides an important window into the processes by which marketized development financial instruments emerged.

Enabling Marketization in Development Finance: The Experience of Germany's KfW

KfW is now one of the world's largest development institutions with an annual volume to developing countries of EUR 8.7 billion (KfW 2019, 6), but it was not originally envisioned as an international development institution. Founded in 1949 as *Kreditanstalt für Wiederaufbau* (Reconstruction Credit Agency) to rebuild Germany after World War II, KfW evolved into Germany's all-encompassing promotional bank; only in 1961 did KfW become the country's primary development institution.[1] Through the 1970s, KfW's development strategy mirrored that of the World Bank. Its dominant perspective was that underdevelopment was the consequence of a lack of domestic savings as well as poor economic policy and infrastructure, both of which inhibited private investment. Therefore, KfW focused on funding key infrastructure and industrial projects to relieve bottlenecks, often with motivations toward supporting German industry, and supported the World Bank's global network of development finance companies (DFCs). A mix of grants and project loans dominated these investments. However, by the early 1980s, assessments of development projects and DFCs revealed serious deficiencies, as many were found to be ineffective, wasteful, and market-distorting.

KfW, as well as other development institutions, had a long-standing conviction that economic development was best achieved by leveraging

[1] Germany's development assistance was originally divided into three institutions. KfW was responsible for financing, GTZ for technical assistance, and BMZ for concessional financing. Over the years, these responsibilities became concentrated within KfW.

the private sector. Since its inception, KfW itself closely followed private investment principles, and even to this day still uses its European Recovery Program (ERP) funds on a revolving basis. Yet even beyond its propensity to rely on private investment processes, KfW possessed a number of unique institutional characteristics that made it well-positioned to be able to experiment and innovate with marketized development financial instruments. First, KfW had strong political and economic backing of the German government. This most notably included being a full faith and credit entity of the German government, meaning that KfW could widely and cheaply borrow on private capital markets. However, it also included a close working relationship with politicians and bureaucrats to co-develop policy initiatives. Second, KfW had greater institutional flexibility than other development institutions. As a bilateral development institution, KfW was not bound by the same restrictions that limited participation in financial intermediaries and instruments within recipient countries, giving KfW much more flexibility in structuring new instruments and maintaining oversight over operations, which helped ensure that development objectives remained aligned with individual incentives. Finally, KfW had extensive experience from its domestic operations using promotional finance instruments and raising capital on private financial markets. Taken together, these three unique attributes laid a foundation of both institutional capacity and flexibility that was necessary in order to create marketized development financial instruments.

However, a series of political crises added urgency to efforts to codify these instruments into policy. First, in 1989, German reunification provided KfW with experience in adapting its domestic programs to a development context and in pushing the German government to embrace risk assumption as a means to expand and expedite fund dispersal. It also demonstrated the need to better coordinate financial intermediaries and manage operations, particularly in challenging macroeconomic environments. Second, the fall of the USSR allowed KfW to apply the strategies deployed in the former GDR to an international context. Moreover, concerns of regional instability convinced the German government to expand its risk-sharing measures in new financial instruments in order to quickly attract private investment. Third, following the Balkan crisis in Southeast Europe in the mid-1990s, which raised apprehensions of new states becoming engulfed in political unrest on the border of the EU, German and European politicians were willing to quickly provide financial resources to stabilize the region. During this period, KfW operationalized its ability to invest in countries without a recipient government guarantee, as well as to create and operate financial instruments within recipient countries. These attributes allowed KfW enormous latitude to combine risk assumption with financial instruments and generated confidence on the part of both governments and private investors that funds were safe investments. Since KfW was unique in these abilities, other national and European development agencies relied on KfW to set up and manage these new financial instruments.

In short, these three critical junctures for KfW illustrate how marketized development financial instruments overcame their initial hurdles and entered the mainstream of economic development practice. Even though KfW had a long-standing objective to mobilize private finance for development investment, as well as a set of unique characteristics that predisposed KfW to an innovating role, it was not until political crises unfolded that required a rapid increase in the size and speed of development assistance that the German government could be convinced to assume risk in these new financial instruments. In particular, this book will focus on two important KfW-facilitated innovations in development finance: microfinance banks and structured finance for development. For each, KfW provided important institutional and financial support that allowed the instrument to develop and thrive.

Crucially, in exchange for this risk assumption, KfW leveraged its capacity to establish and operate the financial instruments within recipient countries. This ensured that fewer moral hazards emerged within financial intermediaries or among end recipients, and that funds were prioritized for high-impact development projects. This capacity had three main features. First, the German government allowed KfW to administer development assistance without a recipient government guarantee. Under the World Bank guidelines, donor governments and institutions were required to obtain this guarantee in order to give recipient countries a stake in the success of a project. By freeing KfW from this requirement, and subsequently transferring project risk away from the recipient country, the German government facilitated a quicker disbursement of financing and provided flexibility into how the instruments could be structured. Second, the German government permitted KfW the ability to create new institutions. World Bank regulations stipulated that development agencies could not establish new institutions within recipient countries in order to avoid issues of sovereignty. However, KfW's ability to control intermediary instruments and institutions meant that it had greater managerial control over them. Third, and closely related, KfW was allowed to maintain a controlling stake in local institutions. The World Bank and IFC were prohibited from having controlling stakes over concerns of sovereignty; however, this also created moral hazards and circumscribed abilities to influence operations. KfW's ability to both create new institutions and maintain controlling stakes over institutions or businesses greatly expanded the flexibility and speed with which it could invest, boosting the appeal to private investors.

As these marketized development financial instruments demonstrated commercial feasibility and positive outcomes, KfW also pursued opportunities to create more complex financial instruments in an expanding list of sectors. Moreover, the successes of these instruments helped convince other development institutions and donor governments that marketized development financial instruments were viable options for implementing development assistance. Over time, marketized development financial instruments would become a pillar of international development policy (Table 1.1).

It is important to note that KfW was not the original creator of the reasoning behind many of these financial instruments, nor was it always the first development institution to utilize them. Nearly all of the financial instruments had been developed within private financial markets before and were in widespread use long before development finance had emerged. Nevertheless, I focus on KfW for two reasons. First, as a full faith and credit entity of the German government, KfW possessed numerous aforementioned advantages over its multilateral development counterparts that made it a fertile testing ground. This included the absence of needing a recipient government guarantee for project financing, the ability to create new financial instruments and institutions within the recipient country, and the ability to retain majority ownership of these institutions and instruments. Critically, KfW did not have to rely on domestic financial institutions or local politicians to administer development assistance, giving it much greater control over in-country operations. When coupled with the risk guarantees of the German government, these advantages bolstered the confidence of private investors and spurred the creation of additional marketized development financial instruments.

Second, even though KfW was not the only institution experimenting with these marketized development financial instruments, the institution

Table 1.1 Timeline of key events for the evolution of marketized development financial instruments, 1944 to present

Year	*Key Event*
1944	The International Bank for Reconstruction and Development (IBRD) is founded
1948	European Recovery Program (ERP, or Marshall Plan) begins
1949	KfW commences operations
1951	The IBRD provides its first loan to a DFC (Ethiopia)
1952	KfW's first SME loans are issued, with its first SME program in 1956
1954	The IBRD's Economic Development Institute (EDI) is founded
1955	KfW begins export financing
1956	The International Finance Corporation (IFC) is founded
1958	KfW's first foreign development loans to India, Sudan, and Iceland
1961	KfW officially becomes responsible for German development assistance
1961	KfW implements first co-financing operation with the World Bank (Roseires Dam, Sudan)
1962	KfW's first loan to a DFC (Pakistan)
1964	KfW's first mixed financing loan
1968	The World Bank is permitted to invest in state-owned DFCs
1971	KfW issues first loan from its own working capital
1978	KfW issues its first foreign currency loan
1979	KfW begins financial support of foreign SMEs
1981	IPC begins local savings bank CMAC in Peru
1986	KfW awarded AAA credit rating
1987	KfW issues its first foreign currency bond
1989	World Bank Development Report highlighting financial sector importance is published
1990	KfW begins operations in the GDR to facilitate unification
1992	KfW begins economic consultations in newly independent states of Central and Eastern Europe through the Transform Programme
1994	The EBRD and KfW found the Russia Small Business Fund (RSBF)
1995	KfW implements its first composite financing initiative
1995	KfW helps establish FEFAD in Albania, the first time an international development organization founded a financial intermediary
1999	MEB Bosnia is the first microfinance bank founded in Southeast Europe
2000	Commerzbank becomes first commercial bank to take an equity stake in a new microfinance bank (MEB Kosovo)
2000	Millennium Development Goals (MDGs) are announced
2005	The European Fund for Southeast Europe (EFSE) is founded as the first structured fund for development

(continued)

Table 1.1 (continued)

Year	*Key Event*
2006	KfW participates in the first on-shore securitization of a microfinance portfolio
2007	TCX is established, which was the first fund dedicated to currency risk
2009	KfW and the IFC initiate the Microfinance Enhancement Facility (MEF)
2009	KfW establishes the Green Growth Fund (GGF), KfW's first fund to focus on sustainability issues in development
2012	African Risk Capacity (ARC) established, one of the first development finance funds to focus on insurance
2014	KfW issues its first green bond
2015	Sustainable Development Goals (SDGs) are announced
2017	The World Bank launches the Maximizing Finance for Development (MFD) strategy

did play an outsized role in the development of two of them. Beginning in the late 1980s, KfW supported the creation and financing of a network of microfinance banks in Southeast Europe in partnership with a private firm, ProCredit. These were far from the first microfinance institutions, but they were notable for their large-scale, commercial basis. It was also unique for a development institution to hold equity stakes in both the microfinance institutions and the consultancy organization ProCredit, two factors that greatly increased KfW's managerial control over operations. Second, KfW was the lead institution in the establishment of structured funds for development, most notably the European Fund for Southeast Europe (EFSE). KfW redirected German aid to serve as the first-loss risk tranche and its own capital market-raised funds into the mezzanine tranche. Private investors were sold the safest senior tranches. Both the commercial-oriented microfinance institutions and the structured funds for development have been replicated worldwide. Both of these innovations demonstrated that financial markets could be harnessed for development objectives.

By analyzing the experience of KfW, I contend that we can better understand how marketized development financial instruments evolved and answer the question of why and how donor governments agreed to assume developing country investment risk. Marketized development financial instruments arose not only out of a long-standing conviction that private investment was the best pathway toward sustainable economic growth, but also out of a political necessity to expediently fund development projects. While growing financial markets provided the possibility for these instruments, KfW, as well as other development institutions, created and promoted marketized development financial instruments to respond to these dual goals. Since KfW had access to both private financial markets and government funds, they did what the private sector could not—create financial instruments that combined public and private money for development projects while simultaneously retaining ownership and investment decision control over the instruments. Over time, marketized development financial instruments diffused to other institutions and sectors, slowly emerging as a pillar of modern development policy. Therefore, understanding KfW's experience not only reveals how development policy was shaped by a relatively unknown actor, but also details the political economy process through which they emerged.

The Road to Marketized Development Financial Instruments

Since the first years of contemporary development assistance in the mid-1940s, donor countries sought to incorporate private investment in development policy. Reconstructing war-torn Europe and developing previously colonized countries was a herculean task to be implemented with public funds alone. As such, emphasis was placed on encouraging private investors to help fund the projects. The International Bank for Reconstruction and Development (IBRD), the progenitor to the World Bank, was an early proponent of mobilizing private capital. As the IBRD's 1947 annual report posited, "development on the scale that is within range of practicability needs financial assistance in amounts which only established credit and the consequent free flow of private capital can provide" (IBRD 1947, 12–13).

From the very beginning, the IBRD acknowledged that it could not—and should not—serve as the only source of financing for developing countries. The IBRD instead argued that its role was catalytic and, more specifically, it should seek to mobilize both domestic and international private capital to complement domestic public funding and development assistance. By the mid-1950s, the IBRD had solidified its intention to focus on private actors. While the majority of its investments still focused on large-scale industrial and infrastructure projects, they were designed to encourage private investment by freeing bottlenecks in the economy.

However, solely financing projects were insufficient to catalyze private investment, particularly to SMEs. One important addition to the strategy was the use of development finance corporations (DFCs) to serve as conduits for IBRD financing. After the first DFC was established in 1949, the IBRD soon set up or invested in dozens more DFCs, and by 1980, had invested USD 6.4 billion in more than 50 DFCs (Hu 1981, 47). To fund these DFCs, the IBRD expanded its involvement with private capital markets and, by 1955, the IBRD had raised USD 852 million from bonds issuances (IBRD 1955, 16).

While the IBRD aimed to mobilize of private capital, development practitioners lobbied for an institution specifically dedicated to the promotion of private enterprise. In 1956, the International Finance Corporation (IFC) was created to support the private sector in developing countries. The IFC was tasked with three principle functions: to invest its own funds, in association with private capital, in investments where there was insufficient quantity for long-term investments on reasonable terms; to act as a clearinghouse for both foreign and domestic private capital; and to improve managerial skill and experience within recipient countries (IBRD 1956, 27). Unlike the IBRD, the IFC was envisioned to deal directly with private businesses without government guarantees, and it targeted investments that would generate additional private participation. By 1970, the IFC had committed a cumulative total of USD 476 million across 43 countries (IFC 1970, 15).

Despite widespread support to foster private investment, the results of the first three decades did not live up to expectations. DFCs were not mobilizing private capital and were themselves reluctant to finance projects that were deemed too risky—precisely the investments they were tasked with fostering (Diamond and Raghavan 1982, 14–16). Projects were criticized for not have quantifiable and comparable assessment metrics. Foreign direct investment (FDI) from developed countries to developing remained anemic; even by 1990, FDI flows into developing countries accounted only for a percentage points of total flows. In order to mobilize private investment, development institutions reemphasized the need to create a domestic financial industry. The World Bank embraced structural adjustment to create stable macroeconomic and governance regulations that, once implemented, would catalyze private sector investment. The 1989 World Development Report codified the shift toward the private financial sector. The report argued for a comprehensive strategy in which developing countries "need to create appropriate financial institutions, develop better systems of prudential regulation and supervision, improve the flow of financial information, develop human skills for managing complex financial operations, and promote good financial habits" (World Bank 1989, 5). It proved to be another turning point for development policy as well.

The shift to a development policy that focused on mobilizing private finance certainly reflected changes in the global economy. The same period witnessed a trend toward the dismantling of trade barriers, the improved provision of legal protection for foreign investors, and the maturation of international financial integration. For development institutions, the deepening of financial markets opened new avenues to distribute the funds. For instance, the IFC pioneered the country investment funds and the Emerging Market Database in the early 1980s in an effort to boost growing investor appetite for developing country investments. These country funds were critical in reducing information costs to private investors who lacked local knowledge of projects, and it also created a monitoring mechanism to ensure that recipients were performing according to regulations (Development Practitioner #44 2016). Yet while private investment was the goal, most international development institutions possessed neither the institutional mandate nor the financial flexibility to redirect development assistance to financial instruments.

While development institutions may have been slow to adapt, other actors began to support entrepreneurs. Originating from a common spirit of self-help, early tests with microfinance emerged from NGOs. Acción, a microfinance-oriented group, began as early as the 1960s, but what would become the first iteration of a microfinance institution did not emerge until the late 1970s, and the first global network of microfinance institutions not until 1983. Concurrently, IPC, another development consultancy, in affiliation with KfW, began to experiment with microcredit loans in Peru (Development Practitioner #56 2017). A few years later, Muhammad Yunus incorporated the Grameen Bank along similar principles. However, until the 1990s, these remained illustrative case studies rather than policy.

By the mid-1990s, the landscape of development had drastically shifted (cf. Gore 2013). Economic crises led development institutions to urge donor governments to try new methods of administering assistance. They pushed for not only greater flexibility in how they interacted with and administered financial instruments, but also asked governments to redirect assistance to mobilize private investment. These actions culminated in the Millennium Development Goals (MDGs), which not only solidified private investment mobilization as the preferred strategy, but also created measures to support their evolution. The results have been far-reaching. In 2014, private financial flows[2] accounted for more than 60% of total international financial flows to developing countries (Development Initiatives 2016, 7). Critical to this transition was the embrace of marketized development financial instruments. In order to facilitate this process, donor governments have assumed an increasing proportion of the investment risk by repurposing assistance to finance the highest-risk portion of financial instruments. It was during this period that marketized development financial instruments gained centrality in development policy.

Defining Marketized Development Financial Instruments

The innovations arising from the desire to harness financial markets and incorporate donor government risk assumption have created a new approach to development that I term marketized development financial instruments. There are four central characteristics—they are financial instruments; they operate according to market logic; and they have a developmental objective. Most importantly, these marketized development financial instruments incorporate donor government risk assumption in order to reduce the risk to private investors.

First, these are financial instruments. By definition, financial instruments are contracts that can be traded between two parties. These instruments can be in the form of securities (stocks and bonds), cash (loans), exchange-traded derivatives (bond futures and stock options), and OTC derivatives (interest rate swaps and forward rate agreements). They can also vary in duration, from short-term debt to long-term debt to long-term equity stakes. Within a development context, the most common instruments have been traditional debt market related: loans and bonds, with some of the more recent innovations stretching into currency swaps and equity futures. Most importantly, financial instruments exclude two

[2] Private financial flows include foreign direct investment (FDI), long-term and short-term commercial debt, portfolio equity, and private finance mobilized via blended instruments.

forms of funding that have defined traditional development assistance—grants and donations. Both provide funding without the expectation of repayment, meaning that they do not operate within financial markets.

Second, these financial instruments must be marketized, meaning that they adhere to market principles. This includes, but is not limited to, paying market-clearing interest rates on borrowed capital and operating in ways that provide a satisfactory financial return based upon risk and portfolio diversification. Marketization is designed to avoid moral hazards on the part of recipients and, according to proponents, achieve a more efficient allocation of scarce financial resources. For development, marketization means projects prioritize bankability—the risks of the projects are considered, a variety of different types of investments implemented, and a revenue stream for investors is present. This also means that rather than directly subsidizing end borrowers, they instead pay market rates that vary according to investment risk.

Third, these financial instruments need to have a developmental objective. What is considered developmental has been subject to interpretation, but broadly this means that these instruments finance projects that are otherwise not independently commercially viable. This normally encompasses market failures—for reasons of excessive risk, information asymmetries, or principal-agent problems—or public goods. Private investors underprovide these projects because they are unable to generate sufficient returns on their investments. These projects therefore become developmental because they are not financed by private individuals but rather by donor governments. These have historically included large-scale infrastructure projects that have high upfront costs, health and education services that provide minimal revenue streams, and microfinance loans whose overhead administration is too costly.

While these three characteristics define the contours of marketized development financial instruments, one aspect appears to be irreconcilable—how can private investors be convinced to invest in commercially unattractive development projects? Therefore, the fourth aspect of marketized development financial instruments is that donor governments assume a portion of the investment risk to incentive private participation. This risk assumption occurs along a continuum—the more that donor governments assume the risk, the greater the number of development projects that become investible. Yet even though donor governments assume a portion of the risk, these instruments still abide by market principles. Loans are disbursed at or near market rates to end-users in developing countries; structured funds require returns on investment and diversify portfolios to attract private investors; and bond issuances for development projects are conducted on international capital markets. In fact, these market operations are essential to their functioning as financial instruments. To avoid market disruption, development institutions often provide only partial subsidization of any one project in order to avoid crowding-out additional private investment, and donor governments often share the burden to diversify risks. Financial intermediaries are created and owned by development institutions to ensure their incentives remain aligned with development objectives. Oftentimes this includes oversight over investment decisions to further mitigate risk. As such, donor government risk assumption does not seek replace the market, but rather facilitate it.

Marketized development financial instruments have existed, in part, for decades. However, the mechanisms of support have become increasingly complex and, over the past two decades, have incorporated more aspects of the financial sector. The OECD (Mirabile et al. 2014, 136–43) has identified three categories of donor government risk assumption:

1. Pooling mechanisms—These combine public and private money, thereby diversifying investment risk for all parties and creating financing schemes larger than either could independently provide. The most common pooling mechanisms are blended loans, syndicated loans, and securitization.[3] Each of these provides a middle ground between pure market and pure public schemes, and can be specifically tailored to a particular project in ways that maximize returns for social benefit. Pooling mechanisms are the oldest form of risk sharing, but contemporary versions are distinguished from previous iterations in their financial complexity and prevalence.
2. Guarantee schemes—These have also been widespread as a way of providing an insurance policy against the risks of investing in unknown countries or enterprises. Advantages include enabling first-time clients establish a positive reputation, reducing the interest rate paid on loans, and helping clients achieve higher credit ratings. These guarantees can be implemented in a number of ways; the IFC, for instance, predominantly issues partial guarantees to promote

[3] See Chapter 11 OECD (2014) for more details.

local financial markets. More recently, these have included underwriting of debt or of bond issuances. However, the use of guarantees, while increasing to over USD 15 billion from 2009 to 2011, has remained below its potential in both quantity and imagination (Mirabile et al. 2013, 14).

3. Equity and mezzanine financing—The most innovative category of development finance has been structured finance, of which equity and mezzanine financing are integral parts. While structured finance has been an important fixture of private investment, it was not until the early 2000s that they were adapted for use in development. Structured finance is arranged with separate tranches that, depending on their seniority, carry different risk profiles. This allows investors to choose a risk profile that best accords with their risk-return preferences. Within development, a government assumes debt or equity[4] that agrees to be repaid only if other investors have been paid in full and is tantamount to a government subsidy of risk. The precise percentage of government first-loss assumption can be adjusted, but instrument designers endeavor to find a balance that encourages appropriate private investment risk-taking without overly subsidizing the investment or crowding-out private investors. Donor governments have assumed the higher-risk equity tranches, while more market-oriented development finance institutions take the mezzanine shares. These two tranches absorb a disproportionately higher amount of risk, which allows private investors purchase the lower-risk senior tranches.

These three ways to incorporate donor government funding into financial instruments have increased in complexity as private financial markets have developed, but they are not the only way. For example, in the case of syndicated loans, development institutions could pass on the savings from their high credit rating to other lenders, effectively reducing the cost for private investors. Donor governments have also provided unfunded liabilities. Finally, there are a host of non-financial instrument measures that lower the cost to private actors. This can include technical assistance,

[4]There are also hybrid forms of investment, such as when debt can be converted into equity, but this distinction, for the purposes of this work, does not add any additional analytical clarity.

management training, pre- and post-investment evaluation and monitoring services, trade finance, and advance market commitments. These lower broader measures of risk, though not investment risk directly. While they are important components of marketized development financial instruments, this book will not specifically examine them.

Two important caveats are warranted. First, while I have coined a new term to describe this phenomenon, there are a range of existing monikers that imperfectly capture this trend. Unfortunately, this has resulted in a disjointed literature on the topic. For instance, blended finance has been used to describe the mixing of public and private funds, but the term itself is not limited to development objectives and omits the myriad of other, indirect ways that governments have more implicitly subsidized financial instruments and markets.[5] Innovative financing is conceptually vague and emphasizes novelty of the instrument rather than the process of mixing public and private funds. Financialization captures the growing importance of financial principles, but is burdened by intellectual opacity and loaded language. Public-private investment and public-private partnerships (PPPs) similarly acknowledge the hybrid nature of the investment, but developmental objectives tend to be more implicit. Therefore, for the purposes of this book, I will refer to the category as marketized development financial instruments that highlights the primacy of tradeable financial instruments, market logic, development outcomes, and government assumption of risk.

Second, donor government risk assumption has long been a feature of development. Development assistance has always been premised on the fact that these projects were not commercially viable and therefore required public subsidization to lubricate the channels for investment. With traditional development assistance, the advantage was that donor governments financially backed development institutions. For instance, the World Bank relies on paid-in and callable capital from donor governments; the model has been replicated in other multilateral development banks (MDBs). By using the creditworthiness of its donor countries, these institutions were able to raise money on international capital markets at a

[5] There is substantial analytical confusion as to what constitutes a blended finance instrument (cf. Development Initiatives 2016). For an in-depth discussion and comparison of various definitions of these financial instruments, see Pereira (2017). This is also distinguished from the raft of exclusively private or charity sources of development, such as Kiva, which are also confusingly labeled innovative aid mechanisms (cf. Jones 2012).

lower price than a developing country could do on its own. These institutions then passed the savings on in the form of discounted interest rates, technical assistance, or grants for projects that were eschewed by private investors. They also included investment in unprofitable infrastructure and industrial projects, usually in co-investment with a recipient country entity. Institutions also provided guarantees for investment, most notably from the Multilateral Investment Guarantee Agency (MIGA), under the auspices of the World Bank Group.

However, I maintain that the scope and intensity of the recent set of marketized development financial instruments extend beyond these previous iterations. The old system of donor government involvement was primarily concerned with subsidization rather than risk assumption. Loans were often administered for development projects with reduced interest rates to the end-user, a fact that created moral hazards. Today, an increasing share of the loans is distributed at market rates, but rather than giving subsidies to the end-users, the financial intermediaries and financial instruments are covered by risk protections. This has two implications. First, market discipline is much stronger and has allowed development practitioners to provide more funding while minimizing moral hazards. Second, the increased participation of development institutions has given them much more flexibility in how investments are implemented. Marketized development financial instruments can be more easily tailored to target certain regions, sectors, and borrowers. The ability to adjust the amount of risk assumption further gives flexibility to incentivize programs at a micro-level. Therefore, I contend that while the mixing of public and private sources of funding are not new, marketized development financial instruments are distinguished by their market operations, development objectives, scope of investment, and flexibility of implementation.

Marketized Development Financial Instruments in Development Policy

Beginning in 2000, there were palpable shifts in development policy that grew to increasingly embrace marketized development financial instruments. The 2000 Millennium Development Goals (MDGs) marked a turning point for this evolution, as it was the first major international agreement on how development assistance should proceed. An ambitious agenda necessitates ambitious funding, and donor countries were asked to increase the amount of ODA they provided in annual outlays.

However, participants acknowledged that private capital would be essential to success.[6] Throughout the initial implementation report, the UN called for private cooperation across numerous sectors and the further deepening of the financial sector, though stopped short of explicitly endorsing any particular financing mechanism (UN 2002).

The MDGs prompted innovations in four financing mechanisms. First, there were mechanisms that encouraged private-to-private flows. These enhanced existing measures to attract FDI and to match private investors with suitable projects. Second, solidarity mechanisms supported government-to-government transfers, such as ODA and other official flows (OOF). This included new funding sources like solidarity levies as well as new distribution mechanisms such as debt swaps. Third, PPPs leveraged or mobilized private finance to assist in the provision of public services, usually in the form of public risk subsidization. Fourth, catalytic mechanisms involved public support for creating an environment that was conducive to private markets. These often had the most complex financial engineering, and gave rise to carbon funds, advance market commitments, and insurance markets (Girishankar 2009, Ch 5). Despite the drive to mobilize private capital, these innovations heavily relied on public funds. Past strategies that focused on solving strategic bottlenecks and liberalizing economic policy subsequently gave way to a raft of new financial instruments. While most of these instruments were not conceptually novel, their application to development policy marked a substantial shift.

In addition, the MDGs gave rise to a series of conferences specifically on mobilizing private financing for development. The first was held in Mexico in 2002 and produced the Monterrey Consensus on Financing for Development. This consensus codified a multifaceted international strategy that was comprised of domestic financial mobilization, increased foreign direct investment, enhanced technical assistance within the financial sector, and harmonization of international trade and investment policies, though the MDGs still relied heavily on donor country aid flows. The Monterrey Consensus was so wide ranging that it covered policies ranging from tax policy to infrastructure to corporate governance (cf. UN 2003).

[6] See Easterly (2009), Saith (2006), and Sachs and McArthur (2005) for an introduction to the broader discussions on the importance and deficiencies of the MDGs.

With a brief pause around the 2008 Global Financial Crisis, in 2015, two more iterations of development financing policy were announced. First, the SDGs succeeded the MDGs. The SDGs further expanded upon the aspirations of the MDGs, yet this also meant that greater quantities of funding would be necessary. The SDGs increased the commitment of donor countries to mobilize private actors (cf. UN 2015c). In 2019, the World Bank further updated its SDGs with the Maximizing Finance for Development (MFD) initiative, which has sought to better coordinate private financing in development projects. Concurrently, the third Financing for Development conference met in Ethiopia to further update and expand the commitment to private mobilization of finance. The outcome of the conference—the 2015 Addis Ababa Action Agenda (AAAA)—created a new financing framework that sought to better align financial flows with development objectives. It went beyond the previous declarations of Monterrey and Doha in that it called for a broader and more integrated approach to sustainable financing that included environmental, social, and governance objectives (ESG). Moreover, the AAAA specifically cited the role of public finance—namely that of regional and national development banks—in supplying financial markets with long-term credit (UN 2015a). The acknowledgment of the important role of public finance marked another critical turning point in development finance.

Today, the proliferation of marketized development financial instruments has altered how development policy is implemented. The numerous access points of finance in the project process—ranging from project conceptualization to evaluation—has enabled development institutions to insert themselves seamlessly into the process. While no comprehensive survey on marketized development financial instruments had been conducted, other definitions provide an indication of the large scope of these instruments. For instance, global totals for blended financial instruments generated an estimated USD 57.1 billion in official flows from 2000 to 2008, or roughly 4.5% of all ODA funding, and an additional USD 11.7 billion in alternative sources of concessional funding (Girishankar 2009, i). From 2009 until 2015, IFC blended USD 385 million in concessional support in 67 projects and mobilized USD 4 billion in third party funding (IFC 2016, 3). This emphasis on leveraging financial markets is also pervasive, and includes domestic and international sources of both public and private finance (cf. UN 2014).

Moreover, efforts to create and harmonize policies among development practitioners have exploded. In 2013, the OECD and World Economic Forum launched the ReDesigning Development Finance Initiative (RDFI) to facilitate the growth of blended financial instruments (WEF and OECD 2015b).[7] At the G20 meeting in May 2017, participants reiterated support for a myriad of policies supportive of financial markets and investment. Not only did this include reaffirming backing for measures to crowd-in private finance, but it also called for enhanced governance and financial risk assessment measures, as well as the promotion of financial inclusion and green finance initiatives (G20 2017a, 3). Individual institutions have also signaled their commitment to marketized development financial instruments.[8] The IFC manages four innovative financing mechanisms, the Global Agriculture and Food Security Program (GAFSP), Blended Climate Finance (BCF), the Global SME Finance Facility, and the Women Entrepreneurs Opportunity Facility (IFC 2016). Structured funds have also become mainstays. The USD 10.1 billion Green Climate Fund (GCF) has brought together donor governments and private enterprise to leverage public funds on international capital markets, and by 2020 aims to mobilize USD 100 billion annually in private investment (GCF 2017, 1). In a 2016 survey conducted by the OECD and WEF, they found that 74 funds and other financial facilities account for USD 25.4 billion in assets and reached 177 million beneficiaries; these funds also posted competitive yields with 5.4% on debt and 16.3% on equity investments (WEF and OECD 2016, 13).

Transformations have also extended beyond the development institutions themselves. Entire new industries have been created. Thirty years ago, microfinance was relegated to small trials of self-help groups in Latin America, but today has grown into an industry worth more than USD 100 billion. New areas of focus for development have also emerged, in no small part due to the flexibility of financial instruments to fund them. Even sectors that were previously imagined to be unbankable, such as drought insurance, have been supported with new instruments. Finally,

[7] This initiative also created the Sustainable Development Investment Partnership (SDIP), a facility that brings together 37 public and private institutions to mobilize USD 100 billion in investment.

[8] For a brief selection of some of the most recent versions, see World Bank (2015a), IFC (2017), OECD (2015), and the United Nations (2014). Multilateral statements have also emerged (EIB 2017; WEF and OECD 2015a).

new financial instruments have emerged that expand the ways in which investment can be conducted. Public-private partnerships (PPPs), which now encompass a complex series of arrangements between governments and private actors, endeavor to reduce government obligations. There are additionally new instruments that include revised cash instruments of grants, loans, and securities, contingent financing, risk mitigation instruments (which include derivatives, insurance pools, hedging products, and swaps), and advisory and technical services.

While development institutions have heralded marketized development financial instruments as the future of development policy, one group has remained a late-adopter—private finance. This is not to say that private finance has not been interested in investment in developing countries; in 2016, FDI to developing countries reached 40% of the global total, and many developing countries now receive more in FDI than in development assistance (Gonzalez et al. 2018, 1). This is also not to say that private finance has not invested heavily in marketized development financial instruments. However, as this book will detail, private investors played a circumscribed role in developing and propagating marketized development financial instruments until the 2000s. Even though donor government risk guarantees greatly reduced their burden, sometimes of up to 50%, private investors remained hesitant of investing in developing projects in which they had little information, and they actually needed to be goaded by development institutions (Development Practitioner #40 2016). Therefore, while private investors today have become ardent supporters in sustaining and expanding these instruments, their role in creating marketized development financial instruments was limited.

In short, marketized development financial instruments have transformed development policy. Rather than relying on the distribution of grants, development institutions have chosen to leverage donor country budgets for private capital mobilization. Key to this strategy has been the risk assumption by donor governments. Pierre Jacquet, President of the Global Development Network, succinctly argued that managing risk was critical: "[R]isk mitigation is at the core of a modernised, reinvented role for ODA. Better risk analysis and coverage is likely to attract private investment and support local entrepreneurship. This is based on the underlying assumption that available market instruments and spontaneous private decisions do not allow for mitigating risks in an effective way, and that this results in under-investment" (Mirabile et al. 2014, 140). The reorientation of donor country funds, particularly those of historically concessional nature like ODA, reflects how profound the shift has been.

The Limitations of Marketized Development Financial Instruments

Given the voracity with which these marketized development financial instruments have garnered attention, there are numerous challenges. For one, the lack of a harmonized definition has meant that there is no consensus on how financial instruments should be structured, which priorities should be pursued, how risk assessments should be administered, and how investment outcomes should be evaluated (G20 2017b, 1). Efforts have been made to standardize procedures and harmonize reporting guidelines through the UN's Financing for Development (FfD) initiative, the World Bank, and the OECD's Total Official Support for Sustainable Development (TOSSD) initiative, but the lack of harmonization has stymied their effectiveness (cf. OECD 2015; UN 2017a). Furthermore, there is no systematic data on these financial instruments. This has further clouded an understanding of precisely what the impact of these new financial instruments has been and how they can be improved. Recently, as part of the 2030 SDGs, the MDBs began tracking how much long-term private capital they either directly or indirectly mobilized. In 2016, the MDBs calculated that they mobilized USD 163.6 billion from private and other institutional investors, with an additional USD 3.7 billion in short-term funding. However, discrepancies over how to count investment remain a contentious endeavor. The lack of consistency has also meant that transparency has been weak (Oxfam 2017, 8–9).

Second, financial instruments are only one component and cannot compensate for poor investment climates, government corruption, and macroeconomic instability. In specifically discussing the use of blended financial instruments, the IFC noted these limitations:

> Blended finance can sometimes be helpful to tip the balance in marginally profitable, risky projects toward attracting commercial investment, but it cannot alter the fundamental economics of an industry. To scale up finance, we need to build an investment climate and regulatory framework that generates robust project structures on a replicable basis. Blended finance can help key investments proceed, but should be seen as a stepping stone to more comprehensive reforms. (IFC 2016, 1)

The UN calls the greater global economic environment the third pillar of modern development strategy, in conjunction with private and public investment (UN 2014, Section 5). Yet as many interviewees cautioned, development instruments themselves only function when embedded in a stable macroeconomic framework and should therefore not be viewed as a panacea for development (Development Practitioner #40 2016; Development Practitioner #52 2017). Moreover, these foreign-initiated instruments may also crowd-out local initiatives within the financial sector.

Marketized development financial instruments have also been the target of critiques that they narrowly emphasize financial markets over developmental impact. NGOs have warned that reliance on these instruments diverts funding to projects that produce revenue streams, such as microfinance and SME finance, at the expense of those that do not, such as healthcare or education (Oxfam 2017, 10). For instance, with regard to PPPs, infrastructure has received the vast majority of funding (USD 68.7 billion), while all other sectors have received only a fraction of that. Demonstrating the difficulties still facing mobilization efforts, additional investment has also remained clustered in high-income countries (USD 92.5 billion), with negligible amounts mobilized in low-income countries (USD 3.6 billion) (World Bank 2017, 7–10). With regard to blended finance instruments, funding has heavily skewed toward middle-income countries; the least developed countries only received 5% of total global mobilized private funds in 2015 (Development Initiatives 2016, 14). With regard to guarantees, more than half have mobilized resources for upper middle-income countries (Mirabile et al. 2013, 6). For donor governments, the fact that they can calculate annual outlays to development funds as ODA has created incentives for governments to use these facilities to fund projects that register as ODA but that are not concessional (Pereira 2017, 15).

Additionally, there is concern that public assumption of risk unduly helps private investors. The goal is additionality, not subsidy. If the aim is also to create recipient country financial independence, artificially subsidizing the market risks engendering dependency and stunting domestic financial institutions. There is skepticism, even within the institutions themselves, of precisely how innovative these instruments have been, particularly in finding new, alternative sources (cf. Girishankar 2009). In one telling example, at a conference assessing the efficacy of microfinance, Robert Cull of the World Bank Research Department bluntly stated that the "notion that we can serve the poorest of the poor without reliance on subsidy is far-fetched at this point," and that microfinance appeared to have only a modest impact on the real incomes of the world's poorest. He continued that few microfinance institutions are profitable, suggesting that even with subsidies, a large market segment is not commercially viable (World Bank 2015b).

Finally, these marketized financial instruments have also drawn ire for the expanding power of the financial sector in development policy. This is in part a suspicion of transferring funding over sectors that have traditionally fallen under the public sector. Numerous advocacy groups have also rejected the notion that developing countries have been transformed into clients (cf. Carroll and Jarvis 2015; Roy 2010). These organizations point out that financial instruments have the potential to reinforce existing economic hierarchies and are primarily concerned with expanding investment opportunities for private actors (cf. Mawdsley 2016). Relatedly, they are also concerned with the potential for these instruments to generate unsustainable debt burdens. This issue has become particularly pronounced in debates over microfinance, which has created billions in debt for poor clients but is exempted from stringent oversight (cf. Aitken 2010; Bateman 2017; Mader 2014). This concern has also expanded to donor countries as well, as public finances would be responsible for the contingent liabilities of developing country default.

While this book does not directly concern itself with these critiques, nor does it attempt to adjudicate whether these instruments are good for economic development, they are important aspects in explaining how marketized development financial instruments transpired. Historically, concerns over private sector capture and market distortion have mattered less simply because the stakeholders in favor—including donor governments, development institutions, and recipient governments—vastly outweighed those with concerns. Nevertheless, they do have important implications for how these instruments might be leveraged in the future and, since these instruments will likely remain important for development institutions in the coming decades, are important to keep in mind.

Contribution and Implications

The evolution to marketized development financial instruments has been complicated. Yet through archival documents and in-depth interviews, this book aims to provide a unique perspective on how development institutions changed development policy and, to my knowledge, is the only scholarship to systematically investigate how and why marketized development financial instruments—in all their forms—emerged to become a central pillar in global development policy. Within this context, I contend that this book makes three particularly important contributions.

First, this book highlights the influential and unknown role that Germany has played in guiding the evolution of international development. Scholarship on the international development regime has zeroed-in on the role of the US and the World Bank, but has often neglected the critical contributions of other development institutions in shifting global strategy. KfW is a curious omission in this analysis, particularly since the institution today is a behemoth in the financial world, with assets in excess of EUR 500 billion, and has an important economic impact not only within Germany, but across the globe. Existing scholarship on KfW, even within the domestic German context, is surprisingly thin, and almost no sources have examined KfW's operations in international development. Therefore, this book endeavors to uncover how this relatively unknown actor has shaped the evolution of a global development paradigm. Through in-depth interviews and archival research, this book documents KfW's contribution in promoting new financial instruments in development over the past few decades, and details both why and how KfW and the German government faced pressured to reform the development process.

Second, I document the emergence and implementation of a new type of financial instruments for economic development. Marketized development financial instruments—which are defined by their closeness to financial markets and risk subsidization from donor governments—have emerged as a cornerstone of contemporary development policy. Yet despite their centrality, current scholarship has focused on individual instruments (e.g., microfinance) but has generally not embedded analyses within a broader paradigmatic shift. I contend that the evolution to marketized development financial instruments was the consequence of a complex political economy of development institutions, donor governments, recipients, and private actors. By contextualizing and identifying the processes of how KfW and other development institutions created and promoted these instruments, I believe that we can better understand why and how marketized development financial institutions became fixtures of the modern development paradigm and where the future may lie.

Third, this book is the only scholarship to document the rich history of the World Bank's global network of DFCs. DFCs were important financial institutions both for developing countries and the World Bank. By 1980, more than 70 DFCs operated worldwide and total cumulative World Bank lending to DFCs exceeded that directly provided to industry, and throughout their existence had been the subject of debate among economists as to whether they were effective or not. It is therefore surprising that DFCs have been omitted from most scholarly accounts of the World Bank. Using hundreds of recently declassified documents, I provide the only academic analysis of how DFCs emerged and operated, as well as why they faced so many hurdles in promoting economic development.

In addition to the academic contributions, this book has three broader implications. First, this book pushes back against the narrative that the United States and the World Bank were at the forefront of marketized development financial instruments, either because of ideological conviction or profit motivation. To be certain, the World Bank had long advocated methods of financing that both supported private entrepreneurs and relied on private financing for funding. However, the World Bank was only part of the equation, and oftentimes was a late-adopter of new instruments. The shift was stymied by the Bank's highly bureaucratic structure, which made changing a pattern of operations difficult, as well as a preference to finance a network of DFCs or directly invest in a project-specific program. Moreover, since the World Bank was required by statute to secure recipient government guarantees, these new financial instruments were incompatible. In fact, it was not until the 2000s that it became active in marketized development financial instruments (Development Practitioner #40 2016). Therefore, while the World Bank undoubtedly played an important role in laying the foundation for these financial instruments, it did not hold a position of centrality in their initial creation or propagation.

Second, I argue that private investors played a relatively circumscribed role in advocating for these instruments. Some scholars have critiqued what they view as a new development paradigm that "is no longer state led or state-centred, but rather financially driven and privately procured" (Carroll and Jarvis 2014, 533). It is true that private investors had long sought to expand their business operations in the developing world. However, not a single commercial bank invested in the first financial instruments in Latin America or Southeastern Europe. There is also scant evidence that commercial banks ever encouraged governments to create these instruments. In fact, as the AAAA declaration lamented, development finance from commercial banks has still not materialized on the scale envisioned. This has been for a simple reason—market access and better information does not change the underlying economics of an investment. Consequently, market forces cannot explain the details of this evolution—who, how, and why marketized development finance instruments developed are afterthoughts to financial market forces. Moreover, an explanation singularly focused on financial markets cannot explain the reasons or timing of donor government assumption of risk. While deepening financial markets provided a necessary condition, they are not sufficient in explaining the details of the evolution.

Third, while this strategy relies heavily on the market, these financial instruments would not exist without extensive donor country risk assumption. While financial markets are heralded as private initiatives, the reality is that non-credit enhanced development projects remain commercially unbankable. Marketized development financial instruments are also able to redistribute risk, but they cannot mitigate risk (Development Practitioner #52 2017). Rather, development institutions have sought to incentivize private participation through a risk transfer from the public to the private sector. First tranche loss risk in structured funds, technical assistance support, and mixed financing are all schemes that combine private investment with government funding. None of the so-called innovative financial instruments were entirely sourced from private actors; in fact, none could operate without government backing. Therefore, while the development model may rely on private actors to function, the entire strategy is operable only because of significant government risk assumption.

Finally, a few important limitations should be noted. First, given the complexity of development assistance, this book does not endeavor to explain the entirety of changes to the development regime. Rather, it tackles a much narrower question of how, when, and why development institutions arrived at system of administering development assistance via marketized development financial instruments. Second, the book relies primarily on documentation and interviews from KfW. I argue that KfW's experience is both important and illustrative of shifts in development and, as such, has implications for understanding how other development institutions operated. KfW is therefore one important experience, but it is not the only. Future scholars should examine the contributions of other development institutions. Finally, this book does not directly address whether or not these instruments were a more effective or more efficient strategy. Development assistance has been notoriously difficult to quantify, and there are persistent disagreements on how to incorporate intangible outcomes into outcome measurements. Nevertheless, this book certainly has implications on those who have benefitted or been disadvantaged by this shift to marketized development financial instruments, which are included throughout.

Structure of the Book

This book proceeds as follows. Chapter 2 analyzes the historical origins of development finance from 1947 through the early 1970s, with particular focus on the experiences of the World Bank. Using a mix of analyst reports and recently declassified archival materials, this chapter examines how the Bank's early experiences reinforced that private investment was the only viable, long-term strategy for economic development. As such, the Bank prioritized catalyzing investment through project loans in strategic investments and privately-owned DFCs. Despite variable successes, this strategy validated a broader perspective that development assistance should be temporary, abide by market principles, mobilize private entrepreneurs, and leverage the domestic financial system for long-term sustainability. These principles laid the foundation for the emergence of marketized development financial instruments.

Chapter 3 explores the breakdown of this development paradigm. In particular, it explores the challenges to early development finance strategies that relied on project loans and development finance corporations (DFCs). Using recently declassified archival documents, the chapter analyzes how a lack of standardized implementation and assessment procedures hampered project loans. DFCs were beset by problems of political interference, improper incentives, and financial dependency. While development institutions, led by the World Bank, sought to improve results by aligning development policy with the discipline of financial markets, reforms were limited. A mix of strict World Bank regulations, internal disagreement, and a lack of political will from stakeholders circumscribed efforts to leverage private markets for development. Instead, the stage was set for another development institution to experiment with marketized development financial instruments.

Chapter 4 explores how KfW came to embrace and promote marketized development financial instruments. KfW's policies before the 1970s matched those of the World Bank, but in the 1980s, KfW received a series of negative evaluation reports and, by the late 1980s, faced pressure from German reunification and the collapse of the Soviet Union to quickly mobilize funding. Given the political urgency, KfW experimented with new instruments that integrated public development institutions with private financial markets. Critically, KfW convinced the German government to guarantee investment risk in these new instruments. These risk-sharing schemes helped KfW to overcome the challenges of providing market-rate development assistance without engendering moral hazards on the part of recipients and provided latitude for KfW to further experiment. Therefore, KfW's institutional flexibility and political support permitted the first iterations of marketized development financial instruments.

Chapter 5 explores how KfW's marketized development financial instruments matured. The 1990s Balkan crisis provided a new opportunity to push forward innovations with German government support. Critically, KfW leveraged its ability to (1) invest in a country without the recipient government guarantee, (2) create a new institution within a developing country, and (3) possess more than 50% of governing shares in any financial instrument. These abilities set KfW apart from other development institutions, and KfW became particularly influential in two innovations of development finance—microfinance banks and structured funds. For both, KfW was able to strictly control the financial instruments through ownership or direct investment control, helping KfW to avoid the creation of moral hazards and to attract private investment participation. Using extensive interviews with development practitioners, I explore in detail how KfW—with the support of the German government—expanded these marketized development financial instruments.

Chapter 6 examines the spread of these marketized development financial instruments from 2005 until the present. The success of a structured fund (EFSE) encouraged KfW to establish additional structured funds in order to mobilize private investment. In conjunction with the same set of European and US development institutions, KfW founded or participated in more than 42 new structured funds with over EUR 1.4 billion in investments. Moreover, KfW continued to support new financial instruments such as insurance funds, green bonds, and securitization of developing country debt. Yet essential to these new innovations was the combination of public funds with private investments, a trend that has reinforced marketized development financial instruments as an important component of development policy.

Chapter 7 concludes with thoughts on the impact of a development system based on marketized development financial instruments. It highlights how current development policy has codified these instruments into formal strategy, as the SDGs, MFD, and AAAA herald them as a critical tool for development policy. The chapter also makes note of how marketized development financial instruments have been embraced by institutions such as the China Development Bank (CDB), highlighting their universal appeal. However, there are also potential shortcomings to the strategy; these include questions about the transparency of financial instruments, the efficacy of these new instruments versus alternative mechanisms, and the potential contingent liabilities to donor country governments. Finally, I discuss the future trends of these instruments.

This book explores the complex process of how development institutions created, managed, and promoted marketized development financial instruments. Key to the feasibility of these new financial instruments was the redirection of donor government assistance to serve as risk buffers for private investors. Development institutions convinced donor governments to absorb this additional financial burden with assurances that these financial instruments were faster and more flexible. These instruments also dovetailed with the development institutions' own convictions that private investment was the best pathway for economic development, but maintained their control over the instruments to avoid creating moral hazards. Over time, marketized development financial instruments evolved into a variety of forms across numerous sectors, but they have nevertheless retained donor government risk sharing as the central ingredient. In the end, a new development finance strategy emerged that sought to increase private investment not through government absence, but rather through the direct participation of development institutions.

References

Aitken, Rob. 2010. Ambiguous Incorporations: Microfinance and Global Governmentality. *Global Networks* 10 (2): 223–43.

Bateman, Milford. 2017. *From Panacea to "Anti-Development" Intervention: The Rise and Fall of Microcredit*. Rochester, NY: Social Science Research Network. SSRN Scholarly Paper. July 18, 2017.

Carroll, Toby, and Darryl S.L. Jarvis. 2014. Introduction: Financialisation and Development in Asia Under Late Capitalism. *Asian Studies Review* 38 (4): 533–43.

———. 2015. The New Politics of Development: Citizens, Civil Society, and the Evolution of Neoliberal Development Policy. *Globalizations* 12 (3): 281–304.

Development Initiatives. 2016. *Blended Finance: Understanding Its Potential for Agenda 2030*. Development Initiatives. http://devinit.org/wp-content/uploads/2016/11/Blended-finance-Understanding-its-potential-for-Agenda-2030.pdf.

Diamond, William, and V.S. Raghavan (eds.). 1982. *Aspects of Development Bank Management*. Baltimore, MD: The Johns Hopkins University Press.

Easterly, William. 2009. How the Millennium Development Goals Are Unfair to Africa. *World Development* 37 (1): 26–35.

EIB. 2017. *Mobilization of Private Finance by Multilateral Development Banks*. Luxembourg: European Investment Bank. http://www.eib.org/attachments/mdb_joint_report_mobilization_2016_en.pdf.

G20. 2017a. Chair's Summary: G20 Finance and Central Bank Governors Meeting. Washington, DC, USA, 20–21 April 2017.

———. 2017b. *Joint MDB Statement of Ambitions for Crowding in Private Finance*.

GCF. 2017. *Status of the Initial Resource Mobilization Process*. Incheon, South Korea: Green Climate Fund.

Girishankar, Navin. 2009. *Innovating Development Finance-From Financing Sources to Financial Solutions*. Washington, DC: World Bank.

Gonzalez, Anabel, Christine Zhenwei Qiang, and Peter Kusek. 2018. Overview. In *Foreign Investor Perspectives and Policy Implications*. Washington, DC: World Bank.

Gore, Charles. 2013. The New Development Cooperation Landscape: Actors, Approaches, Architecture. *Journal of International Development* 25 (6): 769–86.

Hu, Yao-Su. 1981. The World Bank and Development Finance Companies. *Journal of General Management* 7 (Autumn): 46–57.

IBRD. 1947. *Second Annual Report to the Board of Governors: 1946–1947*. Washington, DC: International Bank for Reconstruction and Development.

———. 1955. *Tenth Annual Report: 1954–1955*. Washington, DC: International Bank for Reconstruction and Development.

———. 1956. *Eleventh Annual Report: 1955–1956*. Washington, DC: International Bank for Reconstruction and Development.

IFC. 1970. *IFC Annual Report 1970*. Washington, DC: International Finance Corporation.

———. 2016. *Blending Public and Private Finance: What Lessons Can Be Learned from IFC's Experience?* Washington, DC: International Finance Corporation.

———. 2017. *Blended Finance at IFC*. Washington, DC: International Finance Corporation.

Jones, Sam. 2012. Innovating Foreign Aid—Progress and Problems. *Journal of International Development* 24 (1): 1–16.

Ketkar, Suhas, and Dilip Ratha (eds.). 2009. *Innovative Financing for Development*. Washington, DC: World Bank.

KfW. 2019. *Financial Report 2018*. Frankfurt am Main: KfW.

Mader, Philip. 2014. Financialisation Through Microfinance: Civil Society and Market-Building in India. *Asian Studies Review* 38 (4): 601–19.

Mawdsley, Emma. 2016. Development Geography II: Financialization. *Progress in Human Geography* 41 (3): 1–11.

Mirabile, Mariana, Julia Benn, and Cécile Sangaré. 2013. *Guarantees for Development*. Paris: OECD.

Mirabile, Mariana, Cécile Sangaré, and Claudia Schmerler. 2014. Using Financial Instruments to Mobilise Private Investment for Development. In *Development Co-Operation Report 2014: Mobilising Resources for Sustainable Development*. Paris: OECD.

OECD. 2015. *A How-To Guide for Blended Finance: A Practical Guide for Development Finance and Philanthropic Funders to Integrate Blended Finance Best Practices into Their Organizations*. Paris: OECD.

Oxfam. 2017. *Private-Finance Blending for Development: Risks and Opportunities*. Oxfam.

Pereira, Javier. 2017. *Blended Finance: What It Is, How It Works and How It Is Used*. Oxfam.

Roy, Ananya. 2010. *Poverty Capital: Microfinance and the Making of Development*. New York: Routledge.

Sachs, Jeffrey D., and John W. McArthur. 2005. The Millennium Project: A Plan for Meeting the Millennium Development Goals. *The Lancet* 365: 347–53.

Saith, Ashwani. 2006. From Universal Values to Millennium Development Goals: Lost in Translation. *Development and Change* 37 (6): 1167–1199.

Thomas, Landon. 2018. The World Bank Is Remaking Itself as a Creature of Wall Street. *The New York Times*.

UN. 2002. *Implementation of the United Nations Millennium Declaration: Report of the Secretary-General*. New York: United Nations.

———. 2003. *Monterrey Consensus of the International Conference on Financing for Development*. New York: United Nations.

———. 2014. *Report of the Intergovernmental Committee of Experts on Sustainable Development Financing*. New York: United Nations.

———. 2015a. *Addis Ababa Action Agenda of the Third International Conference on Financing for Development*. New York: United Nations.
———. 2015b. *Consensus Reached on New Sustainable Development Agenda to Be Adopted by World Leaders in September*. New York: United Nations.
———. 2015c. *Transforming Our World: The 2030 Agenda for Sustainable Development*. New York: United Nations.
———. 2017a. *Implementing the Addis Ababa Action Agenda: The 2017 ECOSOC Forum on Financing for Development Follow-Up*. New York: United Nations.
———. 2017b. *Opening Remarks of H.E. Peter Thomson, President of the UN General Assembly at High Level SDG Action Event "SDG Financing Lab."* New York: United Nations.
WEF, and OECD. 2015a. *Blended Finance Vol. 1: A Primer for Development Finance and Philanthropic Funders*. Cologny, Switzerland: World Economic Forum.
———. 2015b. *Blending Capital, Catalyzing Change*. Cologny, Switzerland: World Economic Forum.
———. 2016. *Insights from Blended Finance Investment Vehicles & Facilities*. Cologny, Switzerland: World Economic Forum.
World Bank. 1989. *World Development Report 1989: Financial Systems and Development*. Washington, DC: World Bank.
———. 2015a. *2015 Development Finance Forum*. Washington, DC: World Bank.
———. 2015b. *Does Microfinance Still Hold Promise for Reaching the Poor?* Washington, DC: World Bank.
———. 2017. *Mobilization of Private Finance by Multilateral Development Banks: 2016 Joint Report*. Washington, DC: World Bank.

CHAPTER 2

1950–1970: The World Bank, DFCs, and the Foundations of Private Investment Mobilization

While marketized development financial instruments did not emerge in their current form until the 1990s, development institutions laid the foundation for their evolution decades before. As the only global development institution, the International Bank for Reconstruction and Development (IBRD) played a key role in identifying the challenges facing developing countries. From the beginning, the IBRD acknowledged that financing economic development would be difficult. Developing countries lacked financial resources to fund industrial and infrastructure projects, and sovereign debt issuance was difficult—if not impossible—since they lacked access to capital markets. Through a series of assessment missions, the IBRD concluded that private investment was needed, and hoped to create a virtuous cycle of private investment and economic growth. In order to achieve this, the IBRD followed a three-pronged strategy. First, the IBRD provided loans with subsidized interest rates or extended repayment schedules that targeted large-scale infrastructure and industrialization projects. Second, in order to reach smaller businesses and entrepreneurs, the IBRD channeled financial resources through domestic, privately-owned development finance companies (DFCs). These DFCs would then on-lend to commercial banks and private businesses, providing an important stream of financing for the private sector. Finally, the World Bank established the International Finance Corporation (IFC) in 1956 to directly finance the private sector without the need to interact with

P. Volberding, *Leveraging Financial Markets for Development*,
Executive Politics and Governance,
https://doi.org/10.1007/978-3-030-55008-0_2

developing country governments. The IFC pursued a similar strategy of providing financing for key project loans and DFCs. Eventually, investments in projects and DFCs were envisioned to become unnecessary as the developing country would become financially self-sufficient.

Using a cache of previously classified archival documents, I argue that these early experiences of the IBRD and IFC were critical in the evolution toward marketized development financial instruments because they defined the contours of development policy priorities. First, development institutions identified the absence of private capital as the missing ingredient for economic growth. Second, development institutions viewed financial instruments as a solution to mobilizing private capital. In essence, project loans and DFCs were early iterations of marketized development financial instruments. Both relied on market forces to allocate funding and engender proper incentives on the part of recipients, and both relied—albeit indirectly—on donor government risk assumption to incentivize private actors. Therefore, the underlying logic of development institutions was that they could mobilize private capital by combining donor government aid to reduce risk. However, restrictions on how donor government assistance could be utilized and the inability to monitor the quality of investments meant that these progenitors to marketized development financial instruments disappointed. Nevertheless, these early experiences laid the foundation for these future financial instruments by emphasizing the centrality of private investment and enshrining donor government-backed financial instruments with market discipline as the means to achieve this goal.

The International Bank for Reconstruction and Development (IBRD) and Early Development Finance

As the first international development agency, the IBRD[1] played an outsized role in establishing the long-term trajectory of development policy. Through its initial assessment reports, the IBRD concluded that the mobilization of private investment was the best means to achieve

[1] The IBRD later became incorporated with the International Finance Company (IFC), International Development Agency (IDA), the Multilateral Investment Guarantee Agency (MIGA), and the International Centre for Settlement of Investment Disputes (ICSID) to collectively comprise the World Bank Group.

economic growth, and directed development policy to find ways of serving this purpose. Since developing countries often lacked government budgets and well-capitalized commercial banks to finance transformative investments, development policy was meant to compensate for these shortfalls. The IBRD promoted a dual strategy of project loans and DFCs. These avenues, however, did not always produce the envisioned outcomes, nor did they always mobilize private investment. Nevertheless, the IBRD's experience and perspectives laid the foundation for future marketized development financial instruments.

Established at Bretton Woods in 1944, the IBRD was originally meant to finance European reconstruction. In 1947, the IBRD issued its first loan of USD 250 million for infrastructure and industrial activities in France, and shortly thereafter granted reconstruction loans to Denmark, the Netherlands, and Luxembourg. According to the IBRD's Articles of Agreement, these loans carried interest rates tied to the cost of raising capital, required borrower government guarantees, and were given priority repayment in the event of a default (IBRD 1948, 25–27). Yet shortly after the IBRD commenced operations, an acute capital shortage in Europe and the rise of communist regimes highlighted the deficiencies of the American-led reconstruction program. In response to the impending crisis, the US government announced the European Recovery Plan (ERP), colloquially known as the Marshall Plan, in 1947, to channel funding to reconstruction efforts. With nearly USD 5 billion in initial planned lending capacity, the Marshall Plan dwarfed the financial resources of the IBRD, which through 1948 had lent in total USD 497 million (Kapur et al. 1997, 71). The inundation of subsidized ERP funds to Europe crowded out IBRD loans. Moreover, the IBRD's relatively strict requirements on project assessment, implementation, and reporting further increased the cost to European counterparts to utilize the funds (IBRD 1948, 5). Consequently, only a handful of small loans were issued following the implementation of the Marshall Plan (Mason and Asher 1973, 359).

In order to remain relevant, the IBRD shifted to the promotion of economic development. Under the guidance of the second IBRD President John McCloy, and accelerating in earnest under President Eugene Black, the IBRD transitioned its focus away from European reconstruction and toward the underdeveloped regions of Asia, Africa, and Latin America. Yet adopting the mantle of global economic development necessitated both an identification of the greatest challenges facing underdeveloped countries and a strategy to solve them. Early IBRD operations were therefore dominated by in-depth country assessment missions to determine the barriers impeding economic growth. From 1949 to 1953, the IBRD conducted 11 General Survey Missions primarily to Latin America, but also to the Middle East and South Asia, in order to prepare the institution for its future development objectives.

Even prior to the missions, the IBRD had concluded by 1948 that underdevelopment was primarily a consequence of a severe lack of private capital "to build the necessary productive facilities and buy equipment, to provide schools and shops to train workers in new skills, and to establish housing, public utilities, transportation and other services needed for an efficiently functioning economy" (IBRD 1948, 15). Since developing countries lacked accumulated savings, the IBRD placed particular emphasis on capital formation within the target country and on the creation of healthy—and preferably private—financial institutions. Given the complexities of the economy, this was also thought to be best done through private banks rather than the government. While domestic financial mobilization was the goal, in practice there were numerous obstacles to capital formation. For one, the lack of a sound legal and financial system precluded a strategy of directly loaning money to either commercial banks or consumers, meaning that the IBRD would need to heavily rely on borrower government financing. This made the fledgling bank nervous. The IBRD's trepidation of government financing was not only rooted in its own ideological proclivities, but also in economic realities. The finances of borrower country governments were often in disarray, and suspicions over the capability of new governments raised concerns over corruption. Foreign government assistance was also often used to curry political favor rather than pursuing development outcomes, and the IBRD wanted to adhere to its economic objectives. More problematically, foreign assistance was feared to create financial dependency on international development institutions, a prospect the IBRD desperately wanted to avoid.

The IBRD's conclusion was that private investment was necessary from both foreign and domestic sources. Foreign capital was seen as particularly advantageous since this would not only increase aggregate investment in the economy, but would also facilitate technological transfer to spur industrialization. This mission was deemed so critical that it was codified in the Bank's Articles of Agreement. Accordingly, the IBRD was:

> To promote private foreign investment by means of guarantees or participations in loans and other investments made by private investors; and when private capital is not available on reasonable terms, to supplement private investment by providing, on suitable conditions, finance for productive purposes out of its own capital, funds raised by it and its other resources. (US Treasury 1944, 51)

Attracting foreign capital would also counteract the balance of payments disequilibrium that had emerged between developed and developing countries. Private capital from developed countries would fund projects across the developing world, "thereby assisting in raising productivity, the standard of living and conditions of labor in their territories" (US Treasury 1944, 52). However, given the widespread apprehension of Western corporations to invest in unknown markets, private capital flows were negligible. One last alternative was to prioritize increasing the domestic savings rates of borrower countries with the hope that, in time, a country could rely on its domestic banking sector to provide loans to industry and infrastructure projects. The IBRD posited that "foreign capital cannot be relied upon to do more than supplement local development efforts" and that the developing countries should "take all possible measures to encourage local savings and their investment for productive purposes" (IBRD 1948, 15).

Given these constraints, project loans were determined to be the best strategy. During the first few decades, these were heavily concentrated in infrastructure, which included roads, railroads, ports, and electricity generation, as well as in industrial projects, principally in light manufacturing and natural resource processing. These projects were selected because they had the potential to unlock economic potential of the private economy. The IBRD's first loan was provided to Chile in 1948 for the construction of a hydroelectric dam (USD 13.5 million) and the second for the importation of agricultural machinery and equipment (USD 2.5 million). Shortly thereafter, other loans included a railway in India and electric power generation and transmission in Mexico, El Salvador, and Brazil. By the end of 1950, the IBRD had provided USD 166.3 million across 12 loans (IBRD 1950a, 5).

Since these loans were ultimately guaranteed by donor governments, the IBRD set strict conditions for their disbursement in order to minimize moral hazards on the part of recipients. For one, the loan needed to be guaranteed by the borrower's government; this was thought to increase the likelihood of repayment in the case of default and to incentivize the government to support the project as well. The IBRD also favored projects that could increase a country's exports in order to equalize balance of payments. Finally, the Bank was particularly concerned with strategic projects that would either provide the foundation for growth in a variety of sectors, or that would relieve bottlenecks in the economy. Of course, without extensive experience or knowledge of the particular country, there was always a risk that such investments would simply displace private investment. Yet by 1950, the IBRD brushed the critique aside, noting that it "recognizes, of course, that by financing one particular investment project, it may be releasing resources already available to the borrower for some other investment activity." It went on, however, to say that "this is a principal reason why the Bank seeks to consult with its member countries not only concerning the merits of projects for which a loan is requested but concerning the country's projected investment expenditures as a whole" (IBRD 1950a, 9).

The emphasis on project loans in strategic sectors reinforced the IBRD's underlying perspective that private investment was responsible for producing economic growth. Yet while searching for new avenues of private investment mobilization, the IBRD stumbled upon another inhibiting factor—poor macroeconomic policies. In 1949, the Colombian government asked the IBRD to assess ways to increase its external private funding opportunities. While originally invited to assess the feasibility of supplying loans to Colombian industry and infrastructure, the IBRD delegation encountered a raft of macroeconomic problems ranging from government-induced inflation to an overvalued currency, as well as a paucity of national economic data (Alacevich 2009, Ch 2). The principal mission in 1950 was headed by renowned economist Lauchlin Currie, who concluded in his report that not only did national development primarily depend on the growth of productivity, but also it is intimately interrelated with other non-economic factors. These included education, food production, housing, and public health, all topics that had received limited attention as important facets in development (cf. IBRD 1950c). These results convinced the IBRD that project financing alone was insufficient to produce development (IBRD 1950a, 18). It also strongly reinforced the IBRD's suspicion that governments could harm nascent industries more than it helped.

Following the initial survey missions, the pace of loan disbursement accelerated in 1950. In the 1950–1951 fiscal year, the IBRD issued 21 loans valued at USD 297.1 million, nearly double the previous year's amount, yet still prioritized private-oriented investments. Implementing this, however, was often met with challenges. For instance, the 1953 Annual Report warned that governments should not supply its own financial and technical resources into enterprises where private capital is available, "since that will lessen the resources available for providing basic services and utilities that generally lie outside the scope of public initiative" (IBRD 1953, 10). While it might have been the goal of the IBRD to support greater private sector investment and development, legal restrictions made this effort difficult. The IBRD's Articles of Agreement required that a loan be guaranteed by the borrower government in order to better align the incentives of the government with that of development. If a loan was issued to an organization other than a member government, then it still must be guaranteed by "the member or the central bank or some comparable agency of the member which is acceptable to Bank" (US Treasury 1944, 57). This requirement was possible with government-sponsored projects, which were eager to attract international financing, but problematic when supporting private enterprise. Governments were reluctant to guarantee specific private enterprises because they wanted to avoid accusations of favoritism, particularly when the enterprise was supporting a public project. Private enterprises feared that a guarantee would inevitably lead to greater government interference in their management and operations. The consequence of this policy was that nearly all of the IBRD's initial project loans were to public works. Few involved private enterprises.

To fund the IBRD's growing financial commitments, the institution relied on capital markets. Beginning in earnest in the early 1950s, the IBRD started to raise an increasing portion via bond issuances; by 1967, the IBRD had raised USD 5.7 billion on international capital markets. Yet throughout this process, the IBRD was careful to ensure that money raised through the sales of securities in foreign markets was channeled to productive projects. This was ensured through four provisions. First, that the borrower government guarantees the loan, better aligning business and political incentives. Second, that the borrower would be unable to obtain the loan in the market, in order to prevent crowding out other private financial institutions. Third, that it didn't provide conditions of the proceeds of its loans to be used in any tied manner. Fourth, that project decisions are economic rather than political (IBRD 1968, 97–100). In addition, project assessments were quite rigorous. Emphasis was placed on contribution to broader development rather than pure profitability concerns. Technical assistance was also emphasized, though financial resources to provide technical assistance were constrained. By 1968, the IBRD alone had provided a cumulative total of USD 11.25 billion in funds to 85 countries across 552 separate loans (World Bank 1968, 97).

Though the first two decades were tumultuous, the early experiences of the IBRD laid the groundwork for marketized development financial instruments. The IBRD's assessment missions concluded that private investment was the only path for economic growth, and development policy should facilitate this. When domestic and international private capital was unavailable or insufficient, development institutions should target projects that benefit private investment. The IBRD's loans in practice demonstrated an early iteration of marketized development financial instruments—they were indirectly backed by donor governments via the IBRD and relied on market-based intermediaries to distribute loans. However, these methods were limited in their complexity and were blunt instruments for reaching private entrepreneurs, particularly SMEs. While the IBRD raised money from capital markets, it still struggled to attract any private investors as co-sponsors. As such, two additional avenues of development policy were developed to more directly engage private capital—the IFC and DFCs.

The International Finance Corporation (IFC)

In 1951, the United States International Development Advisory Board and the IBRD jointly floated a proposal to establish an institution fully dedicated to the promotion of private enterprise, a proposition supported by the UN a year later (IBRD 1952, 7). While the IBRD endeavored to indirectly support private investment, development practitioners were eager to create a dedicated institution that could exclusively focus on the private sector. These efforts were initially hamstrung by disagreements over mission scope and financing, but the International Finance Corporation was founded in 1956 to support private enterprises without government intervention. As the IFC's first annual report boldly proclaimed, the IFC "will not invest in undertakings which are government owned and operated, or in the management of which the government participates to any significant extent" (IFC 1957, 2). In its first decade, however, the IFC faced two challenges—first, it lacked sufficient resources to mobilize private investment, and second, operational requirements restricted its ability to control the incentives of financial intermediaries. Two reforms mitigated these challenges and, more importantly, were instructive for the shift to marketized development financial instruments. For one, the IFC was permitted to take equity stakes, giving the IFC much greater control over how the investment was administered. In addition, the IFC was permitted to accept large-scale loans from the IBRD, essentially securing long-term, stable capital. Together, these two reforms provided a crucial stepping stone to implementing marketized development financial instruments.

The IFC and the Mobilization of Private Finance

The IFC was envisioned to serve as a supplementary financer for private enterprise and was meant to lubricate the market by compensating for the illiquidity of the domestic banking sector. Unlike the IBRD, the IFC was mandated to conduct its investments based on a combination of business viability and contribution to the country's larger economic goals. Consequently, investments and loans were meant to be provided at market rates and had no provision for direct subsidization. The IFC had a mandate to promote economic development, but its criteria were broad, and included a spectrum from increasing local employment to generating foreign exchange to developing resource extraction capabilities. The IFC insisted that these two objectives were mutually compatible.

Initial targets were industrial firms and priority would be given to those enterprises located in the least developed member countries. Since financing was intended to be supplementary, the IFC's total investment was never to exceed half of the total value of the enterprise. Its investment participation was also unconventional; rather than providing fixed-interest loans, the investment could instead be a mix of share capital and loans. While at the beginning it was not permitted to invest in equity, the IFC could use programs that possessed quasi-equity features. For instance, the IFC could invest in convertible debt instruments that, upon selling to private investors, could be converted to capital shares. Similar to the IBRD, the IFC had a small amount of funding available for technical and management training, which they used to improve the institutional capacity of the enterprise. However, when the enterprise was sufficiently attractive to private investors, the IFC was supposed to divest.

Perhaps most importantly, IFC investments did not require a government guarantee, thereby avoiding the complications that the IBRD had encountered. The IFC described itself "as a catalytic agent to encourage the flow of private capital into productive enterprise" and that it endeavored "to function as would an experienced private investor, combining caution with adventure and seeking rewards reasonable in relation to the risks" (IFC 1958, 6).

In addition to investing its own capital, the IFC would serve a secondary function as a purveyor of information regarding local market conditions. Aside from the well-known risks of developing country investment—including nontransparent governance, lack of technical capacity, and nonexistent capital markets—private enterprises were also unfamiliar with investment opportunities in developing countries. Assessment of domestic market potential, the regulatory framework, and infrastructure were difficult to complete, because of both cost and distance. The IFC could equalize opportunities: "[The] IFC incurs substantial expense in such investigations and in developing projects to the point where they are suitable for investment. IFC finds that this is a value to private investors interested in the IFC type of financing" (IFC 1959, 10–11). Under this strategy, the IFC could catalyze investment through project pre-approval and assessment, and could signal to investors potentially feasible projects in developing countries, significantly lowering the barriers to doing business. Together with the IFC's own financing capabilities, it was hoped that the IFC could quickly mobilize private investment.

When the IFC was established on 24 July 1956, 31 countries provided a total capital subscription of USD 78 million; by September 1957, this had risen to 51 member countries and USD 92 million. During the first year, the IFC entered into four commitments totaling USD 5.32 million, all of which helped finance private industrial companies in Latin America, and, by the end of the fiscal year, another 25–30 projects were under consideration. By 1958, the IFC had received 235 proposals and disbursed an additional USD 6 million for seven new projects, reinforcing to IFC staff that a pent-up demand for financing existed (IFC 1958, 7). The IFC also managed to register a net income of USD 1.675 million (IFC 1957, 5).

By the end of the 1950s, the IFC functioned more like an investment firm rather than a development institution. Key to this success was that the IFC obtained the authority to make loans in both local and foreign currencies to private firms, in addition to not requiring government guarantees. This combination was perhaps its greatest comparative advantage in its early years (Matecki 1957, 36–39). During this period, the IFC became a more forceful advocate against government management of private enterprises. In 1959, the IFC proudly proclaimed that "powerful economic forces are working towards the expansion of private industrial production in the developing areas of the free world" driven by a "growing realization by governments of many of these countries that the dynamic force of private enterprise is needed into order to utilize adequately their natural and human resources and improve living standards for their people" (IFC 1959, 4). In addition, in pursuit of its role in stimulating the flow of capital, the IFC had also secured a few commercial partners for co-investments, such as for a wood pulp mill in Brazil and a copper mine and smelter in Chile.

The apparent early success of the IFC, however, belied underlying problems. For one, the IFC's proposed initial capitalization was to be USD 500 million, more than 5 times the USD 92 million that materialized. The Articles of Agreement also presented constraints. The IFC was initially prohibited from pursuing equity investments, leaving it with less ability to influence the management of the enterprise in which it had invested. Most critically, the mission of the IFC was contradictory. The IFC was meant to promote national economic development through private enterprise investment in cases where sufficient private capital was not available on market terms. This was a fundamentally problematic proposition—its potential investments were the ones that were already deemed unprofitable by commercial banks yet were still classified as productive for the national economy. Furthermore, the maximum size of investment for any single project was set at USD 2 million, eliminating some investment opportunities. Mason and Asher summarize the challenges that faced the IFC:

> The IFC, in short, had to find investment projects that were marginal to begin with, that were relatively small (and perhaps more likely to have deficiencies of management and other capabilities), that could survive the rigors of the IFC's careful technical examination, and that would emerge (because of the ban on equity investment by the corporation) in forms that were often unfamiliar in less developed countries. (1973, 351)

Even though the IFC managed to profitably grow in the remaining years of the 1950s, the contradictory nature of the IFC's mandate severely hampered its operations.

The IFC also encountered difficulties outside its control. For instance, the envisioned private financial flows did not materialize in ways necessary for transformational economic growth. In developing countries, nationalistic arguments prevented a full embrace of private enterprise, and particularly FDI. These restrictions included limiting foreign control, unsound macroeconomic financial policies, cumbersome government regulations, and high taxation. Persistent difficulties with domestic infrastructure similarly reduced reliability, as replacement parts needed to be shipped from abroad, or government permitting process was often slow. Even when private enterprises invested, the IFC also found that foreign enterprises often over-estimated the growth potential for domestic markets, or at least underestimated the amount of time necessary for market maturation. Yet the IFC was equally critical of industrialized countries for not doing more to facilitate investment. It recommended that industrialized governments should increase "the flow of private investment [to developing countries] by means of tax and similar incentives" (IFC 1959, 7).

The Early 1960s: Reform and Expansion

In an effort to increase the efficacy of the institution, the IFC underwent two critical reforms. First, in 1961, the Articles of Agreement were changed to permit equity stakes. This greatly simplified the investment process and granted the IFC more flexibility when negotiating new deals and underwriting new sales. It could also behave more like a traditional investor; as a shareholder, the IFC could actively participate in the management of the enterprise, imparting its experience and global best practices to the company. In short time, IFC equity investments rapidly increased. By 1967, the IFC's "usual investment consisted of an equity investment together with a long-term loan, and by the end of that year 39% of its disbursed and outstanding investments were held by the Corporation in equity" (IBRD 1968, 96). Second, in 1965, a series of amendments allowed the IFC to borrow from the "World Bank amounts up to four times the Corporation's own unimpaired capital and surplus, or a total at that time of about [USD] 400 million" (IBRD 1968, 96). In October 1966, the World Bank extended a line of credit worth USD 100 million to the IFC, after lifting the USD 2 million project limit. These reforms substantially expanded IFC's operational capacity, particularly in Asia and Africa. Moreover, these reforms foreshadowed the changes that development institutions would later implement in order to operationalize marketized development financial instruments.

Reform 1: 1961 Equity Stakes

The prohibition of equity stakes severely curtailed the IFC's ability to directly influence how private enterprises were managed. The opportunity to hold equity stakes resulted in three broad changes to its abilities. First, the IFC began to participate more actively in private enterprise, occasionally obtaining seats on the Board of Directors. Equity stakes had the added benefit of providing handsome profit margins to the IFC as well. Second, the IFC began to extend beyond industrial investments and into the promotion of domestic capital markets. With greater participation in the firm, it could promote capital markets on a micro-level. Finally, the IFC was permitted to investment in the network of DFCs that the IBRD had been expanding.

First, the IFC was permitted to directly invest in private enterprises. Equity stakes simplified the investment procedure and reduced the need for complex investment negotiations. Greater IFC participation also provided the IFC with a closer working relationship with management and, therefore, more control over the investment. Training and advisory services, particularly when the IFC was able to attract an international commercial banking partner, accelerated the transfer of knowledge (IFC 1963, 3).[2] In short time, equity participation by the IFC had grown substantially. In 1962, 17% of the IFC's total investment portfolio consisted of shares; in 1963, this percentage climbed to 30% and by 1967 had risen again to 40%. 1967 also marked the first year that every new commitment involved equity participation (IFC 1967, 6). At the end of the 1970s, the average annual return on equity investments was 9.8%, slightly higher than the 8.6% return on loans. This amounted to USD 142.5 million in sales receipts, or just over one-quarter of the IFC's total resources (IFC 1970, 15–16).

[2] Nevertheless, the Board of Governors was careful not to give too much power to the IFC, however, putting into the amendment that the IFC "the Corporation shall not assume responsibility for managing any enterprise in which it has invested and shall not exercise voting rights for such purpose or for any other purpose which, in its opinion, properly is within the scope of the managerial control" (IFC 1961, 10).

Second, the IFC expanded into capital market development. The IFC viewed the development of the domestic capital market as critical to deepening the financial sector. However, the IFC possessed neither sufficient capital nor the technological expertise to develop a capital market *de novo*. In the late 1950s, the IFC was engaging in preliminary capital market development activities, including counseling to developing country experts on how to establish a capital market, rewriting government regulations and statutes, as well as providing training on new securities instruments. In addition, the IFC funded facilities that comprise the institutional framework of a capital market, such as "securities exchanges or other facilities for the sale and purchase of securities" (IBRD 1968, 108). These were helpful in improving the government's technical ability, but did little to increase the volume of transactions.

The equity stake reform allowed the IFC to directly promote capital market development through increasing the quantity of securities available for trading. The IFC's equity investment in a private enterprise did more than supply financing—it also demonstrated that an international economic institution was willing to invest in the enterprise. With this vote of confidence from the IFC, the enterprise could more easily raise additional financing in the capital markets and, in some cases, the IFC would often underwrite the shares (IBRD 1968, 96). When the capital market was insufficient, the IFC could also arrange for other financial institutions to directly purchase shares. Moreover, it was envisioned that as enterprises that were funded by the IFC matured, the IFC would sell its portfolio investments into the domestic capital market. This would supply the market with a reputable investment, building trust among investors not only in the enterprise, but also in the larger capital market as well. With the sale of the IFC stake, ownership would then revert back to local investors who would then keep the profits. For the IFC, this would enable it to redeploy its recycled funds, as the principal investment would be recuperated and then reinvested in another private enterprise.

Finally, the IFC was supportive of DFCs because they were easy to finance, required less management than issuing a single-project loan, and would impart long-lasting operational knowledge to the developing country institution. However, in the first five years of operation, the IFC was not permitted to make equity investments, a restriction that extended to DFCs as well. Loans to DFCs were permitted, but until then the IFC had avoided making loans because of limited capital and the inability to participate in DFC management. The 1961 reforms changed this relationship. In particular, the IFC could acquire equity stakes in DFCs, where it could then actively participate in the management (IBRD 1968, 96). During the next four years, the IFC "made a series of equity investments in DFCs and accepted invitations to be represented on the boards of ten of the companies" (Mason and Asher 1973, 352).

The implications of the reform to permit equity stakes were twofold. First, the IFC could lubricate domestic financial markets by increasing the quantity and quality of bonds, through its own direct participation, its guarantees, and DFCs. Second, the IFC had much greater authority to control the financial intermediaries. Both were crucial steps to facilitating private investment and fully embracing marketized development financial instruments.

Reform 2: Greater Borrowing Capacity

The second substantial reform occurred in 1965, when the IFC was permitted to borrow up to USD 400 million in funds from the IBRD. This arrangement was mutually beneficial. The IFC would be able to finance significantly more projects than it otherwise could. This was particularly important because the IFC now acted "for the whole [World Bank] group in the technical and financial appraisal, preparation and supervision of industrial and mining projects" (IFC 1965, 5). The IBRD could solve the difficulties it was having in supporting private investment. Since investment by the IFC did not require a government guarantee, it could more easily attract private partners (IFC 1964, 5). In this way, the IBRD could still promote the private economy while simultaneously circumventing its own restrictions.

The availability of new resources greatly expanded the IFC's loan capacity. From 1956 to 1966, the average size of investments had been USD 1.4 million; in 1967, that rose to USD 4.5 million (IBRD 1968, 96). The IFC also expanded commitments outside of its primary investment area of Latin America, enabling it to have larger projects in Asia and Africa. Even though the IFC was able to expand its growth, a high recovery rate of the Corporation's funds through the sales of commitments obviated the need for the IFC to draw upon IBRD credit by 1970. This was because the IFC was selling its equity stakes in investments, earning interest from loans, and receiving dividends from DFCs. As William Gaud remarked in an internal memo to William Diamond in 1970, "I was greatly interested in your memorandum of January 15 listing the dividends we are now receiving and can expect to receive from development finance companies. I did not know you were making us so rich. Thanks!" (Gaud 1970).

The Late 1960s and 1970s: Expanding the IFC's Mission

The first decade of IFC operations had witnessed substantial change in both scope and operations. The successes of the 1961 and 1965 reforms greatly bolstered the confidence and operations of the IFC, opening new avenues for investment promotion and—crucially—revenue generation. Loans expanded beyond industry and now included agricultural, tourism, food processing, fertilizers, and mining. Equity capital had become nearly half of the IFC's total investments, and a strategy of heavily investing in DFCs was well underway. The financial achievements were impressive. Between 1956 and 1970, cumulative gross commitments had reached USD 476 million. In 1970 alone, the IFC reached a new high of USD 79 million in new loans and USD 32.8 million in new equity investments. The Corporation's net income had reached a high of USD 9.2 million, or an average of 9% across its portfolio, which had also greatly expanded the IFC's assets to USD 415 million (IFC 1970, 3).

The IFC was eager to build upon its successes in the next decade. In 1969, the IFC saw its previous activities of infrastructure as the foundation for industrialization and the growth of commerce, and it was now prepared to translate these achievements into sustained growth. Underpinning this logic was a conviction that a rising standard of living required rising per capita consumption, a process that occured when investment raised productivity levels (IFC 1969, 4). The private sector was believed to be the best way to achieve this. By 1970, fully 95% of the IFC's investments were directed toward industrial development.

During this second phase, the IFC also added flexibility to some of its long-standing policies. Mirroring the changes at the IBRD, the IFC began considering investments in private enterprises in which the government had a minority stake. Additionally, the IFC maintained the previous investment limit of USD 20 million per investment, but also noted that these limits could be "set aside when appropriate" (IFC 1970, 14). The IFC also increased staff in the area of project identification and promotion in an effort to expose more local enterprises to IFC operations. Finally, between 1970 and 1971, the IFC supported, for the first time, privately-owned regional development institutions, Adela in Latin

America and SIFIDA in Africa. The IFC hoped to leverage existing institutional infrastructures to find more bankable projects. The greater local knowledge of the regional institutions also enabled them to pursue investments in entrepreneurial activities, an area that until then had eluded IFC attention.

In 1971, the IFC declared that it was ready to expand into the mobilization and utilization of local capital, noting that it "has specifically sought, through joint ventures, to embrace local investors in the less developed countries in its operations, and so to stimulate the growth and flow of local capital" (IFC 1971, 11). The IFC's objective to catalyze growth via the domestic private sector was no secret. Yet it had taken fifteen years to build sufficient infrastructure and domestic institutions to make this possible. Central to this vision was further empowering local investors. To achieve this, the IFC declared in 1971 that it would only invest "in projects where there is provision for immediate or eventual participation by local investors" (IFC 1971, 11). Previously-implemented policies were also succeeding; cumulative underwriting from 1962 to 1971 had reached USD 50.1 million, with USD 14 million in 1971 alone (IFC 1971, 14). The newly-established Capital Markets Department had also created and supported financial institutions to channel domestic savings into productive investment. The IFC began supporting institutions around the world to perform this task, through which the IFC was able to delegate more of its operations, as well as have a greater impact with fewer staff and less financing.

Yet concurrent with these successes, the early 1970s also proved challenging for the IFC. Externally, the international economic situation had rapidly deteriorated. The erosion of the gold standard between 1971 and 1976 ushered in an era of floating exchange rates that adversely affected many developing country currencies, particularly if they possessed US dollar-denominated liabilities. This was coupled with a series of liquidity crises, the rapid increase in the global price of oil, and a global economic recession. There was also a marked uptick in the number of nationalizations. The IFC saw its investment portfolio growth slow, with both sales and operating income vacillating at lower levels than their highs at the end of the 1960s. Total commitments continued to grow with an additional capital subscription in 1978.

Despite the challenges, the IFC maintained its steadfast dedication to support the mobilization of private finance. Its operations reflected the perspective that underdevelopment could be solved via engaging the private sector in productive investments, and that development institutions could catalyze these transformations. The IFC's reformation provided an early solution to the challenges of using financial markets and instruments in a development context, particularly in ways to directly influence how financial intermediaries operated. While the IFC's investments would still face numerous challenges, it provided an important step to solidifying the shift toward marketized development financial instruments.

Development Finance Companies (DFCs)

Perhaps the greatest step toward marketized development financial instruments came with the advent of development finance companies (DFCs). While the IBRD and IFC were dedicated to private sector promotion, internal regulations and high costs restricted their ability to reach private entrepreneurs and SMEs. DFCs provided a solution to both. Since risk assumption of the institution could be guaranteed to a financial institution rather than the project, DFCs could issue loans with implicit IBRD guarantees or, occasionally, directly with IBRD credit lines. In this way, the IBRD and IFC could reach small, private borrowers. Most importantly, DFCs distributed funding according to market principles in the hope that they would avoid creating moral hazards on the part of recipients. By 1960, the IBRD had supplied over USD 88 million in assistance to DFCs (Boskey 1962, 299), and by 1980 that number had ballooned to USD 6.4 billion through a mix of loans, equity, and technical assistance. As such, DFCs were a progenitor to marketized development financial instruments because development institutions used donor government guarantees and credit lines to facilitate the lending activities of private financial intermediaries. While DFCs encountered numerous challenges, the problems they faced greatly informed how development institutions would revise their strategy for future marketized development financial instruments.

DFCs as a Solution

While the IBRD and IFC desired to support private entrepreneurs, they both lacked the bureaucratic capacity and financial resources to realize this goal. Moreover, the Articles of Agreement required that these institutions obtain a government guarantee, rendering many projects—particularly those that were smaller and privately-operated—impractical to individually administer. DFCs were viewed as an optimal solution. DFCs were specifically designed to complement the commercial banking sector and spur growth through the provision of long-term financing and managerial assistance. The IBRD—eager to provide investments to encourage private sector development—could channel its resources to countries via these local institutions, which were guaranteed by the recipient government. DFCs could also finance smaller domestic projects where it was unfeasible for the IBRD to do so. The IBRD, and in particular William Diamond, spearheaded the efforts to establish a network of DFCs. Since DFCs were required to receive World Bank approval for the disbursement of its loans, the Bank maintained a supervisory role. This could all occur more or less according to market principles—minimal government intervention, a reliance on private initiative, a utilization of near-market interest rates, and a self-help financial system were the foundation for IBRD's DFC strategy.

When the idea for establishing a global network of DFCs was first floated in the early 1950s, economists at the IBRD envisioned five roles for DFCs. First, they could supply long-term capital for industrial expansion. Domestic private commercial banks favored small, short-term loans that were higher margin and lower risk, but these did not satisfy industrial demand. Unlike their commercial banking counterparts, DFCs could plan for loan maturities of 15 years or longer because of the financial stability guarantees from the IBRD. This would enable the construction of capital-intensive industries, such as steel mills, oil refineries, and heavy manufacturing that, in turn, would spark economic growth. In order to avoid competition with existing commercial banks, private banks were encouraged to take equity stakes in DFCs.

Second, a DFC could "effectively encourage the growth of a capital market" (Boskey 1962, 304). This would be achieved in two ways. First, DFCs could introduce new financial instruments such as convertible bonds, preferred shares, and share options, inducing other companies in the country to upgrade their own practices (IBRD 1968, 109). Second, the DFCs themselves could sell bonds in the domestic market. This would raise capital for domestic projects outside of government transfers and expose first-time investors to new financial instruments. DFCs were thought to be attractive investment opportunities because of their diversified risk portfolio, government guarantee, stricter financial practices, and managerial oversight from the World Bank. Firms with NDB-sponsored loans would also face stricter financial reporting standards, thereby increasing fiscal transparency.

Third, DFCs could promote entrepreneurial activity by undertaking "research and surveys to uncover promising industrial fields, perhaps those in which import substitution is feasible, which have export possibilities, or which would make intensive use of indigenous raw materials" (Boskey 1962, 305). DFCs provided an attractive hands-off approach because they could offer financing accompanied with advice, but would not be in the business of founding new enterprises. Nor were they envisioned to even take majority equity stakes in corporations it financed, as "considerations of financial prudence dictated that a DFC should limit its equity exposure to…10% of its own capital for its own capital base for any one venture, and to 100% for its total equity portfolio" (Hu 1981, 49). This would ensure that individuals could engage in economic activities without the fear of government intervention.

Fourth, DFCs provided technical assistance to firms. The IBRD noted that oftentimes limited technical and managerial skills—not the lack of financing or entrepreneurial spirit—prevented the development of the private sector in a developing country. Thus, a DFC "can serve as a nucleus for technical services, available to recipients of its financing or possibly even to industrialists who have not applied to the bank for financing" (Boskey 1962, 306). The Bank especially encouraged technical assistance to SMEs since they lacked the necessary experience in management, financing, and marketing. More importantly, since a DFC had an interest in long-term success rather than short-run repayment, a DFC's incentives would align better with the enterprise than those of the commercial banks.

Finally, DFCs would reinforce domestic institutions and decentralized decision-making. Early conceptions saw DFCs as conduits for IBRD operations. However, soon DFCs were demonstrated to have "institution-building" potential. With DFCs, the IBRD was no longer responsible for each project; instead, "responsibility for project appraisal and supervision was on DFCs. The Bank's activity was concentrated on the evaluation of the institution's performance in these as well as other areas. Decentralized decision-making was at the heart of the institutional approach and the major distinguishing feature of the Bank's DFC operations" (Gulhati 1971, 3). This would enable the World Bank to leverage its impact with relatively little financing.

To the World Bank, DFCs were a win-win strategy. Developing countries received more financing than they could otherwise mobilize from domestic investments or borrow on international capital markets. The World Bank Group could coordinate a global development renaissance without large investments of its own working capital or the assumption of project equity risk. Investments were diversified across many projects and countries. Moreover, it could discourage investment in projects that the Bank deemed undeserving of subsidization—investments were largely prohibited from funding state-owned enterprises (SOEs) or projects that could raise money on its own on the capital markets, such as often in resource extraction. A World Bank publication succinctly summarized their objectives: "The World Bank Group's objective in promoting development finance companies is to help build strong and effective domestic investment institutions which can channel local savings, external capital and local and foreign knowhow into productive private enterprise" (IBRD 1968, 110).

In the early 1950s, the Bank defined the scope of the institutions it was willing to engage with, and through 1968 disproportionately invested—and often created—DFCs along three dimensions. First, many of them were privately owned. Existing national development banks were viewed as lumbering bureaucracies that were as inflexible as they were ineffective. The World Bank argued that ownership should fall to a domestic consortium of large industrialists, insurance companies, and even commercial banks that wanted to spur the domestic economic environment. The Bank's early policies preferred these types of DFCs because of a "belief that the project appraisals and investment decisions of privately controlled institutions would likely be sounder and less politically motivated than those of government entities" (Gordon 1983, 8). Private ownership of an NDB did not render the bank free from government intervention, however, since special permission was often necessary to establish the DFC with exemptions from domestic regulations. Concessional financing—usually through government subsidies or low-interest loans—was ubiquitous and encouraged. In short, "the government was to make a substantial contribution to the capital base of the DFC without assuming corresponding voting power" (Hu 1981, 48). Yet even though there was extensive private capitalization, it was never entirely divorced from government finances and, implicitly, the political and economic objectives of, and possible interference by, the government.

Second, these banks were restricted to financing private enterprises. State-owned enterprises were not eligible for World Bank-sponsored funds. To Bank officials, the frequent lackluster performance of state-owned enterprises raised too many questions about perverse incentives and government intervention. It also reflected a larger ideological conviction that private actors operated with better incentives to pursue economic growth (Hu 1981, 48). In an effort to mobilize private financing of private enterprises, the World Bank often required DFCs to find domestic partners as a precondition to obtain World Bank loans. For instance, DFCs in Ecuador, Morocco, and Turkey sought matching private partners for their investments (Gordon 1983, 16). These remained requirements of Bank-sponsored loans until 1971.

Finally, these banks specifically targeted the private industrial sector. This belief diverged considerably from the commonly accepted rationale for national development banks. Existing NDBs—such as Germany's KfW and Brazil's BNDES—historically provided financing to large infrastructure projects and agricultural development, in addition to industry, in order to alleviate bottlenecks in the national economy. This often included the large-scale financing of SOEs. However, since the World Bank already provided project loans to large-scale infrastructure projects, the objective of the DFCs was specifically to prioritize industry-oriented DFCs out of a conviction that industrialization via private entrepreneurs was the most efficient way toward economic, and tacitly political, modernization.

Aside from the Bank's proclivity to support the expansion of private enterprises through DFCs, two other factors help explain the Bank's support for DFCs. First, according to the Bank's charter, any loan made to a non-governmental borrower was required to have a government guarantee. However, private industrialists often refused government guarantees because they thought it would invite unwanted interference into their business affairs. Conversely, governments often hesitated to directly invest in private firms out of fear of demonstrating favoritism to any one enterprise, or to private industry over public investment projects. Therefore, DFCs served as an important conduit through which the World Bank could directly finance small private industrial projects in countries either without appropriate appraisal mechanisms or with large distrust between the private sector and the government. Second, DFCs served as an important intermediary institution that would undertake a detailed technical and creditworthiness appraisal for the Bank, thereby reducing administrative costs for the Bank (Boskey 1959, 4). Projects that utilized

Bank funding, even when administered through the national development bank, still required approval from the World Bank to ensure that funds were used productively and properly, as well as to educate the development bank in techniques of project appraisal and implementation.

The resulting strategy offered numerous advantages. Local industrialists were more likely to trust financing from the Bank via a DFC than from a local commercial bank. Lending through a DFC was also more palatable than a government, which bore only ancillary risk and was removed from any of the political problems associated with the borrower. Practically, the localization of financing meant that the DFC would be in a more advantageous position to assess the potential and creditworthiness of investments, and correspondingly reduced the burden on the World Bank to assess and monitor projects. Moreover, this also enabled the Bank to fund an increasing number of small industrial projects that would have otherwise been too risky or costly (Boskey 1962, 300). Outside of the operational advantages, the World Bank noted that DFCs could maintain the Bank's continued influence in the domestic industrialization process (Diamond and Gulhati 1973).

1950–1968: The Growth of DFC Partnerships

The Bank's first experience with DFCs was in Ethiopia and was formed following a request from Ethiopian officials to attract private financing (Diamond 1984, 9). Shortly after, the World Bank concluded a similar agreement with Turkey at the request of the Turkish government and private industry (cf. Yazici 1962). Much like the Ethiopian DFC, the Turkish bank was designed to incentivize private investment and foster the development of a securities market (IBRD 1950b, 4). Over the next few years, the World Bank participated in the formation of the Industrial Credit and Investment Corporation of India (ICICI, founded in 1955) and the Pakistan Industrial Credit and Investment Corporation (PICIC, founded in 1957), as well as loans to DFCs in Finland, Malaysia, and Thailand in 1964 (World Bank 1964, 9). However, the World Bank Group observed that the financial and technical support of DFCs was not always sufficient to achieve their development goals. A 1956 internal report found that credit operations in Turkey were very successful, yet only modestly impactful in Ethiopia and negligible in Mexico (IBRD 1956, 1–2). One impediment was the relatively low level of economic management knowledge within the bureaucracies. This included both the staff and executives of the DFCs as well as government ministries. Support emerged for an institute that could satisfy both the Bank's financial training and research needs.

The Economic Development Institute (EDI) was founded by the Bank to serve these functions. In 1954, the Ford Foundation and Rockefeller Foundation agreed to provide the budget for the EDI for the first three years. Alec Cairncross, then a professor at the University of Glasgow, was selected as the first director of the EDI. It was decided that a group of bankers and government ministers should be selected to attend a six-month course in Washington DC to both learn and share their experience. The first class was held from January through June in 1956. In 1960, in partnership with the Rockefeller Foundation, the EDI provided English-language books, articles, and reference materials to developing governments. They were chosen for their usefulness for practitioners in solving problems of economic development (IBRD 1968, 66). As the demand for project preparation increased, the EDI added shorter curriculums of two and three months. These were targeted to the preparation and evaluation of projects in specific sectors of industry, agriculture, transportation, and education.

In an effort to create a collaborative forum for DFCs, the Bank hosted in 1958 a meeting of 12 representatives of DFCs. The Bank staff was particularly heartened by the uniformity of policies that the banks had adopted—all financed financially sound projects, provided loans in duration of 5 to 15 years, and required security for their loans. Unproven programs such as import substitution policies, entrepreneurial investments, underwriting, and capital market development were largely eschewed (Rao 1958). However, the World Bank also noticed a dilemma because all of the DFCs "wanted to make the maximum contribution to industrial development, yet, on the other hand, they wanted to make the maximum contribution to the development of their own banks as financial instruments for development" (Demuth 1958, 4).

In 1962, the Bank also restructured how DFCs related to the institution. For the first decade, special consultants assessed and implemented most of the Bank's promotional work on DFCs. For instance, George Woods, who would later become president of the World Bank, was the chief consultant on the organization of ICICI, PICIC, and the Private Development Corporation of the Philippines. In January 1962, all of the work relating to DFCs was transferred to a Development Finance Company Division housed within the IFC. The DFCD was headed by

DFC enthusiast William Diamond, and the staff worked on all aspects relating to DFCs on a full-time basis (Mason and Asher 1973, 325). It was during this period of IFC coordination that the DFCs received the most amount of financing. Originally, the DFCD was limited to promotion, technical assistance, and policy guidance, but over the years accumulated the responsibility of managing all operations and relations between the Bank and DFCs. This included considering "proposals for the establishment of new industrial development finance companies predominantly private in character, or for financial and technical assistance to such companies" (IFC 1963, 4). Expansion in Latin America became a central objective operation (Kapur et al. 1997, 821).

Both the change to the IFC charter that permitted equity investments by the institution and the transfer of DFC coordination further spurred investments in DFCs. The IFC's first investment following the 1962 restructuring was a USD 2 million loan to both the Corporación Financiera Colombiana de Desarrollo Industrial and the Corporación Financiera Nacional in Colombia. These investments enabled them to expand their activities to equity participation, long-term financing, and underwriting. Later that same year, the IFC supported a cement plant in conjunction with PICIC, which had obtained its funds from a World Bank loan (IFC 1962, 11). Also in 1962, the Bank and IFC provided the first combined financial assistance to a Moroccan DFC, marking the beginning of coordinated strategy by the World Bank Group to provide the right mix of loans and equity stakes (IFC 1963, 18). Expansion accelerated in the next year, as the IFC invested in 7 DFCs and helped in the capitalization of 13 others. It also participated in the foundation of new DFCs in the Philippines and Nigeria. Consequently, the financial support from the Bank and IDA began to decrease, and by 1964, they had provided USD 282.9 million, primarily in support of ICICI and PICIC, or roughly 3.3% of the total cumulative operations (World Bank 1964, 40). Funding remained focused on industry, housing, and agricultural projects. In 1962, funding to development banks was 7.5% of total DAC funding, most of which was US funding. USAID authorized 57 loans worth USD 386 million to 49 different institutions in 32 countries. Other European countries provided the remaining amounts, with particular support from the UK, France, and Germany (OECD 1964, 13). In 1963, George Woods, the new president of the World Bank, softened the Bank's strict policy against lending to industrial projects in the public sector, though it remained official policy to not lend to public enterprise until 1968 (Mason and Asher 1973, 373–74).

For its part, the IFC provided a growing list of services, and within two years of beginning, its coordinating role for DFCs "helped to interest local sponsors in a number of these projects, assisted in drafting corporate charters, advised on capitalization, gave guidance in questions of policy and operating methods, helped find experienced personnel, and recruited the support of outside investors" (IFC 1964, 9) (see Table 2.1). With its equity investments, the IFC was also able to assign board members to BNDE, NIDB, PICIC, IFC of Thailand, MIDF, and Venezolana de Desarrollo. Yet of critical importance to the IFC was to maintain the national character of the domestic institutions, with the belief that "domestic shareholdings should be as widely distributed as is consistent with the potentialities of the local capital market" and that the IFC, if necessary, should sell only to domestic interests to ensure that "these institutions are not controlled from abroad and that the autonomy of national interests is preserved" (IFC 1963, 5).

Table 2.1 Total IFC investment in DFCs, 1969

DFC	*Country*	*Total IFC investment (USD)*	*IFC share %*
Caldas	Colombia	885,666	10.4
Colombiana	Colombia	13,125,891	14.9
Nacional	Colombia	9,695,100	11
Norte	Colombia	4,239,186	17.7
Valle	Colombia	7,932,252	9.5
COFIEC	Ecuador	560,000	9.8
IFF	Finland	14,000	3.6
NIBID	Greece	100,000	7
BIDI	Ivory Coast	140,000	7.1
KDFC	Korea	270,000	14.3
LBIDI	Liberia	100,000	24.9
MIDF	Malaysia	250,000	10
BNDE	Morocco	400,000	24.7
NIDB	Nigeria	2,000,000	25
PICIC	Pakistan	5,000,000	4
BANDESCO	Spain	420,000	8.3
IFCT	Thailand	50,000	8
SNI	Tunisia	300,000	20
TSKB	Turkey	130,000	10.8
CAVENDES	Venezuela	400,000	15

Source Diamond (1969a)

Even in operations in which there were no private domestic stakeholders, the IFC was careful to not act only as a replacement for the private sector. It also sought to mobilize additional investments, particularly from the private financial sector of the developed world, but these institutions were often shielded with smaller equity shares and higher class shares. The IFC further encouraged domestic banks, insurance companies, and leading industrialists to become shareholders. Foreign institutions, such as the IFC, EIB, KfW, and the Asian, African, and Inter-American regional banks, were encouraged to take up minority stakes (Gordon 1983, 8).

The World Bank was also not alone in its investments. USAID and the Commonwealth Development Corporation of the UK found numerous joint ventures with the World Bank in DFCs. Two German institutions—DEG and its parent, KfW—were also active. Hermann Abs, the former head of KfW, was also present on the IFC's external advisory board. Yet unlike the World Bank, these institutions lacked the ability to impact overall economic policy or institution building, and instead supported the conclusions of the World Bank (Thiebach 1970). Funding was often limited to a project or a share smaller than that of the World Bank. Nevertheless, the banks found comfort in mutual engagement. For example, in 1970, the World Bank arranged meetings between its Division heads and Mr. Willi Engel of KfW to discuss potential investment opportunities in DFCs (Diamond 1970a). Joint investments between three or more were common, such as the joint World Bank, USAID, and KfW investment in the Ethiopian Agricultural and Industrial Development Bank (AIDB) (Kpognon 1971).

In the first two decades of DFCs, there was substantial evidence of the success of DFCs (see Table 2.2). By 1969, the IFC alone had supported 21 private DFCs with USD 29 million in commitments (IFC 1969, 12). As a proportion of total DFC shares, the IFC held the highest amount in Nigeria's NIDB (25%), Liberia's LBDI (24.9%), and Morocco's BNDE (24.7%) (Diamond 1969b). Twelve of these DFCs were required by charter to only fund private enterprise, and an additional two were only permitted under special circumstances (Mathew 1970b). The IFC also had representatives on the Board of Directors of 13 of these institutions (World Bank 1969, 2). The IFC even went so far as to find senior staff for DFCs when qualified candidates were unavailable (Diamond 1970b). Additionally, William Diamond, an early supporter of DFCs, noted that DFCs "began to see themselves, not as isolated institutions, but as parts

Table 2.2 Total IDA, IBRD, and IFC investment in loans and equity, through 31 December 1971

DFC	*Country*	*Total amount (USD)*
IVK	Austria	23,288,654
BNB	Brazil	25,000,000
DFCC	Sri Lanka	5,316,343
CDC	Taiwan	52,334,880
CFC Bogota	Colombia	2,023,216
CFN Medellin	Colombia	2,041,966
CFC Caldas	Colombia	701,403
Financieras	Colombia	102,500,000
Del Norte	Colombia	431,282
Del Valle	Colombia	431,282
SOCOFIDE	DRC	15,756,345
COFIEC	Ecuador	8,251,371
DBE	Ethiopia	4,000,000
IFF	Finland	63,151,779
NIBID	Greece	58,219,082
ICICI	India	259,756,143
IMDBI	Iran	154,446,465
ICC	Ireland	10,000,000
IDBI	Israel	60,000,000
BIDI	Ivory Coast	204,081
KDFC	South Korea	55,702,043
LBIDI	Liberia	248,950
MIDF	Malaysia	8,660,204
BNDE	Morocco	97,640,370
CIH	Morocco	10,000,000
NIDB	Nigeria	17,399,516
PICIC	Pakistan	183,875,233
IDB	Pakistan	20,000,000
PDCP	Philippines	64,910,154
DBS	Singapore	5,000,000
BANDESCO	Spain	585,351
IFCT	Thailand	1,429,037
SNI	Tunisia	25,930,096
COFITOUR	Tunisia	9,986,582
IDB	Turkey	128,997,573
CAVENDES	Venezuela	12,836,183
IICY	Yugoslavia	2,000,000
ADELA	L. America	10,000,000
SIFICA	Africa	500,000

Source IBRD (1971)

of an integrated financial community. That is, they began to see that the short-term money market is linked by laws, customs and conceptions of risk to the longer-term capital market, parts of a single system" (Diamond 1981, 14). Thus, at least according to Diamond, the DFCs were impacting private investment mobilization.

Redefining the Relationship Between the World Bank and DFCs

The encouraging results of the 1950s belied some emerging challenges. Of particular concern was how the IFC implemented its strategy in developing countries. Worries began to circulate that IFC economists paid scarce attention to how Bank financing impacted a developing country's comparative advantage and the operations of other industries. Additionally, the rapid growth of Bank lending to DFCs was not seen as to be the appropriate realm for the IFC, which was both a smaller partner of the World Bank Group and whose objectives centered on private investment, not necessarily the banking industry. Incoming World Bank President Robert McNamara concluded that a reformulation of policy may be necessary, especially with regard to DFCs. In particular, two events in the late 1960s helped change the course of the World Bank's relationship with DFCs. First, the World Bank changed its policies vis-à-vis Bank support for government-owned institutions, as the Bank was permitted to invest in SOEs. Second, the Pearson Commission made specific recommendations for the governance and distribution of Western aid. The Commission noted that Western aid operations were insufficient and poorly managed, and recommended that local institutions be granted greater operational autonomy.

First, in June 1968, the World Bank governing board relaxed the requirement that only private DFCs could be funded. Instead, the Bank was permitted to invest in government-controlled DFCs, provided that "their management was sound and autonomous in day-to-day decision-making" (World Bank 1969, 3). Instead of only focusing on the manufacturing industry, they may also fund multi-purpose companies including tourism, housing, and other productive activities. Between 1968 and 1969, the IFC helped create two new companies that were devoted to promoting new enterprise and providing investment services, rather than finance. This increasing flexibility reflected "the importance which the Group attributes to institutions which can mobilize capital, allocate it for productive purposes, promote investment and generally act as intermediaries in the investment process" (World Bank 1969, 3). Furthermore, these changes allowed the financing of SOEs, though prior to disbursement approval and an ad hoc amortized repayment schedule was necessary (Diamond 1970b). While the extension to SOE investment reflected the broader shift within the World Bank, it did further neuter the IFC's claim to DFCs, which did not have to be private. As a result, Bank President Robert McNamara transferred the industrial projects division of the Technical Operations Department of the Bank back to IBRD authority, which only four years prior had been given to the IFC. The limitations of the private market in developing countries also spurred action. The Executive Directors approved the policy change on 24 May 1971, and in November 1971, the World Bank approved its first loan to support public-sector enterprises via the Tanzania Investment Bank (Diamond 1971).

Second, in 1968, then World Bank President Robert McNamara commissioned former Canadian Prime Minister Lester Pearson to assess the achievements of the Bank. The Pearson Commission, as it would become colloquially known, highlighted the numerous shortcomings of the existing international aid regime, particularly emphasizing decreasing donor commitments and the lack of a coordinated strategy among developed countries. While the Commission avoided adjudicating the economic and financial performance of specific DFCs, it did recommend that "aid-givers should provide greater help to development banks and similar institutions in developing countries" (Pearson 1969, 190). Yet the support for local DFCs was rooted in a larger perspective that viewed local decision-making as a better alternative to development economists. In particular, the Commission recommended the utilization of programmatic aid, rather than project aid, to allow recipient countries to fund recurrent costs, refurbishment and expansion projects, and smaller investment projects. It was imagined this would localize development decisions, providing greater autonomy for developing countries and enhancing the aggregate benefit.

The recommendation for programmatic aid impacted the development strategy of the World Bank. According to an internal draft document, the World Bank interpreted this as a way to mitigate the inefficiencies of the conventional project approach as it "tend[ed] to be biased in favor of large-sized investments to the detriment of the relatively small and scattered productive enterprises" (World Bank 1969, 1). Instead, these DFCs could increasingly serve as conduits for increased World Bank Group aid to institutions with knowledge of the local conditions, allowing funds to be used faster and at a localized level. The report also acknowledged the contribution of DFCs to facilitating savings and investment, as well as promoting financial intermediation. Therefore, the original objective of localizing development decisions resulted in the World Bank delegating additional responsibility to financial markets and DFCs.

These two changes to DFC policy prompted a wider reconsideration of how the Group should manage the DFCs, particularly on financial and assessment matters. First, the Bank realized that it needed to provide more assistance in the pre-assessment and implementation phases. To address a growing number of projects in both the private and now public sectors, Chief Economist Ravi Gulhati argued that a standard model could not work for all projects, and that more decision-making authority should be delegated to localities. In addition, he argued for the establishment of a broader framework that "will require changes in governmental policies—tariff, quotas exchange rate, fiscal incentives and the like. The Bank should undoubtedly play a part, as it has in the past, in influencing government decisions in these areas" (Gulhati 1971, 2). Gulhati expressed hope that these DFCs could play a constructive role in remaking government policy, and even recommended that the Bank review its support for a DFC every two years, in case they fail to produce tangible governance outcomes.

Seeing as the Bank viewed the DFCs as another mechanism to influence domestic governance, it was important to have them well trained as well. The Bank used the EDI, arranged for special training of DFC personnel, and assisted the review of specific projects (Gulhati 1970d). By the second half of 1971, the World Bank directly reviewed 60 projects across 9 DFCs (IBRD 1972). While there were disagreements over the minimum thresholds as to when the World Bank needed to be notified when a DFC invested in equity, the Disbursement Division thought that the DFCs "could become lax and not require the necessary documentation from their borrowers as developed with the Industrialization Fund of Finland" (Bladen 1971).

Additionally, the Bank worried that if the financing cost provided to DFCs was too low, this would create adverse incentives for DFCs. The borrowing costs to the Bank were low because it was backed with capital from donor countries and had a AAA credit rating. The advantage was that developing countries were channeled urgently needed capital at rates lower than the market would provide them. Yet, there was a risk that if "the lending rate is too low, allocation of resources will not take place in the most economic manner and a DFC's capital might be used to finance uneconomic projects" (Development Finance Companies Department 1969, 2). Diamond noted that "the presence of low-cost capital (and the hope of getting more of it in the future) may in some cases have deprived a DFC of the discipline of raising capital on market terms and may thus have diminished its potential role as a mobilizer of private savings" (Development Finance Companies Department 1969, 5). One economist already determined that the mobilization of additional private investment has been limited: "An examination of their sources of funds shows that they have operated predominantly as institutions through which foreign funds and domestic budgetary funds have been channeled into private industry" (Kamarck 1969). Another economist argued that the opportunity cost of such capital had never been discussed, and that this quasi-equity distorted the market forces by emboldening DFCs to support less efficient enterprises (Goffin 1969, 1). Moreover, these investments were never reviewed by the government who might want to use it for other projects.

In order to finance these DFCs while minimizing the moral hazard, the Bank attempted to adhere to a structure where low-cost or interest-free loans were only available for the long term and as subordinated to the DFC's other debt. These implicit subsidies enhanced profitability and operational capital, assuring immediate income and better return to private shareholders. As quasi-equity, it was able to be leveraged for additional funds and allowed DFCs to take more risks in investments. However, it was also necessary to monitor the operations of DFCs to ensure that cost savings were passed on to final customers. An internal Bank memo argued that a review of the interest rates charged was warranted, in order to encourage these banks to raise more money from the domestic and private capital market. However, another economist argued against the new stringent regulations on interest rates, nothing that "policy in general dismisses as unacceptable the use of interest incentives by a government to influence the direction of investment" and could actually be "weakening their competitive position by not offering the same incentives." He recommended that the Bank either provide more financing to technical assistance or work with the UNDP or UNIDO to create training programs since talent loss is highly problematic in DFCs (Mathew 1970a).

There also existed other financial problems. There was substantial internal discussion on how much debt service coverage a DFC should maintain and the degree of subordination necessary for a quasi-equity loan to be considered part of the borrowing base, as well as the exclusion of quasi-equity loan maturities from the loan base (cf. Gustafson 1969b; Hasan 1969). Some changes had a deleterious impact on the functioning of DFCs. In March 1969, the Bank announced changes to its currency repayment policies. The Bank would select the currency (or currencies) of disbursement and the repayment schedule, and DFCs would be obliged to repay in those currencies. This was designed to give the Bank more flexibility in the choice of its assets to maximize return, but this change caused problems for DFCs because of higher currency risk. The resulting foreign exchange risk—if not covered by a government guarantee—could possibly create enormous losses for DFCs. Conversely, an upward appreciation of the currency could lead to DFCs making enormous profits, but make sub-loan recipients worse off in real terms (Gustafson 1969a). As one employee lamented, "I do not think to be fitting the Bank's development goals to force losses on DFCs or private enterprise or to allow them making windfall exchange gains as a result of the Bank's repayment practices" (Miraki 1969, 1).

Finally, the Bank had difficulty in measuring the impact of DFCs. As late as 1964, there was no systematic overview of how these disparate DFCs were operating. In 1964, the OECD conducted a comprehensive investigation and found that development banks suffered from the lack of high-skilled labor that could analyze, implement, and evaluate DFC investments (OECD 1964). The Bank had not developed a test for either the financial or, more importantly, the economic return of investment capital by end-users, and what little data they possessed only measured nominal numbers. One economist noted the difficulty of assessing outcomes without standardization: "Without a clear concept of the past and proposed influence of a development finance company on sectoral policy and growth, institutional appraisal is at best incomplete. At worst, it encourages the setting up, or the perpetuation, of an ineffective resource allocation mechanism" (Picciotto 1969). Ravi Gulhati, the World Bank's Chief Economist, noted that the viability criteria with which to adjudicate DFCs were flawed. A DFC is viable when its financial position is able to attract private investors, but, as Gulhati notes, such viability may quickly evaporate if the government were to remove its lending and tax privileges or concessional financial aid from abroad is reduced (Gulhati 1970a). Moreover, the absence of systematic data on DFCs has meant that both time-series and cross-sectional data were absent. He noted that limited comparisons based on socioeconomic indicators and operational structure—such as between the Indian and Pakistan DFCs—would help establish analytical traction.

In an effort to improve understanding of the DFCs, the World Bank developed a more rigorous appraisal process for the DFCs. Gulhati argued for the incorporation of alternative measures outside of financial indicators (Gulhati 1970d) and a more vigorous cost/benefit analysis in order to select projects that had maximal benefit (Gulhati 1970b). He noted that standard financial analysis might not be a suitable guide when the cost-price structure is distorted by an overvalued exchange rate, quantitative import restrictions, or tariff regimes, and provided an initial tool to measure government protection (Gulhati 1970c). Another proposal that Gulhati made was to systematically survey the DFCs regarding their subloans, in particular "to calculate the economic rates of return on Bank loans to development finance companies" (Gulhati 1971, 2). The survey templates included questions regarding the value-addition of the project, the amount of employment generated, the yield from direct taxes, and the net foreign exchange earned per unit of investment (Gulhati 1970e). However, others noted that this still may not go far enough to understanding the problem. As one said, what is needed is "a method to quantify the project's rate of return to society in order to compare it with the financial rate that measures the firm's profitability" (Sanchez-Marco 1970).

While the problems were often identified as those arising from the Bank's policies, the internal memos recognized that borrower country governments were complicit. Diamond noted that the principal responsibility for mobilization and allocation rested with recipient governments, as DFCs can "do little to assure effective mobilization or allocation of resources where policy is not conducive in the first place; nor can they by analytical techniques fully compensate for the distortions which government policies might create" (Development Finance Companies Department 1969, 1). Governments must create the institutional and legal framework; without that, DFCs and more complex financial instruments cannot salvage a project. It also sheds light on the fundamental contradiction—success depends on the ability to create synergies between the international aid agency and the government. If the borrower country is unwilling or unable to perform its part, the development institution has only limited recourse, primarily because of the ire that direct intervention in domestic laws raises. Since even privately-operated DFCs were intimately interrelated with borrower governments, the Bank was often delicately balancing autonomy with development outcomes.

The impact of the 1968 changes was mixed and occasionally contradictory. On the one hand, there was little diversion of World Bank funds to state-owned enterprise investments. In the Europe, Middle East, and North Africa division, for example, only in Morocco (BNDE) and Tunisia (SNI) was Bank financing used for SOE investments by 1971; the rest of the DFCs maintained their policy of exclusively financing private enterprise (Pollan 1971). Part of this was because while DFCs were permitted to support SOEs, they were only allowed to use a minor portion of World Bank loans to state enterprises. This was intended to prevent government pressure on the DFC to finance SOEs with subsidized funding. There also remained continued suspicion on the part of the Bank that DFCs still were dependent on the broader context of investment. As a 1975 DFC policy paper noted, "the innovative impact of any DFC will, however, also largely depend on the quality and vision of the management of the institution; given this, there is no ready-made formula or model that will easily produce dynamic promotional DFCs" (IBRD 1975, v). Yet just the next year in 1976, the emphasis on private investment disappeared from operational statements in the IFC and was replaced by the Bank's growing interest in supporting SOEs (Kapur et al. 1997, 835).

While there may have been disagreements about the particulars of DFC implementation, Bank support for DFCs remained strong. According to the Bank's own Five Year Program, commitments to DFCs from 1969 to 1973 were targeted at around USD 1.5 billion, compared with USD 483 million in the preceding five-year period. Growth was targeted at Latin America and Africa, where the possibility of loaning to government-controlled DFCs was greater. Most importantly, they were able to expand their total investment portfolios. From 1966 to 1970, 17 of the DFCs exhibited portfolio growth of greater than 20% per year, despite strong economic headwinds (Diamond and Gulhati 1973, 49). The IFC was particularly active. By the end of the 1970 fiscal year, the IFC had invested USD 42.5 million in 24 DFCs across 19 countries. Also in 1970, the IFC helped establish two more DFCs—the International Investment Corporation of Yugoslavia (IICY) and Société Congolaise de Financement du Developpement (SOCOFIDE) in the Democratic Republic of the Congo—with a similar joint investment with the IDA, IBRD, national governments, domestic commercial banks, and foreign commercial banks (IFC 1970, 6–8). By 1972, the World Bank had associated itself with

45 DFCs, though with significant heterogeneity (Uecker 1967, M2). Approximately two-thirds of all World Bank lending to the industrial sector during the 1960s were conducted through the DFCs, a quantity that totaled USD 1.7 billion in loans, credits, and equity. Most importantly, most DFCs managed to stay financially solvent, as well as being able to provide a significant amount of funding to fledgling industries, professionalize their bureaucracy, and promote development along a wide range of dimensions including innovation, productivity, and total output (Diamond and Gulhati 1973, 49).

Conclusion

The experiences of the IBRD and IFC through the 1970s are instructive because they laid the foundation for the shift to marketized development financial instruments. As the leading development institution at the time, the IBRD concluded through its assessment missions that private investment was the key to economic development, and that development policy should use limited donor government funding to mobilize private investment. This perspective has shaped the contours of modern development policy. In essence, project loans and DFCs were an early iteration of marketized development financial instruments. DFCs foreshadowed the emergence of financial instruments as they were designed with similar parameters—they were to be quasi-state-backed institutions, promote private enterprise, and, in order to minimize moral hazards, operate according to commercial principles. Reforms at the IFC to maintain equity stakes was another crucial step toward marketized development financial instruments.

Despite the efforts of development institutions, these instruments were unable to mitigate the moral hazards that they created, and both project loans and DFCs suffered from the inability of the IBRD and IFC to directly control investments. Commercial investors were interested in expanding their investments, but development institutions struggled to convince them to take a co-investing role. Nevertheless, these early involvements with project loans and DFCs provided important experience into how development institutions could more effectively mobilize private investment. For development institutions, these critical experiences of the World Bank suggested that donor assistance could be better integrated with financial instruments, so long as moral hazard was reduced and investment oversight enhanced.

References

Alacevich, Michele. 2009. *The Political Economy of the World Bank: The Early Years*. Stanford, CA: Stanford University Press.

Bladen, John. 1971. Disbursements to Development Finance Companies.

Boskey, Shirley. 1959. *Problems and Practices of Development Banks*. Baltimore, MD: The Johns Hopkins Press.

———. 1962. Industrial Credit Institutions. In *Methods of Industrial Development*, ed. Albert Winsemius and John Pincus. Paris: Organization for Economic Co-operation and Development (OECD).

Demuth, R.H. 1958. Statement of R. H. Demuth, Director of Technical Assistance and Liaison, to Meeting of Executive Directors on June 12, 1958, Regarding Conference of Development Bank Representatives.

Development Finance Companies Department. 1969. Interest Rates Charged by Development Finance Companies and Terms of Government Loans to Such Companies.

Diamond, William. 1969a. *Total Shares Outstanding Versus IFC's Shareholding in Development Finance Companies, as of October 31, 1969*. Washington DC: International Bank for Reconstruction and Development.

———. 1969b. Office Memorandum with Mr. William Gaud.

———. 1970a. Letter from William Diamond to Dr. Willi Engel.

———. 1970b. Use of Borrowed Funds for Investments in Share Capital by Development Finance Companies.

———. 1971. Development Bank Policy Changes.

———. 1981. *Reflections on the Performance of Development Banks and the Challenges Ahead*. National Bank of Egypt.

———. 1984. Transcript of a Taped Statement by William Diamond, East Asia and Pacific Department, Industrial Development and Finance Division Retreat.

Diamond, William, and Ravi Gulhati. 1973. World Bank's Experience with Development Finance Companies. *Economic and Political Weekly* 8 (23): M47–56.

Gaud, William S. 1970. IFC Investments in Development Finance Companies.

Goffin, P.C. 1969. Development Finance Companies—Comments on Mr. Diamond's Memorandum of September 12, 1969.

Gordon, David L. 1983. *Development Finance Companies, State and Privately Owned: A Review*. Washington, DC: The World Bank.

Gulhati, Ravi. 1970a. A Few Thoughts on Present Bank Policies Regarding Development Finance Companies.

———. 1970b. Appraisal Reports on Development Finance Companies.

———. 1970c. Economic Appraisal of DFC Projects.

———. 1970d. Economic Aspects of Development Finance Companies Project Appraisal—Dec 30.

———. 1970e. Questionnaire on DFC Sub-Projects.
———. 1971. A Few Thoughts for 1972.
Gustafson, Douglas. 1969a. Currency Repayment Provisions on Bank Loans to Development Finance Companies (DFCs).
———. 1969b. Four General Points on DFC Lending Policy.
Hasan, Zamir. 1969. Some Thoughts on Your Four General Points on DFC Lending.
Hu, Yao-Su. 1981. The World Bank and Development Finance Companies. *Journal of General Management* 7 (Autumn): 46–57.
IBRD. 1948. *Third Annual Report to the Board of Governors: 1947–1948*. Washington, DC: International Bank for Reconstruction and Development.
———. 1950a. *Fifth Annual Report to the Board of Governors: 1949–1950*. Washington, DC: International Bank for Reconstruction and Development.
———. 1950b. *Report and Recommendations of the President to the Executive Directors on the Industrial Development Bank of Turkey Loan Application Guaranteed by the Republic of Turkey*. Washington, DC: International Bank for Reconstruction and Development.
———. 1950c. *The Basis of a Development Program for Colombia*. Washington, DC: International Bank for Reconstruction and Development.
———. 1952. *Seventh Annual Report to the Board of Governors: 1951–1952*. Washington, DC: International Bank for Reconstruction and Development.
———. 1953. *Eighth Annual Report to the Board of Governors: 1952–1953*. Washington, DC: International Bank for Reconstruction and Development.
———. 1956. Some Concluding Remarks on the IBRD Development-Bank Operations.
———. 1968. *The World Bank, IDA and IFC*. Washington, DC: International Bank for Reconstruction and Development.
———. 1972. Project Appraisals Reviewed by Development Finance Companies—Div. II.
———. 1975. DFC Policy Paper.
———. 1971. International Bank for Reconstruction and Development, International Development Association, International Finance Corporation: Summary of Operations—Development Finance Companies. Washington, DC: International Bank for Reconstruction and Development.
IFC. 1957. *First Annual Report 1956–1957*. Washington, DC: International Finance Corporation.
———. 1958. *Second Annual Report 1957–1958*. Washington, DC: International Finance Corporation.
———. 1959. *Third Annual Report 1958–1959*. Washington, DC: International Finance Corporation.
———. 1961. *Fifth Annual Report: 1960–1961*. Washington, DC: International Finance Corporation.

———. 1962. *Sixth Annual Report: 1961–1962*. Washington, DC: International Finance Corporation.
———. 1963. *IFC Annual Report: 1962–1963*. Washington, DC: International Finance Corporation.
———. 1964. *IFC Annual Report: 1963–1964*. Washington, DC: International Finance Corporation.
———. 1965. *IFC Annual Report: 1964–1965*. Washington, DC: International Finance Corporation.
———. 1967. *IFC Annual Report 1967*. Washington, DC: International Finance Corporation.
———. 1969. *IFC Annual Report 1969*. Washington, DC: International Finance Corporation.
———. 1970. *IFC Annual Report 1970*. Washington, DC: International Finance Corporation.
———. 1971. *IFC Annual Report 1971*. Washington, DC: International Finance Corporation.
Kamarck, Andrew. 1969. Paper for Board on Some Aspects of DFC Policy.
Kapur, Devesh, John Prior Lewis, and Richard Charles Webb. 1997. *The World Bank: Its First Half Century*. Washington, DC: Brookings Institution Press.
Kpognon, Stanislas. 1971. Ethiopia: AIDB Lending Program.
Mason, Edward S., and Robert E. Asher. 1973. *The World Bank Since Bretton Woods: The Origins, Policies, Operations, and Impact of the International Bank for Reconstruction and Development and the Other Members of the World Bank Group: The International Finance Corporation, the International Development Association [and] the International Centre for Settlement of Investment Disputes*. Washington, DC: Brookings Institution.
Matecki, Bronisław. 1957. *Establishment of the International Finance Corporation and United States Policy*. New York: FA Praeger.
Mathew, P.M. 1970a. Changes in Policies and Practices.
———. 1970b. Development Finance Companies in Which IFC Has Participated, That Can Make Equity Investment in Majority Government-Owned Enterprise.
Miraki, J.Z. 1969. Comments on Mr. Gustafson's Memorandum of May 12, 1969 on Currency Repayment Provisions in the Bank's Loans to DFCs.
OECD. 1964. *Intermediate Financial Institutions*. Paris: OECD.
Pearson, Lester B. 1969. *Partners in Development: Report of the Commission on International Development*. New York, NY: Praeger Publishers.
Picciotto, R. 1969. DFC—Government Financing and Return on Capital.
Pollan, Hans. 1971. Financing of State Controlled Enterprises by DFCs.
Rao, Badri. 1958. Proceedings of the Meeting on Development Banks Held at the Economic Development Institute from May 5, to May 9, 1958.
Sanchez-Marco, Carlos. 1970. Economic Appraisal of DFC Projects.

Thiebach, G. 1970. Activities of Kreditanstalt Fuer Wiederaufbau (KFW), Germany, in Chile, Paraguay and Uruguay.

Uecker, Roland. 1967. Forms of Organization in the Development Bank Field. In *The Role of Development Banks in Economic and Social Development*, Berlin: German Foundation for Developing Countries.

US Treasury. 1944. *Articles of Agreement: International Monetary Fund and International Bank for Reconstruction and Development*. Washington, DC: US Treasury.

World Bank. 1964. *World Bank and IDA Annual Report 1963–1964*. Washington, DC: World Bank.

———. 1968. *World Bank Annual Report 1968*. Washington, DC: World Bank.

———. 1969. Draft Paper on Pearson Commission Recommendations Regarding Development Finance Companies.

Yazici, Bulent. 1962. The Industrial Development Bank of Turkey. In *Methods of Industrial Development*, ed. Albert Winsemius and John Pincus. Paris: Organization for Economic Co-operation and Development (OECD).

CHAPTER 3

1970 to 1990: Development Finance in Crisis and the Search for a New Paradigm

The World Bank Group saw lending grow from USD 1.9 billion in 1971 to USD 7.6 billion in 1980 (World Bank 1980, 66). Concurrently, the count of DFCs rose from 45 in 1970 to over 70 by 1980, and cumulative Bank lending to DFCs (USD 6.4 billion) had exceeded direct lending to industry (USD 5.3 billion) (Hu 1981, 47). Despite these impressive numbers, the Bank's strategy of loans and DFCs encountered serious problems. First, the absence of a rigorous and standardized methodology for project evaluation meant that little was known about the impact. Second, DFCs had little appreciable impact on fostering the growth of domestic capital markets and had not attracted significant amounts of private capital. In fact, many DFCs were still dependent on subsidized financing (Shin 1968). DFCs had also created numerous moral hazards on the part of developing countries, and the World Bank was beginning to question their utility. Finally, despite growing international financial markets, private investment remained anemic across the developing world.

The lackluster outcomes pushed the World Bank—and development institutions more broadly—to rethink how they administered development assistance. The Bank's key conclusion was that DFCs and other financial instruments disappointed because they did not abide by market discipline. Partial integration with financial markets had created adverse incentives: recipient government guarantees led to political interference,

P. Volberding, *Leveraging Financial Markets for Development*,
Executive Politics and Governance,
https://doi.org/10.1007/978-3-030-55008-0_3

subsidized credit misallocated scarce financing, and development institution credit lines created moral hazards for financial intermediaries. Consequently, many in the World Bank, led by the DFC Department and the IFC, sought ways of mobilizing private investment that maintained proper incentives. In essence, they argued for a transition to the logic of marketized development financial instruments—more private financing, stronger adherence to market rates, and better control over the investment decisions. There was just one problem—the World Bank was unable to transition to these financial instruments. The World Bank's Articles of Agreement restricted how it could reorient development assistance, particularly for private financial instruments. Moreover, the World Bank lacked political consensus from stakeholders on how to reform the system. Combined with its inherently bureaucratic nature, this meant the World Bank had neither the political support nor the flexibility to realize marketized development financial instruments.

Therefore, even though the World Bank was the largest and most influential development institution, it was circumscribed in its ability to fix the problems that plagued project loans and DFCs. Despite strong voices within the World Bank, their efforts were not enough to overcome bureaucratic inertia and political vacillations. Tepid support from the private financial sector for development instruments further hampered efforts. Instead, another development institution with decisive political backing and greater institutional flexibility would need to spearhead marketized development financial instruments.

Disappointing Development Outcomes

While World Bank project aid totals reached record highs (World Bank 1973b, 1), the purported sanguine results overlooked numerous problems. A large part of the overly optimistic conclusions was that there was little assessment of development projects after completion, meaning that the conclusions were largely based upon guesswork. Until the mid-1970s, rigorous evaluations of projects were often of secondary importance, if conducted at all. In order to improve knowledge, development institutions began a concerted effort to establish robust project assessment guidelines. However, reports confirmed the suspicions of economists—project loans were falling short of transformational impact. Moreover, nearly four decades of development aid had produced little in the way of financial independence, including the lack of development of domestic capital markets, meaning that donor countries needed to routinely replenish funds (World Bank 1979, 7–8). Even though development institutions recognized the problems, internal divisions and the absence of political will stymied efforts of reform.

DFCs were also discovered to be fraught with their own challenges. As archival materials reveal, DFCs had limited impact on the development of local capital markets, were still financially dependent on government sources for injections of capital, and had failed to achieve promised development outcomes. In one positive outcome, DFCs were discovered to be mostly profitable, but this was a consequence of subsidized financing and low-risk taking in investment ventures. In addition, both the World Bank and DFCs themselves had little information on DFC project assessment and no standardized assessment methodology. For instance, in an internal World Bank analysis of 36 economic and appraisal reports of investments by DFCs, only 10 contained any data disaggregated by sector, and none at the project-level (Shin 1969). This inadequacy of data made generalizations on the problems of development finance impossible for the World Bank. The failures of these two strategies, however, highlighted how development institutions needed to reform them, a necessary step toward fully embracing marketized development financial instruments.

Evaluation Programs and Rethinking of Project Loans

Project loans formed the cornerstone of World Bank operations because they were the simple to implement; a development institution provides all or most of the required capital for a specific project, and projects could be individually selected. Since project loans were administered from abroad, a functioning domestic capital market was not a prerequisite. Yet the reasons for the predominance of loans were also that it enabled donor countries control over the process, theoretically removing opportunities for corruption (Development Practitioner #44 2016). This control allowed development institutions to demonstrate their impact on important domestic constituencies. It also was aimed at boosting the confidence of private investors that saw donor governments as trustworthy partners.

However, three challenges plagued these project loans. First, individually managing a project was costly—finding bankable projects, assessing risk, and implementing and evaluating the investment took effort. Crucially, this incentivized development institutions to select safer projects that were financially prudent; these tended to be larger investments that reduced the marginal administrative cost of implementation and mitigated risk assumption. The smallest projects, such as SMEs, were completely ignored. One World Bank employee summarized the problem: "The problem with project lending is that it biases the flow of investment funds into large, mainly urban and public sector projects, and against small rural enterprise and social development schemes" (Nevin 1985, 429). Second, project aid often imposed administrative burdens on developing countries. Another employee noted the World Bank was particularly guilty in burdening developing country administrations, saying that "the perfect project can only be attained by making other projects very imperfect; the technical and administrative resources do not exist for both" (McCarthy 1978, 92). Third, it was unclear whether these projects generated development benefits. The tendency to fund the flashiest projects often did not equate with the most beneficial projects. Until the late 1970s, many development projects were selected to benefit industry from the donor country or a policy objective. The United States, through its Export-Import Bank, pursued an aggressive policy-driven financing program for Brazil in the 1950s, mostly to dissuade Brazilian politicians from forging strong ties with the Soviet Union (cf. Becker 2003). KfW's first project loans in the 1960s were aimed at iron ore mining and exportation facilities that could ensure raw materials to German industry (Harries 1998, 86).

Yet the absence of a rigorous evaluation system limited knowledge of performance in early projects, and it was not until the 1970s that evaluation became more important within development institutions. The Bank's first internal assessment was not conducted until 1964, and it was not until 1971 that Robert McNamara established an evaluative function within the Bank, an institution that later evolved into the Operations Evaluation Department (OED) a few years later (Grasso et al. 2003, 4–6). The OED also developed a set of reporting guidelines for reviewing projects and advocated for greater amounts of self-monitoring and flexibility in project design. In order to disseminate these guidelines to other agencies, the OED published its procedures in 1979, and they soon became a highly influential set of internal operating guidelines among development institutions. The World Bank's relatively large budget allowed it to conduct a number of assessment reports. Other international institutions similarly became active in project assessment. In 1982, the OECD published its *Compendium of Aid Procedures*, with the goal that "the report will support efforts already under way in many DAC countries to re-examine their own aid-giving procedures in order to make them as effective as possible" (OECD 1981, 8). The *Compendium* was the first comparative review of aid procedures.

Despite these new procedures, challenges persisted. One concern was that while the proportion of failed projects was small, the same mistakes were repeated across institutions. Evaluation periods were also limited to project completion and a short period thereafter, meaning that development institutions had little knowledge of what transpired a few years later. The limitation of ex-post assessments meant that projects were often ill-prepared for operational responsibilities. The authors therefore recommended that development institutions strengthen cooperation in evaluation and implementation procedures, adopt a common standard for evaluation, and take a broader and longer-term perspective of impact.

In addition to problems of evaluation, developing countries were underperforming in their bid to attract private capital. Between 1980 and 1984, developing countries attracted USD 12.5. billion in FDI, or approximately 25% of total global FDI flows. However, the distribution was highly unequal. The 10 largest FDI recipients received nearly 75% of total developing country FDI receipts, while the least developed countries received a scant USD 190 million, or 0.4%, of the total (UNCTAD 1991, 11). A main reason was that developing country investments were not as attractive as ones in developed countries, particularly during times of global economic turmoil. Fledgling international financial markets also impeded progress. Yet the structure of the international financial system also made it difficult for developing countries to rely on external private funding. The most common form of debt was general obligation credit, which was typically in the form of floating-rate bank loans. Between 1974 and 1983, fully 80% of the total net external financing for non-petroleum exporting developing countries consisted of this financing. As Lessard (1986, 15–16) noted, floating-rate debt loans were not necessarily problematic, but these were problematic when they became the *only* form of financing.

These challenges of both project loans and the attraction of private capital became well known to development institutions. However, two factors stymied the ability of development institutions—and in particular the World Bank—from pursuing more systematic reforms. First, there was a lack of political will on the part of donor countries to substantially change procedures. Concerns about geopolitics, control over investment decisions, and political visibility of investments made many countries hesitant to alter aid procedures. Even untying aid—that is, disbursing assistance without conditions—took decades of efforts by the OECD (Führer 1996, 57). Moreover, domestic support for development assistance had been eroding, which led to a decrease in donor government support in real terms. Second, bureaucratic slowness and disagreements between World Bank staff limited the pace of reforms. Of particular contestation was whether or not to make the World Bank function more closely to the tenets of private finance (Development Practitioner #44 2016). Ultimately, the World Bank would choose to add greater conditionality to its loans with the infamous structural adjustment programs (cf. Gibbon 1993), but these did not circumvent all of the problems associated with project loans.

DFCs Falter

From the beginning, development finance companies (DFCs) were envisioned as a tool to mobilize private investment, as DFCs could serve as an intermediary institution to finance small enterprises and could facilitate the development of a domestic capital market. However, while they were to operate as commercial intermediaries with a developmental objective, DFCs were plagued with moral hazards. Critically, the challenges of DFCs on how to provide credit lines, reach small private entrepreneurs, and mobilize private investment would provide important lessons for a revised strategy based on marketized development financial instruments.

By 1980, the World Bank had supported over 70 different DFCs across 40 different countries. DFCs were envisioned to be financially self-sufficient, to promote local ownership of financial resources, and to foster the development of the industrial and financial sectors within the domestic economy. Initial reports regarding DFCs were quite positive. Supporters emphasized that judging by financial health, DFCs were fiscally sound. From 1967 to 1971, the average annual profit on assets for World Bank Group-affiliated DFCs was nearly 3.5%, with no single DFC registering a loss (see Table 3.1). The KDFC exhibited the best financial performance of any of the DFCs, achieving an 11.8% annual return on investment. Gordon (1983, 49–50) estimated that of the 53 World Bank-affiliated DFCs surveyed in 1979, only four had negative net profits as a percentage of average net worth. The margins were highest in the privately-operated *financieras* in Colombia, with profits consistently between 25 and 40%, as well as in more developed nations, like Israel and South Korea. Nevin's (1994, 256–57) own calculations similarly found that EIB-related DFCs

Table 3.1 Profitability of DFCs funded by the World Bank, 1943–1973

DFC	*Full Name*	*Country*	*Year*	*Profit %*[a]
ADELA	ADELA Investment Company S. A.	L. America	1964	2.6
AIDB	Agricultural and Industrial Development Bank	Ethiopia	1970	–
BANDESCO	Banco del Desarrollo Economico Espanol	Spain	1963	2.7
BAPINDO	Bank Penbangunan Indonesia	Indonesia	1960	–
BIDI	Banque Ivoirienne de Developpement Industriel	Ivory Coast	1965	3.2
BNB	Banco do Nordeste do Brazil	Brazil	1953	6.5
BNDE	Banque Nationale pour le Developpement Economique	Morocco	1959	2.2
Caldas	Corporacion Financiera de Caldas	Colombia	1961	2.4
CAVENDES	Compania Anonima Venezolana de Desarrollo	Venezuela	1963	4.8
CDB	Cyprus Development Bank Limited	Cyprus	1963	–
CDC	China Development Corporation	Taiwan	1959	3.6
CFN	Comision de Valores - Corporacion Financiera Nacional	Ecuador	1943	4.2
CIH	Credit Inmobilier et Hotelier	Morocco	1920	3
COFIEC	Ecuatoriana de Desarrollo S.A. Compania Financiera	Ecuador	1966	3.6
COFITOUR	Compagnie Financiere et Touristique. S.A.	Tunisia	1969	–
Colombiana	Corporacion Financiera Colombiana	Colombia	1959	3.7
DBM	Development Bank of Mauritius	Mauritius	1964	1.7
DBS	Development Bank of Singapore Limited	Singapore	1968	2.5
DFCC	Development Finance Corporation of Ceylon	Sri Lanka	1955	3.8

(continued)

Table 3.1 (continued)

DFC	*Full Name*	*Country*	*Year*	*Profit %*[a]
DFCNZ	Development Finance Corporation of New Zealand	N. Zealand	1964	3.5
EADB	East African Development Bank	East Africa	1967	4.6
ICC	The Industrial Credit Company Limited	Ireland	1933	2.5
ICICI	The Industrial Credit and Investment Corporation of India	India	1955	2.6
IDBI	Industrial Development Bank of Israel Limited	Israel	1957	5.3
IDBP	Industrial Development Bank of Pakistan	Pakistan	1961	2.2
IFCT	The Industrial Finance Corporation of Thailand	Thailand	1959	3
IFF	Industrialization Fund of Finland Limited	Finland	1954	2.7
IICY	International Investment Corporation for Yugoslavia	Yugoslavia	1969	–
IMDBI	Industrial and Mining Development Bank of Iran	Iran	1959	3.4
IVK	oesterreichische Investitionskredit Aktiengesellschaft	Austria	1958	1.4
KDFC	Korea Development Finance Corporation	South Korea	1967	11.8
LBIDI	Liberian Bank for Industrial Development and Investment	Liberia	1965	2.8
MIDF	Malaysian Industrial Development Finance Berhad	Malaysia	1960	5.3
Nacional	Corporacion Financiera Nacional	Colombia	1959	6.5
NIBID	National Investment Bank for Industrial Development	Greece	1963	3
NIDB	Nigerian Industrial Development Bank Limited	Nigeria	1964	3.8

(continued)

Table 3.1 (continued)

DFC	*Full Name*	*Country*	*Year*	*Profit %*[a]
Norte	Corporacion Financiera del Norte	Colombia	1963	4.6
PDCP	Private Development Corporation of the Philippines	Philippines	1963	5.2
PICIC	Pakistan Industrial Credit and Investment Corporation Ltd	Pakistan	1957	3.4
SIFIDA	Societe Internationale Financiere pour les Investissements et le Developpement en Afrique S.A.	Africa	1970	–
SNI	Societe Nationale d'Investissement	Tunisia	1959	2.2
SOFIDE	Societe Financiere de Developpement (SOCOFIDE)	Zaire	1970	–
TSKB	Turkiye Sinai Kalkinma Bankasi A.S.	Turkey	1950	3.9
TTDFC	Trinidad and Tobago Development Finance Company	Trinidad and Tobago	1970	–
Valle	Corporacion Financiera del Valle	Colombia	1961	5.8

[a]Profit before tax as a percentage of average total assets since the date founded
Source Diamond and Gulhati (1973)

were largely profitable. Of the twenty African DFCs surveyed, sixteen had positive returns, with the majority earning less than 5%; only four had registered net losses in 1984.[1]

Early challenges were a consequence of a mixed mission. While DFCs were intended to be privately-owned and finance private projects, their scope broadened considerably. DFCs became a potential avenue to fund

[1]The survey also concluded that privately-owned and privately-operated DFCs performed slightly better than the government ones, with an average profit rate of 10.4%. In both cases, unprofitable DFCs were the exception. However, when they were unprofitable, DFCs were also likely to fail spectacularly. The worst disaster was the Uganda Development Bank, which in 1984 had net losses of 114.3% of the value of its own funds.

SMEs, a constituency that had been underserved by traditional development finance. They were also used as a low-cost vehicle for the transmission of technical skills and international best practices. When the World Bank eliminated the private ownership requirement in 1968, DFCs also adopted a greater role in public policy implementation and, in some cases, they developed responsibilities in export promotion and regional development. Yet this scope expansion brought its own challenges. First, a more complex mission created a more complex operational environment. Three stakeholders participated in financing DFCs—the government, private enterprise and banks, and international development agencies—an ownership structure that created conflicts of interest. This institutional design put DFCs in an awkward position, since their broad benchmark for projects created a constant tension to balance development objectives with financial prudence. Further confusion was added following the 1968 reforms, when the World Bank Group also expanded its support to state-owned DFCs and, in particular, supported intermediary financial institutions that were frequently state-owned as well. The permission to invest in state-owned enterprises blurred the lines between the public and private spheres, and removed clarity from their mission (DFC Department 1975).

By the 1970s, there was widespread indication that DFCs were encountering problems. In 1974, a World Bank study found that government-owned agricultural lending institutions had average loan arrear rates of 41% (Caprio Jr and Demirguc-Kunt 1997, 2). Reports also showed that DFCs often served protectionist purposes. For instance, 38.7% of investments made by the Turkish TSKB and 44.5% of those made by India's ICICI had effective rates of protection over 100% (World Bank 1973a, 2), and people in the Bank were suspicious that their experiences were representative (Vibert 1973). Mayer (1989) described a situation that indicated DFCs had failed to achieve fiscal solvency: "Very few [DFCs] are self-supporting. About one-third are in serious financial difficulties. By 1983, almost half had more than 25 percent of their loans affected by arrears and one-quarter had more than 50 percent of their loans in arrears" (1). DFCs also had an unclear financial impact. From 1964 to 1968, the Bank provided USD 491 million in funding, while USD 645 million was provided from other sources; however, the majority of these funds were from public sources (Kalmanoff 1969a).[2] While DFCs themselves were not necessarily meant to be financially solvent, they at least needed to be effective (UNIDO 1979, 5).

Even by non-financial metrics, DFCs disappointed. Their role in developing local capital markets was perhaps the greatest deficiency. While it was envisioned that DFCs would sell their own securities, or underwrite those of companies that they funded, domestic financial markets never materialized in ways to sustainably fund DFCs (Gordon 1983, 7). The Industrial and Mining Development Bank of Iran, to which the Bank had committed USD 205 million, was the only example of a DFC expanding a domestic capital market and establishing a domestic stock exchange. However, other instances of DFC-provoked institutions never materialized and most were beset by delays and inaction. The ICICI of India waited over 15 years—until 1965—to issue its first debt security. Pakistan's PICIC and Turkey's Industrial Development Bank had not issued any debt securities by the early 1970s (Mason and Asher 1973, 369). With weak or nonexistent domestic capital markets, mobilizing private investment remained difficult.

DFCs were similarly unsuccessful in sparking widespread industrialization. Given the strict limits on lending to state-owned enterprises, the majority of industrial lending by the Bank prior to 1965 went to projects in developed nations; Japan and Australia received the majority of this money (Mason and Asher 1973, 371). Even on broader measures of development, which included total technology transfer, institutional strengthening, and public goods provisions, the record of DFCs was mixed. The amount of additional employment created was also unclear because of the relatively high cost per job created, suggesting that DFCs were relatively inefficient distributors of capital. Finally, as late as 1980, there lacked a systematic methodology. At the conclusion of a conference on development banking in the 1980s, the evaluation of DFCs was grim: "The consensus was that operational and institutional self-evaluation would be crucially important for the next decade. At the same time it was felt that there had been little progress in the area of self-evaluation and that there was an urgent need for guidelines" (UNIDO 1979, 154).

[2] The breakdown was as follows: USD 206 million from domestic public sources, USD 183 million domestic private sources, USD 178 million from foreign public sources, and USD 78 million from foreign private sources.

Observers highlighted five reasons for DFC inadequacy in development finance—the lack of a need to create DFCs, high risk aversion in DFC lending, continued dependence on subsidized financing, the influence of greater macroeconomic policy, and high levels of government interference. All of these factors, while trying to leverage finance and market discipline for development outcomes, ultimately stymied attempts to mobilize private finance.

No Need for New Institutions
Proponents of DFCs argued that domestic commercial banks were less responsive to the long-term credit needs of the industrial sectors because of their inadequate local currency deposits and high level of risk aversion. This led commercial banks to favor short-term loan commitments for tangible assets, such as import-export credits or inventories. DFCs were designed to fix this failure—through the financial backing of the government, DFCs would be more willing to take riskier, long-term assets. Yet by the 1980s, World Bank economists questioned the rationale for why a new institution needed to be established when commercial banks could have been transformed (Gordon 1983, 4). This perspective was reinforced by the fact that many DFCs adopted characteristics of commercial banks. The pressures of competition led some DFCs to accept deposits, and some banks, "concerned with the problems confronted by clients, were led increasingly to provide financial and managerial consulting services from their own staff resources"; other development banks created money market companies, leasing companies, mortgage and merchant banks, and venture capital companies (Diamond 1981, 12). For instance, South Korea's KDFC was converted into the Korea Long-Term Credit Bank; two institutions in the Philippines, PDCP and PISO, linked with commercial banks to undertake securities and provide consultancy services (Gordon 1983, 17–18). By the 1980s, observers were already warning that DFCs would become irrelevant. H. F. G. Leembruggen, general manager of the Malaysian Industrial Development Finance Corporation, warned that unless linkages between DFCs and policy were strengthened, developing banks would be "adulterated and lost as the development banks metamorphose into marginal financial lenders as a consequence of normal competition" (UNIDO 1979, 35).

At the same time, recipient governments were becoming increasingly participatory in both the commercial and development banking sectors. Several privately-established DFCs, such as Pakistan's PICIC, Sri Lanka's

DFCC, and Nigeria's NInB, were all effectively nationalized. In 1980, only 23 out of 139 DFCs remained entirely in private hands; by contrast, 64 were entirely government owned, with another 28 at least majority owned by the government (UNIDO 1979, 34). Even if the private DFCs remained private, many received government loans or guarantees for additional funding. As such, the differences between DFCs and commercial banks narrowed, raising questions as to the utility of continuing to support new long-term credit institutions, or, in the case of nationalizations, whether they could still be trusted.

Risk Aversion

Despite the intention that DFCs should fund riskier projects, in practice DFCs were just as risk averse as their commercial counterparts. This was a consequence of two problems. First, the mission statement of DFCs was contradictory—to promote socially-beneficial development projects while remaining themselves financially solvent. By definition, projects that DFCs were assigned to were ones that were not commercially bankable, rendering the second objective difficult. Moreover, not only did the World Bank pressure DFCs to remain operationally lean, but the capital markets also forced DFCs to maintain their financial reputation if they wanted to borrow money in the future. As noted by Hu (1981), "in the absence of explicit and clear instructions to the contrary, this means a preference for safe, well-proven technologies, to be supplied by well-known reputable sources, and to be operated by reliable project" (55). Consequently, DFCs tended toward projects that supported cash flow positive enterprises that were larger, well established, and technologically conservative, precisely those projects that DFCs were designed to avoid (World Bank 1973b, 5).

Second, DFCs often lacked the technical and institutional capacity to assess new projects (Uecker 1967, H10). One early internal World Bank assessment report described the breadth of operational mismanagement:

> Some recent negative observations as example: a development bank branch did not know where the estate of its borrower was located; one development bank was unaware that the buildings for the machines, financed by the bank, had not yet been erected and that the machines had been stored in the open for 9 months; another had taken as security a rubber plantation which did not exist at all and realized this only when trying to make use of it; another did not know that the completed plant, financed by it, had not started production after one year's time. (Engel 1967, D2)

The absence of staffing and resources ultimately led DFCs to avoid seeking higher impact development projects. This created an incentive for DFCs not only to seek out more easily managed projects, but also ones that would gain quick approval.

The consequences of a reduced appetite for risk were widespread. SMEs were particularly susceptible to underfunding. Their small-scale operations and lack of financial history made them high-cost and risky investments, as each loan needed to be individually assessed, making the per unit cost of investment relatively high. In a 1972 World Bank study, less than 10% of the total volume of DFC lending was directed to enterprises with less than USD 100,000 in assets; more than 30% went to enterprises with assets greater than USD 1 million (IBRD 1975, 14). Moreover, the tendency to fund financially attractive projects may have also led to the support of profitable but ineffective import substitution industries. And despite the attempt to broaden the investment portfolios, the large industries still provided the most solid investments, undercutting the stated DFC goals of promoting grassroots private entrepreneurs. That DFCs also were close to politicians and existing commercial industries and finance did little to make investment decisions independent. Efforts to fix this never materialized (cf. Loganathan 1971; Nougaim 1971).

Financial Dependence on World Bank or Government Financing
While DFCs were meant to be financially sustainable, in practice this was more complicated. As of 1973, 16 of the World Bank-sponsored DFCs received more than 80% of their total available resources from World Bank Group financing that was originally envisioned to be temporary (Diamond and Gulhati 1973, 51). Moreover, only a handful of DFCs received a majority of the funding. Until 1974, five DFCs (ICICI in India, IMDBI in Iran, KDFC in Korea, SNI in Tunisia, and TSKB in Turkey) accounted for more than 40% of all World Bank lending to DFCs (World Bank 1974). As such, "while they no longer depend on the Bank, most do not yet 'stand on their own feet' in market terms" (IBRD 1975, 19) (see Table 3.2).

There were four main reasons why DFCs were unable to diversify financially. First, recipient governments were reluctant to cede influence over institutions they viewed to be domestic. For government-owned DFCs, this meant that funding diversification would dilute their influence over the management (World Bank 1973b, 6). Second, foreign

Table 3.2 Sources of total financing of DFCs as of 31 December 1967 (% of total resources)

DFC	*Country*	*Private*		*Public*		*World Bank*	*% Private*	*% Public*
		Domestic	*Foreign*	*Domestic*	*Foreign*			
IVK	Austria	42.1	23.4	18.3	–	16.3	65.5	34.6
DFCC	Sri Lanka	12.5	11.9	75.6	–	–	24.4	75.6
CDC	Taiwan	11.3	1.6	33.4	9.7	44	12.9	87.1
Caldas	Colombia	47.7	9.9	35.5	–	6.9	57.6	42.4
Colombiana	Colombia	24.8	32.9	32.4	0.5	9.4	57.7	42.3
Nacional	Colombia	28	16.5	42.6	–	13	44.5	55.6
Norte	Colombia	27.5	32.6	29.4	–	10.5	60.1	39.9
Valle	Colombia	32.6	11.9	52.5	–	3.1	44.5	55.6
DBE	Ethiopia	–	–	65.1	14.7	20.2	0	100
IFF	Finland	21	1.5	27.1	–	50.4	22.5	77.5
NIBID	Greece	55.3	15.5	23.9	2.1	3.2	70.8	29.2
ICICI	India	8.8	3	39.3	7.2	41.7	11.8	88.2
IMDBI	Iran	10.3	4.3	56.1	2.6	26.8	14.6	85.4
IDBI	Israel	16.3	28.3	32	15	8.4	44.6	55.4
BIDI	Ivory Coast	5.4	12.6	70.6	8.8	2.6	18	82
LBIDE	Liberia	0.6	19.9	59.6	6.5	13.4	20.5	79.5
MIDF	Malaysia	3.7	17	52.2	3.5	23.6	20.7	79.3
BNDE	Morocco	17.4	1.9	25.4	1.6	53.6	19.3	80.7
NIDB	Nigeria	1	22.9	64.8	1.5	9.8	23.9	76.1
PICIC	Pakistan	7	4.1	10.5	30.1	48.4	11.1	89
PDCP	Philippines	19.6	8.3	–	22.8	49.3	27.9	72.1
Bandesco	Spain	84.9	5.8	8.2	–	1.2	90.7	9.4
IFCT	Thailand	10.3	13.5	41.6	22.8	11.7	23.8	76.1
SNI	Tunisia	26.2	2.4	51.6	0.8	18.9	28.6	71.3
TSKB	Turkey	9.8	0.2	42.7	14	33.2	10	89.9
Cavendes	Venezuela	18.9	46	11	16.1	8	64.9	35.1

Source Kalmanoff (1969b)

development institutions wanted to maintain control over the implementation of projects. Donors suspected that DFCs were either inefficient or corrupt, and in order to maintain domestic support for continued financing, they required substantial oversight into their investments (cf. OECD 1981). Third, there was insufficient private capital to entirely fund DFCs. Ultimately, this meant that DFCs were never able to generate the multiplicative impact that its original creators planned. Finally, the mission of DFCs was often contradictory, since they were required to provide below market-rate financing to their projects, but secured private financing at market rates. This squeezed the operational margins of DFCs such that they sought ways to lower the cost of financing they received. On the borrowing side, the slow development of domestic capital markets hampered the ability of DFCs to raise money from private sources. Ultimately, this meant that in order to achieve their increasingly ambitious development goals while maintaining solvency, DFCs needed to find subsidized sources of financing or to run significant budget deficits. Since the latter was highly frowned upon by both the market and governments, DFCs heavily relied on public financing from governments and aid institutions.

However, the subsidized foreign credit meant DFCs did not need to seek private funding. The lack of pursuit of private funds also limited the size of DFCs, which, in turn, restricted how much lending the DFCs could provide. This correspondingly reduced the effectiveness of their industrialization and development programs (Gordon 1983, 6–7). Moreover, the natural inclination of DFCs was to purchase imported equipment, raw materials, and other inputs, and tacitly discourage local subcontracting or the development of local equipment industries (Hu 1981, 54). This outcome was counter to the objective of fostering a local supply chain network. It also incentivized continued financial dependence on sources of cheap foreign credit, even though the denomination in foreign currency created a potential liability during a local currency devaluation. These were hardly the envisioned outcomes.

Dependence on Macroeconomic Conditions

World Bank economists also realized that the macroeconomic environment often swamped the positive effects of long-term DFC lending. Despite their powerful international financial supporters, DFCs in only a handful of countries surpassed 10% of total industrial lending (Diamond and Gulhati 1973, 49). Outside of political capriciousness, established policies were similarly detrimental. For instance, in an era of fixed exchange rates, government policy tied the hands of DFC managers. DFCs were themselves dependent on foreign investment for continued financing, and their investments domestically relied on economic growth and export competitiveness. Of particular concern was a sudden currency devaluation, which could scare off potential private investors to DFCs, and even the perception of macroeconomic instability could greatly increase a DFC's borrowing rates. A devaluation could drastically increase the real value of foreign currency-denominated debt. This was enormously problematic, since DFCs were primarily funded with US dollar-denominated World Bank loans (Nevin 1994, 255–56).

Similarly, the central bank interest rate policy profoundly impacted DFCs. For one, governments often promoted a low interest rate environment to spur growth; however, these "policies favoring low interest rates prevailing in many African countries in the late 1960s often resulted in DFCs in those countries being dependent on bilateral loans with low rates of interest" (World Bank 1976, 12). In order to maintain a DFC's promotional nature, the government often restricted the upper limits of the rates that could be charged for onward lending, a number that was frequently established at below market rates. DFCs were also not permitted to charge varying interest rates based on a borrower's risk profile. With interest rates unreflective of the quality of the loan to the enterprise, DFCs favored projects that were the least risky, accelerating the trend of only financing established enterprises. A predetermined interest rate also made it difficult for DFCs to pursue a development policy independent of politics, since "institutions which are unable to lend at market rates will be largely dependent on credit facilities obtained on their behalf by the government. This can potentially affect overall resource mobilization in an economy; at a minimum it means the DFC involved will be a captive of its government's financial decisions" (IBRD 1975, 16).

The consequence of DFC dependence on macroeconomic policy was therefore negative. DFCs could never attain creditworthiness because of macroeconomic mismanagement outside of their control, which would simultaneously erode the reputation and underlying financial strength of a DFC, thus raising its borrowing costs. DFCs occasionally even had to charge above market interest rates in order to attract the same amount of private capital. Rising inflation rates, below-market lending rates, and currency volatility eroded the DFCs' capital base. A World Bank report noted the "state of international capital markets, combined with country creditworthiness issues, has closed access to foreign funds for some DFCs which, on their own strength, might otherwise have been suitable borrowers" (World Bank 1976, 12). Therefore, the challenges of government economic policy squeezed the finances of DFCs, as even the best operated DFC could not overcome the impact of a sudden currency devaluation, poor government management, or mercurial market interest rates.

Susceptible to the Same Political Pressures

Even though the privately-owned and operated DFCs were designed to be institutionally separate from the government, in practice both formal and informal links persisted. DFCs still required government permission to operate as a financial institution. Often DFCs funded projects that were of great importance to the government that still required the necessary permitting and approval from the government. The management of DFCs also hailed from bureaucratic sources, as was the case in India, Pakistan, Singapore, South Korea, and a host of other countries (Diamond 1957, 75). When private capital or international development aid was insufficient to cover the operating costs of a DFC, the government often provided subsidized funding through government-issued channels, including long-term loans or joint investments. Occasionally, the government even guaranteed DFC debt obligations through the central bank, providing another avenue of government influence and political leverage.

Moreover, the original promoters of DFCs overlooked the political economy of most developing countries. Large industrial enterprises were disproportionately owned and operated by powerful families, who they themselves were politically well connected. They also were often interconnected with the nascent commercial banking sector and possessed their own motives and viewpoints of how to best utilize financing. As Gordon (1983) bemoaned, private DFCs were "susceptible to undue influence by 'insiders,' that is, the bankers or business groups that frequently control them" (9). In fact, many private firms invested not only to earn profit, but also because they gained access to the country's inner financial and political circle. Conversely, for those corporations that were not politically well-connected, there was a hesitance to partner with DFCs for fear of the loss of business secrets. When faced with limited options for disbursing credit, it "resulted in practice that subsidised rates of interest for the fortunate borrowers, so that DFCs have tended to settle into the role of much-sought-after dispensers of privileged credit to priviledged *(sic)*" (Hu 1981, 48). Taken together, this indicated that private ownership could not guarantee that DFCs operated according to development outcomes, nor was it free from recipient government interests.

Lessons from DFCs

Ultimately, DFCs were difficult to leverage as tools of development for private investment as many of the policies and organizational structures engendered poor incentives. However, there were efforts to better align the incentives of DFCs with development objectives. A 1973 internal memo argued that the World Bank should redefine its relationship with DFCs in three important ways: (1) avoid the financing of economically inefficient projects, (2) reorient investment to SMEs, and (3) reduce the use of concessional finance. These changes were to be achieved through a dual approach of persuasion—convincing DFCs with examples from other banks—and control—making the World Bank's own requirements stricter (World Bank 1973b, 2). Gulhati (1971) further recommended a more rigorous appraisal procedure that included economic rates of return and a deeper analysis of the socioeconomic impact. Despite the changes, the World Bank and other development institutional lost interest in DFCs. In response to the dueling pressures of the government and the market, and the persistent pressure to improve development outcomes, DFCs also naturally began to extend their financial services beyond basic lending to leasing services and insurance (Ligeti 1985, 317–18).

By the end of the 1980s, DFCs were not sustainable from the perspective of the World Bank. By the end of the decade, loans to all development financial intermediaries fell from 11% of all new World Bank Group credit in 1989 to only 2.4% in 1993 (Caprio Jr and Demirguc-Kunt 1997, 3). Moreover, a sample in 1989 showed that nearly 50% of the DFC loans were in arrears (World Bank 1989, 60). Yet the experiences from DFCs provided important lessons. First, recipient government guarantees and subsidized credit lines were demonstrated to be insufficient avenues for ensuring market discipline or expanding private capital engagement. While DFCs were envisioned to operate with financial markets, development institutions struggled to provide financing that reached its targeted end-users. These half-market, half-government strategies created too many moral hazards. Second, and as a result, the conflicting incentives of DFCs meant that private investments were never mobilized. DFCs never had an incentive to reach out to private investors, and private investors never had sufficient trust in the system to warrant new investments. Consequently, the message to development practitioners was clear—if development objectives were to be achieved with financial intermediaries, donor country funding needed to complement, and not distort, financial markets.

The Search for a New Development Model

The strategy of project loans and DFCs was insufficient to mobilize private investment, but how to modify it into new development procedures was uncertain. Development institutions like the World Bank were cognizant of the ways that subsidized funding created perverse incentives for recipient governments, private institutions, and DFCs. They were also aware of the dilemma that projects that were the most financeable often had relatively low developmental impact. Any revised effort should therefore seek to encourage private investment while maintaining the proper incentives on the part of recipients. What remained constant was the desire to keep private investment at the center of any revised strategy. Initially, programmatic aid was favored, but implementation challenges led development institutions to look more seriously at integrating further with financial markets.

While deeper cooperation with financial markets was the goal, development institutions struggled to devise a coherent strategy. As the largest development institution, the World Bank faced a threefold challenge. First, private investor interest was growing, but it would not be until the early 1990s that they would become serious players in financing developing projects abroad. By 1989, developing countries collectively accounted for 16.9% of total global FDI flows (UNCTAD 1991, 11). Second, internally, the World Bank had differing factions on how fast and how deep integration should be with financial markets. Moreover, the World Bank's Articles of Agreement prohibited it from taking equity stakes or creating new financial instruments. Finally, donor governments provided only modest support for World Bank reforms on development financial instruments. Without strong political backing for changes, the World Bank was unable to pursue dramatic reforms to align development policy with financial markets.

The Desire to Harness Private Investment

While attempts to mobilize private capital via loans and DFCs created lackluster outcomes for private investment, it did not erode the underlying conviction that private capital was essential, and that self-sufficiency in capital accumulation and private investment was the ultimate goal. As such, financial markets continued to provide a pathway forward. Development practitioners argued that, despite the challenges with the existing institutions and instruments, allocative efficiency was maximized and moral hazard reduced with market discipline. One World Bank executive noted that development banks "should constantly evolve as they mature in the direction of raising their resources in the domestic and international capital markets" and that "each of them should establish for itself the goal of achieving...full independence from reliance upon governmental and intergovernmental financial support" (UNIDO 1979, 30). Yet despite repeated calls from development institutions to replicate this model in the developing world, these outcomes never came to fruition.

If anything, the frustrations with DFCs and project loans reinforced the notion of market discipline. The travails of project loans were often assigned to individual project characteristics rather than the financial instrument. Recipient government mismanagement—either through corruption, political interference, or an unconducive investment environment—was often identified through project assessment reports as the principal cause of disappointing outcomes. The emphasis on self-responsibility among development economists reflected the perspective that culpability rested primarily with recipient countries (e.g., Heussen et al. 1987). DFCs, for their part, were not primarily ineffective because they lacked private financial resources. Instead, blame was levied against governments, whose macroeconomic policies inhibited the operations of DFCs, or that DFCs grew dependent on subsidized credit. International development agencies had provided financing and training, but it was the responsibility of the DFCs to implement these projects. To international development bankers, financial prudence, market mechanisms, and individual initiative would need to be harnessed.

The implications of this perspective on development policy were twofold. First, greater attention needed to be paid to the environment in which these financial operations occurred. One possible solution was the World Bank and IMF's structural adjustment loans, which were provided with stringent conditionality on macroeconomic governance. These, however, were normally issued only during severe economic turmoil, and they proved to be highly unpopular interventions. Second, it validated the claim that market discipline was essential to guiding development policy. The decision-making process had become too complex for a single institution to coordinate and projects had become too diffuse for centralization. Market-based mechanisms reduced the administrative cost while simultaneously mitigating allocative inefficiencies. It was imagined, for instance, that market-determined interest rates encouraged a rationalization of credit that was impervious to political interference. Eliminating subsidies for DFCs also reduced the moral hazard of DFCs to remain dependent on government-provided funds, even when commercial alternatives were available.

The main problem, therefore, was implementation. In 1979, a joint conference between UNIDO and the Bank brought together bankers and academics to discuss the future of development banking. In the introduction to the symposium, the Executive Director of UNIDO, Abd-El Rahman Khane, relayed the significance of the meeting and alluded to the coming iterations of development finance:

> This symposium might well turn out to be a starting point for a new concept and new dimensions in industrial development financing. Each one of us present here is conscious that the restructuring of the world economy must, in fact, coincide with both the restructuring of world industry and its financing...For the future we expect a more widespread application of new industrial financing methods, for example for international subcontracting, export leasing, compensation and buy-back arrangements. These non-conventional banking techniques will be a new challenge for the industrial banker; they will diversify the scope of traditional development banking activities, and they will require a considerable personal capacity for judging risks and implementing innovative ideas. (UNIDO 1979, 1)

In part, the changes were provoked by the rapidly changing and development of the international banking sector. No longer was international financing limited to a few institutions; commercial banks and development banks alike had developed a vast network of operations and subsidiaries across the globe, opening up new opportunities for investment.

Concurrently, foreign investment in developing countries continued to face shortfalls. The Lima Declaration and Plan of Action required substantial amounts of financing in order to achieve its investment goals by 1985; conservative estimates put the total foreign exchange requirement at USD 20 billion per year in 1980. There were also calls to expand the scope of financing. Industry and infrastructure had accounted for the vast majority of development aid in the postwar era, but other sectors such as health, education, and agriculture were argued to also need funding, particularly in order to raise industry into higher value-added production. However, these sectors were perceived to be the least bankable. Development institutions still favored larger and less risky projects and, much like difficulties encountered with DFCs, were unenthusiastic about these projects.

Programmatic Assistance—Different Method, Similar Challenges

One possible solution to deliver financing schemes was to expand programmatic lending. Unlike project loans, which would focus on one project, programmatic lending was distributed to either a government agency or a DFC, which would then on-lend the funds to other actors. The principle advantage of this method was that it defrayed the cost of implementation to national or local actors, who presumably had more information on the local economic conditions and individual enterprises. Nevin argued that programmatic lending was more flexible, as a single loan could be approved prior to the selection of projects and could be "applied more flexibly for all forms of capital expenditure, including expenditure on working capital, the replacement and rehabilitation of existing capacity, and small expansions and development schemes" (Nevin 1985, 429). Additionally, programmatic aid allowed donor countries to better allocate resources, especially when a country was near the capacity to absorb additional investment. Finally, conditions which were attached to the disbursement of aid, if properly determined, "can help transform a badly run into a well-run sector or economy, and in the process remove a number of difficulties under which aid projects labour" (Cassen and Associates 1986, 150). Programmatic aid can also serve a complementary role to project aid by supplying supporting services.

The enthusiasm of development institutions to give project aid, however, was tepid. The influential Pearson Report initially advocated for programmatic aid as a way to increase funding, reduce administrative costs, and empower local governments (cf. Pearson 1969). But by 1978, only SIDA (Sweden) and NORAD (Norway) had devised a set of aid procedures to finance projects via programmatic aid (McCarthy 1978, 92). Larger institutions found it much more difficult to reorient financing away from entrenched methods. Bureaucratic momentum at the Bank combined with management hesitancy to change financing slowed the transition process, as did the desire to fund projects that were visible to the recipient country. Other large institutions, such as Germany's KfW, also were slow to embrace programmatic aid. The fact that any programmatic aid was administered was principally a consequence of necessity rather than desire. For one, there was little need for new project financing when the existing projects were often in desperate need of maintenance or had high operating costs. The sudden devaluation of developing country currencies further added to the troubles, and programmatic aid was one way of pooling currency risk in an uncertain environment (Pearson 1969, 150–51).

Additional barriers existed as well. First, development institutions needed to be willing to finance sectoral programs that consisted of many smaller projects. In order to do this effectively, discretion needed to be granted to the local implementing agency—be it the government or another institution—to select projects that would adhere to the pre-established standards. In particular, the devolution of project responsibility would allow institutions to support small loans without the accompanying administrative costs (McCarthy 1978). Development institutions were hesitant to trust local institutions, particularly after the negative experiences with DFCs. Second, since development institutions were often reluctant to relinquish direct oversight, it was necessary to accompany capital assistance with technical assistance. This could include more rigorous training programs for staff members, assistance with financing, or education programs for the end borrowers themselves. This would help ensure that, in the absence of an international institution, investments would be implemented efficiently. The World Bank Group already had limited amounts of funding available for technical assistance, and the EDI was in charge of training new development bankers. Nevertheless, funding was limited for most technical assistance projects, in part because it provided little in the way of tangible outcomes.

Third, the implementing agencies needed flexibility in executing a project. This required that development agencies abandoned their burdensome and highly restrictive procurement and tendering rules. Historically, development assistance was tied to a donor country's economic interests, yet even after most tied aid rules were officially abolished, there remained a tendency for recipient countries to favor enterprises originating from the donor country. For example, in a 1966 World Bank survey, approximately "87% of German capital assistance loans to development banks has been used for purchases in Germany even though no tying restrictions were imposed. This evidently shows that the recipients felt it was in their interest to buy German goods" (Lamby 1967, G2). Finally, there needed to be simplified disbursement procedures. To discourage corruption, development institutions required extensive reporting and accountability measures that complicated and delayed disbursement. If the objective was to reduce the administrative burden and encourage on-lending to otherwise unreachable clients, development institutions needed to trust their partners.

Finally, the pitfalls of programmatic aid were similar to those of project aid and DFC financing. There was no established methodology for determining the rate of return on an investment, even with financial measures (Cassen and Associates 1986, 151). The scaling up of financing also complicated administration costs. The lack of coordination between development agencies risked project ineffectiveness. The consequences for development assistance were less clear. If development institutions wanted to ensure that development funding was administered effectively, programmatic aid did not provide the most advantageous way forward without invasive procedures. One possible solution involved providing significantly more technical assistance to DFCs or other domestic development institutions in the hope that they would be able to serve as independent intermediaries for programmatic financing. Given the lackluster record of World Bank attempts through the EDI, this proved to be an unpopular solution. The other possibility involved greater participation in the operations of the institution. Michael Nevin of the EIB posited this idea: "A preferable approach would be to adopt a more active role: taking shares and assisting with the institutional development of DFCs, particularly alongside other institutions such as Caisse Centrale of France, DEG of Germany, FMO of the Netherlands and CDC of the United Kingdom" (Nevin 1994, 264). This active role would allow greater control over the management of the institution and could help guard against political interference. Development institutions could provide more extensive training of the staff members or loan out their own employees for a predetermined period of time. However, limitations in financing and the World Bank's inability to hold equity stakes made this option unviable.

A Renewed Embrace of Financial Markets for Development Outcomes

Given the constraints of DFCs, project loans, and programmatic aid, development institutions began to look anew to deepening financial markets. Unlike previous attempts, the maturation of global financial markets presented new opportunities. To be certain, development institutions were already inextricably linked to financial markets. The MDBs relied on bond issuances to raise capital for investments, and the World Bank had supported policies that strengthened the maturation of local financial markets. Yet the MDBs' attraction of financial markets during this period was different in their scope and their ambition, and extended beyond previous iterations where financial markets played a passive role.

On the funding side, development institutions could increase the amount that they leveraged in the capital markets; bond issuances slowly became more commonplace. Development institutions also hewed more closely to the operations of commercial banks.

Additionally, development institutions began to more comprehensively integrate with financial markets. For one, the promotion of the financial sector became a foundation for development policy. The World Bank's watershed 1989 *World Development Report* signaled the shift. Second, development institutions began to more closely abide by financial markets to improve the behavior of financial intermediaries. This included eliminating Bank-subsidized finance and working more closely with commercial banks. Finally, development institutions also began to experiment with new financial instruments in new sectors. The increased attention to SME and microfinance signaled the first shift to focusing development assistance toward individuals rather than large projects.

Revisions of Existing Strategies via Markets

A growing perspective was that financial markets could be leveraged for the purposes of development. Rather than subsidies, lending to intermediaries at market rates was seen as the least distortive. Those that could be financially viable at market rates should either be privatized or combined with commercial banks (World Bank 1989, 106). On the lending side, there was growing consensus that loans to end borrowers should be administered at market rates. This logic rested on the fact that a profit motive for DFCs was beneficial to incentivize responsible lending. International development institutions had already incorporated market rates into their efforts in project aid. Moreover, the provision of artificially below-market interest rates led to an overconsumption of loans by fiscally healthier enterprises. In this way, the most financially stable enterprises crowded out funding for smaller and riskier enterprises.

Yet even with the proposed market changes, the widespread disillusionment with DFCs provoked another prescription that the focus of global development loans should be toward commercial banks. Commercial banks theoretically have better incentives to operate with financial prudence since, unlike their DFC counterparts, they would not be financially rescued when their capital was depleted. However, most developing country commercial banks lacked adequate capitalization, were subjected to the same vicissitudes of the macroeconomic policy environment, and often lacked skilled employees. A new approach emerged in the early

1980s in Latin America to bolster the operations of commercial banks. Since the region already had a relatively well-developed banking sector, DFCs had always played a less significant role in financing. Instead, development institutions had channeled funding through the commercial banking sector to reach borrowers. In order to facilitate these on-lending programs, development institutions also began to support commercial banks with project appraisal and accounting skills, particularly when dealing with SMEs. These initial programs provided the inspiration for how the existing DFC model could be improved; in addition to a greater reliance on the commercial banking sector, development institutions should also seek to strengthen their capacity and, critically, their business environment (Cassen and Associates 1986, 137). The removal of interest rate subsidies and a more comprehensive integration with commercial banks were the early steps to eliminating the moral hazard of financial intermediaries and formed an important stage in the transition to marketized development financial instruments.

A Shift in the Focus of Development

These revisions to existing development policy were also accompanied by a much more ambitious desire to shift the focus of development. While industrialization and infrastructure projects formed the core of traditional policy, more efforts were directed to fund individual entrepreneurs. In order to enable entrepreneurs, there was a growing conviction within the development community that SMEs were a potential pathway forward. For one, they reinforced the view that economic growth should be based upon individual initiative rather than heavy-handed government programs. Skepticism of government institutions to facilitate SMEs encouraged development institutions to seek alternative ways to directly finance end recipients. There was also concern that while industrialization and infrastructure projects were important, they increasingly concentrated the wealth in the largest cities, providing little benefit for those living in rural areas. Finally, there was hope that development finance could reach those projects that were, in fact, unbankable. The maturation of the commercial banking sector both domestically and internationally meant that it was sufficiently capable of handling larger industrial projects, a development that shifted the need of financing toward smaller borrowers. SMEs, it was assumed, faced a financing problem, and financial markets gave development institutions the tools to solve chronic underfunding.

Until the 1980s, there was very little development institutional financing for SME projects. The World Bank had only financed five SME projects through 1975, and three of those projects (in the Philippines, Colombia, and Cameroon) began that same year (World Bank 1976, 27). Yet SMEs were not ignored because of the lack of support, but rather because of the difficulties of implementation. Until the 1980s, financial technology was simply not advanced enough to administer SME loans on an individual basis, and World Bank policies required recipient government guarantees, an infeasible task with small loans. Restrictive interest rate policies, the lack of borrower history, and the absence of extensive electronic communications meant that extending loans to an entrepreneur was a risky and time-consuming affair. This was not feasible for SME loans as the administration costs would be exceedingly high.

Some early innovations in SME financing arose from institutions other than the World Bank. In the early 1980s, the Netherlands Development Finance Co (FMO) experimented with a new mechanism to support SMEs that adhered to the tenets of market liberalism. This early iteration was designed to solve many of the moral hazard problems that plagued development finance (Development Practitioner #30 2016). It also was a manifestation of the market discipline that had formed the foundation for early development finance—it emphasized the commercial banking sector, validated the distribution of finance through market mechanisms, and was closer to achieving financial sustainability than a subsidized government institution.

From the perspective of development institutions, this proved to be a promising option. First, rather than working with government institutions, development institutions could instead leverage the commercial banking sector. Second, since commercial banks were ostensibly free of bureaucratic restrictions, development institutions could take a much more active approach to governance. Third, by charging market rates for loans, the commercial bank could eliminate the moral hazard of enterprises seeking subsidized finance. Macroeconomic risks of currency devaluation were consequently priced into the interest rates, as were individual company risks. Finally, development institutions could take advantage of innovations in capital markets. One was the development of a more marketized version of syndicated credit, which allowed development institutions to share financial risk through jointly financing projects. As one World Bank employee described, "innovations of this kind can be classified into two groups: those designed to provide flexible payments schedules for borrowers and those designed to satisfy lenders' needs for greater liquidity in their assets" (Saini 1986, 6).

Nevertheless, there was still significant resistance. The World Bank was reluctant to fully abandon the model of project loans and DFCs, if for no other reason that it would be a tacit admission that a cornerstone of its historical development strategy was flawed. Bureaucratic inertia similarly slowed the process. Donor country politicians were also hesitant to remove the recipient government guarantees out of fear that the loss of risk protection would hurt them politically during loan defaults, similar to what happened during the Latin American debt crises of the 1980s. Even within development institutions, there was debate as to the merits of abandoning a development aid model that had persisted for decades. Some worried about the potential loss of influence, since commercial banks rather than government institutions would serve as intermediaries. Some were concerned about the inability of commercial banks to reach or choose to serve those that are neediest. Others were simply ideologically opposed and were uncomfortable with the idea that market forces would dictate the distribution of aid (Development Practitioner #23 2016).

For the World Bank, it was not until 1989 with the release of the watershed *World Development Report* that an official embrace of a new strategy was codified. In the report, the World Bank reiterated the connection between savings, the financial sector, investment, and economic growth; the difference was the policy prescription. It still maintained an orthodox perspective on reforms that, "[t]o operate efficiently, financial institutions and markets have to be guided primarily by market forces rather than government directives" (World Bank 1989, 111). Yet the Bank conceded that government intervention in the financial sector may have been necessary under certain circumstances, and that direct government allocation of credit was highly problematic for the commercial financial sector. The numerous banking crises in the 1980s led to a series of recommendations from the Bank—the creation of stable legal and regulatory environments, the formalization of the informal financial sector, and a continued liberalization of financial policy. To the surprise of many, the World Bank also backed away from some of the most hardline positions. It signaled its support for smaller, more informal financial instruments, such as savings cooperatives or lending small sums of money without collateral, in order to encourage further development in the world's poorest countries. Moreover, the World Bank certainly endeavored to privatize the financial sector, but noted that this should be done cautiously; only after the balance sheets had been improved should they be permitted to operate entirely on commercial terms (1989, 130).

Perhaps the best summarization of the shifting prospects of development assistance came from William Diamond. In a speech to the National Bank of Egypt, Diamond outlined possible future roles for DFCs. One possibility was to use DFCs in the promotion of structural adjustment. DFCs had extensive accumulated knowledge of the on-the-ground economy and had the ability to work with governments to identify structural defects, which not only included interest rate policy and taxation, but the establishment of securities markets and new financial institutions as well. Additionally, since they played a financial role, DFCs could also provide advisory services and reformulate investment proposals. However, even Diamond recognized the limitations of DFCs. In what would ultimately become a prescient statement, he elaborated on the future of development finance:

> The crux of the problem of resource mobilization is, therefore, how to tap new, unofficial sources of finance, and thus progressively to reduce the predominance of official sources. Developing alternatives to official sources of finance, both domestic and foreign, call for coming to grips with the market. So far as domestic resources mobilization is concerned, this means helping to create a market, adapting a development bank's financial policies to that market's requirements, and promoting new institutions. (Diamond 1981, 22)

Diamond continued that development institutions should seek commercial sources of financing, specifically recommending co-financing schemes. He also noted that there was a wide range of potential combinations with international financial institutions, particularly via equity capital. As such, he suggested that governments and development institutions alike should "call for devising new financial instruments suited to the varied requirements of local savers, and for leadership in establishing more services and perhaps new financial instruments" (Diamond 1981, 22). By the end of the 1980s, development institutions wanted to translate this into practice.

The implementation of these changes within the World Bank was difficult. In order to realize Diamond's vision, the World Bank needed to reform its operations, particularly in the way that the institution directed investments. However, there were numerous obstacles to reforming the World Bank. For one, private banks were interested in expanding their investments, but were extraordinarily hesitant to do so in developing countries. The IFC had had success in creating country investment funds, but these were only for the most profitable projects (Development Practitioner #44 2016); traditional World Bank projects were not immediately profitable, nor were they located in the most business-friendly environments. The World Bank was prohibited from taking equity stakes, controlling the management of the intermediary institutions, or directly creating new partner institutions, and these factors impeded the Bank from attracting private co-investment. With no authority to set up new partner institutions or control their investment decisions, the World Bank was forced to partner with subpar DFCs as their local conduits. Unsurprisingly, few private investors showed interest.

Second, the World Bank was internally conflicted over how much it should integrate with financial markets. Diamond's DFC Department and the IFC were strong supporters of greater marketization because they saw it as a way to fulfill a long-term position that private investment should bear a greater responsibility for economic development (cf. Diamond 1981). Others, namely from the traditional development assistance and grant departments, were hesitant of the Bank leaving its long-standing role as a purely development organization (Kapur et al. 1997, Ch 7). Without a coherent position on financial instruments, the Bank could not muster the necessary political support for institutional reform. By the mid-1980s, the World Bank had settled on a different strategy of engendering private investment through structural adjustment policies (cf. Gibbon 1993). The inability of the World Bank to create and operate new institutions inevitably led it to pursue other ways of risk management.

Finally, donor governments themselves were uninterested in reforming the World Bank. Beginning in the 1970s, donor governments had become suspicious of project loans and DFCs, and had begun to view them as ineffective, corrupt practices. Partly a consequence of this, donor government assistance as a percentage of GDP had waned in the 1970s and plateaued in the 1980s (OECD 2011, 9). In particular, the largest stakeholder—the United States—demonstrated remarkably little interest in pursuing financial instruments for the purposes of development. Instead, the United States supported the World Bank's shift to structural adjustment loans as a way of encouraging private investors. With neither its largest stakeholder nor a strong collection of other donor governments willing to support the necessary institutional changes, another development institution would need to blaze the trail.

Conclusion

Despite the persistent efforts of development practitioners to administer assistance via project loans and DFCs, together they produced lackluster outcomes. Project loans were beset with complications of improper incentives and political interference, an outcome exacerbated by the inability of development institutions to systematically assess the results. DFCs, which were originally envisioned as a government-guaranteed financial conduit for foreign development assistance, were equally problematic. DFCs had little operational autonomy, were subjected to government meddling and politicking, and were unable to counteract deleterious macroeconomic environments. DFCs further failed to mobilize additional private investment. Moreover, they had contradictory mandates of fiscal solvency and socially-beneficial projects, a mission that kept them dependent on public financing. By the end of the 1980s, the World Bank had rescinded financial support for DFCs and many were privatized, combined, or entirely shut down.

Yet the challenges of this strategy had a more profound impact on the future of development policy. The mobilization of private investment remained the primary objective, and development institutions explored using financial markets for development purposes. Unwilling to repeat the mistakes of the previous decades, development institutions acknowledged that recipient country incentives that were properly aligned with development outcomes would be key to success. However, the largest development institution—the World Bank—had numerous limitations in how it could reorient development assistance for use in financial instruments. Waxing global financial markets provided the potential for further experimentation, but the World Bank was unable to combine donor government development assistance in ways that adhered to market discipline. Together with the lack of political will to change, the Bank was unable to push forward drastic changes that better aligned development projects with financial markets. Nevertheless, these early forays into financial markets laid the foundation for a shift to marketized development financial instruments. With a growing consensus that financial markets provided a future for development policy, all that was needed was an impetus strong enough to overcome bureaucratic hurdles and a development institution flexible enough to use financial markets for development objectives.

References

Becker, William H. 2003. *The Market, the State, and the Export-Import Bank of the United States, 1934–2000*. Cambridge, UK: Cambridge University Press.

Caprio Jr, Gerard, and Asli Demirguc-Kunt. 1997. *The Role of Long Term Finance: Theory and Evidence*. Washington, DC: World Bank.

Cassen, Robert, and Associates. 1986. *Does Aid Work? Report to an Intergovernmental Task Force*. Oxford: Oxford University Press.

DFC Department. 1975. *DFC Policy Paper*. Washington, DC: World Bank.

Diamond, William. 1957. *Development Banks*. Baltimore, MD: The Economic Development Institute: International Bank for Reconstruction and Development.

———. 1981. *Reflections on the Performance of Development Banks and the Challenges Ahead*. Cairo: National Bank of Egypt.

Diamond, William, and Ravi Gulhati. 1973. World Bank's Experience with Development Finance Companies. *Economic and Political Weekly* 8 (23): M47–M56.

Engel, Willi. 1967. Credit Control by Development Banks. In *The Role of Development Banks in Economic and Social Development*. Berlin: German Foundation for Developing Countries.

Führer, Helmut. 1996. *The Story of Official Development Assistance*. Paris: OECD.

Gibbon, Peter. 1993. The World Bank and the New Politics of Aid. *The European Journal of Development Research* 5 (1): 35–62.

Gordon, David L. 1983. *Development Finance Companies, State and Privately Owned: A Review*. Washington, DC: The World Bank.

Grasso, Patrick G., Sulaiman S. Wasty, and Rachel V. Weaving (eds.). 2003. *World Bank Operations Department: The First 30 Years*. Washington, DC: World Bank.

Gulhati, Ravi. 1971. A Few Thoughts for 1972.

Harries, Heinrich. 1998. *Wiederaufbau, Welt und Wende: Die KfW–Eine Bank mit öffentlichem Auftrag*. Frankfurt am Main: Knapp.

Heussen, Hejo, Bernd Breuer, and Lore Wellmann (eds.). 1987. *Promotion of Self-Help by Savings Banks: A Dialogue Programme; St. Blasien, Bonn, 25.5. - 5.6.1987*. Berlin: ZWS.

Hu, Yao-Su. 1981. The World Bank and Development Finance Companies. *Journal of General Management* 7 (Autumn): 46–57.

IBRD. 1975. DFC Policy Paper.

Kalmanoff, George. 1969a. Bank Group Assistance to Development Finance Companies, Compared to Other New Resources Mobilized by the Companies.

———. 1969b. *Selected Basic Data on Development Finance Companies*. Washington, DC: World Bank.

Kapur, Devesh, John Prior Lewis, and Richard Charles Webb. 1997. *The World Bank: Its First Half Century*. Washington, DC: Brookings Institution Press.

Lamby, Werner. 1967. The Role of Regional Development Banks. In *The Role of Development Banks in Economic and Social Development*. Berlin: German Foundation for Developing Countries.

Lessard, Donald R. 1986. *International Financing for Developing Countries: The Unfulfilled Promise*. Washington, DC: World Bank.

Ligeti, Sàndor. 1985. Development Banks in the Developing Countries / Les Banques De Dèveloppement. *Savings and Development* 9 (3): 297–323.

Loganathan, C. 1971. The DFC Department of the Bank and Its Role in Small Developing Member Countries.

Mason, Edward S., and Robert E. Asher. 1973. *The World Bank Since Bretton Woods: The Origins, Policies, Operations, and Impact of the International Bank for Reconstruction and Development and the Other Members of the World Bank Group: The International Finance Corporation, the International Development Association [and] the International Centre for Settlement of Investment Disputes*. Washington, DC: Brookings Institution.

Mayer, Colin. 1989. *Myths of the West: Lessons from Developed Countries for Development Finance*. Washington, DC: World Bank.

McCarthy, Stephen. 1978. The Administration of Capital Aid. *Development Dialogue 1*: 90–95.

Nevin, Michael. 1985. Dilemmas in Development Banking. *Savings and Development* 9 (4): 421–40.

———. 1994. The European Investment Bank and African Development Finance Companies. In *The European Economy in Perspective: Essays in Honour of Edward Nevin*, ed. Jeffery Round. Cardiff: University of Wales Press.

Nougaim, Khalil. 1971. Assistance to DFC Clients Through Management Consulting Firms.

OECD. 1981. *Compendium of Aid Procedures*. Paris: OECD.

———. 2011. *Measuring Aid: 50 Years of DAC Statistics—1961–2011*. Paris: OECD.

Pearson, Lester B. 1969. *Partners in Development: Report of the Commission on International Development*. New York: Praeger Publishers.

Saini, Krishnan. 1986. *Capital Market Innovations and Financial Flows to Developing Countries*. Washington, DC: World Bank.

Shin, B. H. 1968. Sources of Finance of Development Finance Companies as of December 31, 1967.

———. 1969. On the Flow of Funds in Industrial Sector in Selected Countries.

Uecker, Roland. 1967. Forms of Organization in the Development Bank Field. In *The Role of Development Banks in Economic and Social Development*. Berlin: German Foundation for Developing Countries.

UNCTAD. 1991. *World Investment Report 1991: The Triad in Foreign Direct Investment*. New York: UN Conference on Trade and Development.

UNIDO. 1979. *Development Banking in the 1980s: Selections from the Proceedings of the UNIDO/World Bank Symposium, Zurich, June 1979*. Vienna: United Nations Industrial Development Organization.

Vibert, Frank. 1973. 'The World Bank and Development Finance Companies' Minutes of Staff Review.

World Bank. 1973a. Annex–Conclusions of the DFC Case Studies.

———. 1973b. The World Bank and Development Finance Companies.

———. 1974. DFC Special Studies: Principal Findings.

———. 1976. *Development Finance Companies: Sector Policy Paper*. Washington, DC: World Bank.

———. 1979. *Operations Evaluation: World Bank Standards and Procedures*. Washington, DC: World Bank.

———. 1980. *World Bank Annual Report 1980*. Washington, DC: World Bank.

———. 1989. *World Development Report 1989: Financial Systems and Development*. Washington, DC: World Bank.

CHAPTER 4

KfW and the Early Stages of Marketized Development Financial Instruments

By the 1980s, development assistance was undergoing a substantial transformation. Assessment missions revealed the shortcomings of project loans and DFCs, yet practitioners remained committed to the idea that private investment mobilization was the appropriate path for development policy. However, while the World Bank struggled to integrate development policy with financial markets, other development institutions began to experiment with new financial instruments. I argue that KfW, Germany's development institution, was an important innovator and promoter of these new instruments because of its underlying institutional characteristics—including strong political backing, institutional flexibility to own and operate financial instruments, and extensive domestic experience with financial instruments—as well as its strong German government support for risk-sharing mechanisms that emerged following key political junctures.

Through the 1980s, KfW's operations closely mirrored global development trends. After adopting the mantel of Germany's development assistance in 1961, KfW supported a standard mix of project loans and DFCs, often to the benefit of German industry. Yet after 1980, following a stinging set of internal evaluation reports, KfW became increasingly concerned with matching incentives with development outcomes. Like its international counterparts, KfW shared the view that development assistance should adhere to market discipline, a conviction that mirrored its

P. Volberding, *Leveraging Financial Markets for Development*,
Executive Politics and Governance,
https://doi.org/10.1007/978-3-030-55008-0_4

own private sector-oriented domestic promotional business. Yet applying its domestic experience to a developing country context was not straightforward, and KfW initially encountered the same institutional roadblocks as the World Bank. However, two crises—German reunification and the collapse of the Soviet Union—proved to be critical junctures in enabling KfW to overcome these barriers. In particular, through these crises, strong German government support enabled KfW to leverage two critical advantages that allowed it to better experiment with marketized development financial instruments. First, the German government agreed to guarantee investment risk of these instruments in recipient countries in order to expedite implementation. Second, KfW convinced the German government that, in order to reduce moral hazard that had plagued earlier funding mechanisms, KfW needed to have greater authority not only to create new financial instruments, but also to maintain control over their operations. This institutional flexibility over financial instruments, combined with government risk assumption and an expanded technical assistance capacity, allowed for KfW to more effectively experiment with marketized development financial instruments and better align private financial markets with development projects.

KfW and the Crisis of Development

The initial two decades of KfW reflected those of other development aid agencies. Its operations in the mid-1950s centered on providing export financing credits to enable developing countries to purchase German industrial equipment or to finance projects that supplied German industry with natural resources. KfW's first international development activity was in India with a debt restructuring agreement and the provision of industrial credits for the construction of a steel mill in Rourkela (Harries 1998, 86). From 1958 to 1960, KfW funded projects in Pakistan, Mexico, Chile, Guinea, Sudan, Turkey, Spain, and Greece. In 1961, KfW also supplied DM 208 million in credits to the Liberian government to import high-quality iron ore, its largest loan internationally to date (KfW 1960, 55). That same year, KfW officially adopted the mantel as one of Germany's international development aid agencies that allowed the institution to tap official lines of credit for development purposes (Harries 1998, 80).

KfW had succeeded in jostling for the title over other domestic economic agencies, a shift that was critically important for the survival of KfW itself as well. After all, the *Wirtschaftswunder* (economic miracle) had ushered in a period of unprecedented economic growth in West Germany, undermining KfW's purpose as a reconstruction agency. The rehabilitation of KfW highlighted the fact that the German government desired to maintain its presence in the economy, particularly with regard to the *Mittelstand*, or Germany's numerous SMEs (Grünbacher 2001, 77). The implications for development were also clear as the German government desired to leverage KfW for political purposes. The Cold War politicized development finance, and the United States was eager to have West Germany join the fray against the spread of communism. Adenauer's government also saw development finance as critical to bolstering its claim as the sole legitimate German government and utilized KfW-supplied development assistance as a way of enticing countries away from recognizing East Germany (Grünbacher 2005, 236). Economically, the accumulation of foreign capital reserves also pushed the West German government to seek offshore investment. When combined with the clamoring of German companies to increase the markets for their industrial exports, rebranding KfW's funding as development assistance made both political and economic sense.

During this period, KfW's development priorities reflected the standard mixture of project loans and financial support for DFCs. From 1961 to 1971, capital loans accounted for 72% of total KfW contribution to developing countries (KfW 1971a, 70). Loans and grants for manufacturing and infrastructure projects transitioned to a modest increase in support for socially beneficial projects and increased funding for World Bank-sponsored DFCs. In 1973, German aid became completely untied to German suppliers (KfW 1976a, 35).[1] A full policy for joint financing projects with other development agencies was also established in 1973 (KfW 1973c), though worries still persisted that the objectives of KfW did not entirely align with those of the World Bank (KfW 1975b). Mirroring global trends, in 1975, KfW began to seek measurements of aid effectiveness; total employment created from investments provided the first measure of broader social impact as it was the easiest quantifiable number (KfW 1975a, 83). Concurrently, KfW favored capital aid loans for critical infrastructure and industrial projects. However, given the relatively small

[1] Even though there was no official requirement, German suppliers retained a majority of contracts. By 1982, German suppliers accounted for 77% of KfW's supply contracts (KfW 1982).

scale of KfW's operations—in 1980 KfW provided DM 3.594 billion in grants and loans to developing countries (KfW 1980a, 35)—financing partnerships with the World Bank remained an important component (Lamby 1967, G2).

In addition to project loans, KfW also supported DFCs. From 1962 through 1981, KfW provided lines of credit to 81 DFCs across 49 countries (see Table 4.1). KfW provided DM 3.6 billion in loans to DFCs, comprising just under 10% of KfW's total outlays to developing countries. The largest loan was to India's IFCI, an amount that totaled DM 227.5 million in 1981. By 1973, KfW had redoubled its efforts to finance projects via development banks, particularly in the agricultural and SME sectors with a stronger oversight to ensure end-credit users benefit (KfW 1973a), and in 1977, KfW created an audit guide for evaluating DFCs (KfW 1977). In 1980, KfW cooperated with BMZ to reform the "Guidelines for the Bilateral Financial Cooperation with Development Banks" to provide much clearer policies on credit line limits, financial health of development banks, project assessment, and reporting requirements (KfW 1980b). Updated guidelines were issued in 1985 (KfW 1985b).[2] Yet lurking within the DFC data were problems. For one, numerous KfW employees reported that investments in DFCs were often poorly managed, had little developmental impact, and had internal reports of widespread corruption (Development Practitioner #40 2016; Schmidt 2016). Additionally, KfW's DFC investments were heavily skewed to middle-income countries, undermining the argument that DFCs encouraged private investment in the world's poorest regions. Asia dominated total KfW financing to DFCs (mainly in India, Pakistan, and Israel), receiving fully 56% of total investments. As a percentage of total German assistance, DFCs in Latin America received the greatest share, amounting to 22% (KfW 1982, 59). In both cases, the most underdeveloped countries in Asia and Africa received disproportionately little assistance.

From 1958 to 1980, development assistance at KfW closely mirrored trends of the World Bank. Political considerations determined aid allocations and a mix of project loans and support for DFCs comprised the principal investments. A similar desire for private investment mobilization guided policy. However, KfW also began encountering challenges to its

[2] "Orientierungsrichtlinien für die bilaterale Finanzielle Zusammenarbeit mit Entwicklungsbanken," BMZ-Papier 222-T 9121-9/80.

Table 4.1 KfW investments in DFCs, 1962–1981

DFC	*Country*	*Year of first investment*	*Amount (million DM, 1981)*
BSB	Bangladesh	1974	56.2
BSRS	Bangladesh	1974	19.4
		1963	179.5
IFCI	India	1963	227.5
NSIC	India	1964	67
ARDC	India	1980	100
BAPINDO		1976	11
IMDBI		1972	24.5
IDBI		1965	474
Lemelacha	Israel	1972	26
IBA	Israel	1975	80
YAAD	Israel	1978	12.5
NIR	Israel	1978	10.5
Otzar La'taasiya	Israel	1978	83
IB	Israel	1980	140
LADB	Israel	1981	10
IDB	Jordan	1972	38
ACC	Jordan	1978	21
JCO	Jordan	1978	16
SMIB		1965	33.8
KDB	South Korea	1966	50
MIDF		1971	5
NIDC	Nepal	1964	7
	Pakistan	1962	187.6
IDBP	Pakistan	1962	130.7
IFCT		1963	51
AIDB		1964	10
BNDE	Burundi	1974	2.8
BIDI	Ivory Coast	1968	30
BNDA	Ivory Coast	1974	20
BGD	Gabon	1970	3.9
NIB	Ghana	1968	20
BHC	Ghana	1978	15
BCD		1963	9.8
KIE	Kenya	1966	33.6
CBK	Kenya	1979	5
LBDI	Liberia	1965	4

(continued)

Table 4.1 (continued)

DFC	*Country*	*Year of first investment*	*Amount (million DM, 1981)*
BNM	Madagascar	1969	2.2
MDC		1965	0.3
BDM	Mali	1975	15
CNCA	Morocco	1973	103.4
MCCB	Mauritius	1975	3
BDRN	Niger	1966	2
BND	Burkina Faso	1972	4
BRD	Rwanda	1974	6.5
SOFISEDIT	Senegal	1977	10
ABS		1976	5
TRDB	Tanzania	1973	5
TIB	Tanzania	1975	25
BTD	Togo	1972	2
STB		1968	50.3
BDET	Tunisia	1973	38.3
FOSDA	Tunisia	1974	7
SOFIDE	DRC	1973	28.5
BND	CAR	1965	3.7
BOAD	Multilateral	1981	9.1
BISA	Bolivia	1971	3.8
BNDE		1965	171.1
Banco do Brasil	Brazil	1965	61.7
CORFO		1965	81.3
FIDE	Dominican Republic	1975	7.5
CV-CFN	Ecuador	1969	18
BNF	Ecuador	1980	15
JDB	Jamaica	1975	4.2
BR		1966	44.2
IFI	Colombia	1971	10
CFP	Colombia	1977	8
BND		1969	15.5
BNF	Paraguay	1964	51
CAH	Paraguay	1979	5
BIP		1980	12.5
BROU	Uruguay	1975	12
BCIE	Multilateral	1970	59

(continued)

Table 4.1 (continued)

DFC	*Country*	*Year of first investment*	*Amount (million DM, 1981)*
	Multilateral	1975	16.5
	Multilateral	1977	15
ETBA		1969	22.5
NIBID	Greece	1977	40
ABG	Greece	1977	80
BFN		1981	27
		1969	304
	Cyprus	1969	14

Source KfW (1982)

KfW. 1982. *Projektfinanzierung in Entwicklundsländern*. am Main: Kreditanstalt für Wiederaufbau

assistance system, chief among them the absence of a systematic evaluation system and moral hazards with DFCs. Based on its own domestic experiences, KfW attempted to apply market discipline in a development context, though this would be a long evolution.

Increasing Challenges for KfW

During this period, a number of factors complicated the role of KfW. First, Germany's aid regime was fragmented among three institutions. KfW was officially tasked with financing development projects, but the Federal Ministry for Economic Cooperation and Development (Bundesministerium für wirtschaftliche Zusammenarbeit und Entwicklung, BMZ) was responsible for selecting—or, at the very least, approving—projects and coordinating with German policymakers. GTZ[3] provided the technical assistance for projects. This division of labor, however, inhibited coordination and slowed implementation of projects (Development Practitioner #34 2016). It also created competition between GTZ and KfW for project leadership, a dynamic that would often stymie project implementation. Later, a stagnating German development budget made the competitive situation worse (OECD 1998, 50).

[3] Deutsche Gesellschaft für Technische Zusammenarbeit, or German Corporation for Technical Cooperation, was later merged into Deutsche Gesellschaft für Internationale Zusammenarbeit (GIZ).

Second, KfW was reaching a similar conclusion that the traditional strategy of relieving bottlenecks was ineffective at mobilizing private investment. Instead, KfW began to look at ways of supporting private enterprises outside of the largest cities. This meant financing rural infrastructure, agriculture projects, and entrepreneurs of SMEs and reflected a "self-help" perspective that was based on Germany's own economic renaissance (cf. DSE 1986; Mathéy 1982; Ullrich and DSE 1982). For KfW, this meant that technical assistance was crucial to empower individuals and institutions, and, as the 1970s progressed, technical assistance outlays to governments and businesses became increasingly prevalent in KfW's development assistance (cf. KfW 1975a).

Finally, there were growing suspicions that German development assistance was ineffective. Like their multilateral counterparts, KfW underwent a similar process of evaluation. The growing evidence that existing programs in agriculture (KfW 1974, 88) were in trouble suggested that greater resources should be devoted to project assessment. However, while such evaluation programs were conducted on domestic SME credit lines, KfW had not developed a standardized methodology (Development Practitioner #26 2016). As one internal document noted, "[i]n Kreditanstalt we have always been hesitant to supply forms of *formulars*, as we feel there is no specific American, German, Indian, or Brazilian way of project appraisal. If anything, certain aspects are emphasized more than others by way of tradition or because of the demands of a particular situation" (Wabnitz 1967, E7). And it was not until 1991 that a comprehensive and comparative project evaluation report was undertaken (cf. KfW 1991).[4]

Prior to the systematic evaluation, there had been limited independent evaluation reports of German assistance, and most had been commissioned by BMZ. For DFCs, KfW under the direction of Dr. Willi Engel had supported the policies of on-lending via traditional NDBs. Only one independent assessment of these DFCs had occurred, an assessment of the *financieras* in Colombia, and concluded that inappropriate macroeconomic policies hampered their efforts (cf. Nitsch 1970). The first official assessment specifically of these development financial institutions was commissioned by BMZ in 1971 on the DFCs in Colombia.

[4]The first comprehensive evaluation report was commissioned in 1988–1989 in coordination with the Financial Cooperation (Finanzielle Zusammenarbeit) program. There were five iterations of the report.

The report found widespread inefficiencies in the disbursement of aid, but the German development institutions were resigned to the results because of the lack of alternative investment mechanisms. The *Abschlussdruck*, or pressure to utilize all available funds during the calendar year, only added to the predicament of disbursing the funds without proper assessment (Development Practitioner #57 2018).

In 1973, KfW called a meeting of employees involved in financing DFCs to discuss these ongoing challenges. While KfW endeavored to increase domestic savings rates and ensure that its credit lines reached SMEs, it struggled to eliminate the arbitrage opportunities for financial intermediaries between subsidized credit lines and government-set interest rates (KfW 1973b). Additionally, lethargy in reform was also a consequence of KfW's own reluctance to drastically reform its policies to support more market instruments. Some segments within KfW still looked suspiciously at using private finance for development. Yet most had the perspective that KfW's responsibility was to disburse the money to projects and DFCs, and there was a sense of resignation that better behavior could be induced from recipients (Development Practitioner #40 2016).

The tepid interest in KfW for reform, combined with the lack of political will to reconceive of development, meant that assistance policies remained virtually unchanged for the following decade (Development Practitioner #7 2016). Nevertheless, pressure had been mounting within the German ministries to gain better insight into the effectiveness of aid (Development Practitioner #57 2018). In 1980, BMZ again ordered an independent evaluation of German-sponsored projects abroad. The focus of the effort was DFCs, but also encompassed a wide range of German government assistance programs. This time, third-party academics were sent to the three regions—Latin America, Africa, and South Asia. Each was tasked with evaluating the impact of development assistance on its economic and social impact merits, as well as confirming that funds were being used according to German regulations (Schmidt 2016). Parallel missions examined the end recipients of these on-lent grants (Development Practitioner #56 2017).

The results of surveys were uniformly negative. The Africa report was critical of KfW-supported development institutions, and the institutional quality of these financial intermediaries was found to be insufficient (Development Practitioner #40 2016). The report, however, was less forthcoming with recommendations. The South Asia group's report was tepid in its overall outcomes, but one member, Jan Pieter Krahnen, wrote a dissenting opinion that accorded with the findings of the Africa report (Krahnen 2016). But it was the Latin America report that was the most scathing in its criticism. Professor Manfred Nitsch, a well-known German development political economist on Latin America, agreed to survey three countries—Nicaragua, Colombia, and Ecuador—with the assistance of Claus-Peter Zeitinger and Reinhardt Schmidt. Prior to visiting the countries, Nitsch was already familiar with the problems that had plagued development institutions in Colombia since a similar report he conducted in 1973 concluded that development institutions were often ineffective for development outcomes (Nitsch 1973). However, the new findings surpassed all expectations.

The situation uncovered in Nicaragua proved to be the most revealing about the deficiencies of the existing development strategy. Nicaragua had been specifically selected because the overthrow of the Somoza regime in 1979 led the auditors to believe that the current Sandinista government would have no incentive to lie about previous misdeeds. However, it was quickly apparent that widespread financial malpractice had occurred, and the current Sandinista regime was equally corrupt. Upon arrival in Nicaragua, the assessment group was met by the German ambassador who attempted to dissuade their investigation on account of an almost certainly negative report. Yet since Nitsch was also slated to present at the Ebert Foundation, the mission proceeded undeterred, even though the group had lost the official mandate from the German government (Development Practitioner #56 2017). In the submitted report, the authors relayed, in excruciating detail, how German development assistance was misused. In Nicaragua, the report detailed tales of corruption, fraud, and collusion with the Somoza regime, and evidence that KfW and BMZ were aware of the problems. Most notably, the report found that the two DM 10 million loans that KfW provided had—to the last cent—been misused by the previous Somoza regime (Development Practitioner #56 2017). The experiences in Colombia and Ecuador were better, but the report still found the institutions undercapitalized and ineffective (Nitsch et al. 1981a).

The impact of the three assessment reports was substantial. For BMZ and KfW, these reports were embarrassing as it highlighted their inability to administer development assistance in accordance with German legal requirements. In response to the draft report, BMZ wrote a letter detailing the authors' errors and noting once more that since the research in Nicaragua was conducted outside the auspices of the German government, the findings could not be publicly published (BMZ 1982). The final version eliminated any reference to Nicaragua and avoided issues of corruption and ineffectiveness of NDBs, providing instead a saccharine version of German development assistance (Nitsch et al. 1981b). Nitsch and Schmidt were also blacklisted from many German government contracts for future consulting work (Schmidt 2016). Yet there was also a more profound impact on the way that practitioners began to conceive of development. The incident sparked a decade-long internal debate within KfW about whether the institution should continue to support financial intermediaries within developing countries with adjustments or whether to scrap the traditional model and begin with a new strategy (Development Practitioner #26 2016). Their new, competing vision encompassed a greater embrace of growing global financial markets to induce proper behavior on the part of recipient countries (Development Practitioner #7 2016). This in no small part incentivized further investigation in areas such as microfinance and SME financing.

Early Experiments with Financial Markets

KfW's perspective was that financial logic should inform development. Its earliest strategy codified "commercial prudence" in the General Agreement in 1966, and KfW's initial funding through the ERP was used on a revolving basis. Since 1957, the domestic *Mittelstand* program funded SMEs, and KfW had issued DM-denominated bonds for domestic projects (Harries 1998, 49). This approach translated to development assistance as well. From early on, members of KfW thought that private-based mechanisms reduced the biases and corruption in investment decision-making (Voigt 1967, F2). Moreover, research reports such as the North-South Commission identified financing gaps as one of the largest obstacles for developing countries. Poor credit ratings had burdened developing countries into unsustainable debt loads, if they could even secure international private financing at all. KfW posited that ODA had an important role in providing non-repayable grants or loans on soft terms, but that private investment and market-rate alternatives were also important. KfW estimated that in 1980, USD 4 billion was provided in development assistance on market terms, and another USD 4 billion was mobilized on non-market terms. It was the responsibility of development to mediate lending and reduce the risks and information costs to the private sector (KfW 1980a, 88–91).

However, KfW's domestic experience was not easily translated into international operations. The initial forays into financial markets took two forms. First, KfW began to increasingly rely on capital markets to obtain financing for its development projects, and included simple versions of mixed financing whereby German government capital was mixed with KfW's. Second, KfW concluded that a robust domestic financial sector was key to achieving self-sufficiency in economic growth. This dovetailed with KfW's long-time support for SMEs via DFCs, but this rarely translated into direct assistance to the financial institution itself. As such, there were some limited experiments in the 1980s with directly supporting recipient government banking sectors through the provision of financing, increased technical assistance, and an improvement of macroeconomic policy, experiences that would form the foundation of KfW's embrace of marketized development financial instruments.

Leveraging Private Capital Markets

Within the domestic economy, KfW had long relied on domestic German bond issuances to provide funding for its operations. While KfW attempted its first capital market issuance in 1949, it was not until 1957 that KfW felt that domestic capital markets had matured sufficiently. In 1958, KfW successfully issued DM 100 million in long-term bonds, specifically earmarked for SMEs (Grünbacher 2005, 93). That same year, KfW had its first financial innovation of medium-term fixed-rate notes (*Kassenobligationen*), and, by 1960, KfW had issued more than DM 500 million (Harries 1998, 52). The trend to increased financing from capital markets expanded precipitously over the next two decades. In 1970, KfW issued a then record-breaking amount of DM 650 million in bonds (KfW 1970, 43), and a decade later, DM 45.2 billion (KfW 1980a, 24). These funds were used to finance KfW's extensive support for German SMEs, export credits, environmental projects, and domestic infrastructure and industrialization projects. The Ministry of Finance was particularly eager about providing these financing mechanisms.

When KfW expanded its activities to international markets in 1961, KfW transferred its experience to the development sector. KfW was an early proponent of mixing private and public finance: "Private funds from various sources, such as the banking sector, institutional investors (insurance companies) and the capital market, are added by Kreditanstalt to an apportioned core of budget funds. The risk of a private development loan is thus reduced for the lender to an internal capital market issue" (KfW 1967b, 2). However, KfW was also forced to make a delicate balance in how it applied its funds raised on capital markets to developing countries. In particular, there were concerns about using Germany's stellar credit rating on behalf of other countries: "The KfW Board of Management wished to tap the capital market primarily in the interest of promoting domestic trade and industry and of the expanding export financing. The Board was afraid that the KfW might forfeit the trust of its creditors if too much of their funds was transmitted to developing countries" (Harries 1998, 79). The underlying projects of KfW's international development programs were not often commercially bankable, so no revenue would be available to repay loans. As such, KfW rebuffed the initial proposals from BMZ that wished KfW to refinance capital aid for development. According to Hermann Abs, the head of KfW at the time, the volumes, maturities, and interest rates were not conducive to success in the capital markets; rather, KfW argued that bridging loans and interim financing functions were the most that could be provided with market resources (Harries 1998, 84). For the 1960s and 1970s, funding for KfW's development operations was sourced from its own annual budgets or via grants provided by the German government to maintain the institution's high creditworthiness. At the same time, KfW was to support a network of foreign branches, offices, and participating interests of German enterprises, but this yielded only modest results (cf. KfW 1980a).

Nevertheless, KfW still tried to use private credit markets to fund development projects. The easiest way was to utilize the German government's wide array of guarantee instruments for capital exports to developing countries, which could be complemented by financial credits.[5] In theory, this was meant to encourage private financing of development projects abroad, particularly by German industrial companies, but in reality it exclusively served to secure raw material imports (Harries 1998, 77). While these export financing credits facilitated German industrial interest in developing countries, it did little to help KfW attract additional private

[5] The Hermes cover (Hermesdeckung) is an export credit guarantee and was introduced in 1949 as a way of protecting German companies in the event of non-repayment on the part of foreign debtors. Its main target was SMEs.

investment within the country. There was a distant hope that capital assistance would lead to increased private investment, however KfW's limited budget could come nowhere close to closing the financing gap across the developing world. For instance, in 1975, KfW explicitly noted that greater private investment, particularly through mixed forms of capital aid loans and export financing, would be the most beneficial pathway forward (KfW 1975a, 91). However, precisely how these public sources of funds could be mixed with private ones within the international realm remained elusive, and there was little optimism that financial markets within recipient countries could cover the shortfall.

Mixed financing provided one way of diversifying investment risk and incorporating private partners, and served as the earliest form of KfW's financial instruments. Under this scheme, KfW mixed German government-backed export credits with its own capital assistance program. As early as 1961, KfW co-financed the Roseires Dam in Sudan with the World Bank with a contribution of USD 18.4 million (IBRD, IDA, and KfW 1961); concurrently, KfW co-financed textile and dam projects with the newly established European Investment Bank (EIB) (Harries 1998, 92). Beginning in 1964, KfW also began to actively engage in mixed financing with German financial partners. BMZ had published a framework entitled "Financial and Technical Cooperation of the Federal Republic of Germany" whereby public funds marked as ODA could be mixed with KfW's own resources to provide subsidized rates of capital to developing countries. In 1967, KfW proved that mixed financing could be implemented with commercial banks. KfW itself provided DM 450 million for the construction of an UNINSA steel mill in Spain, while the remainder was financed by a syndicated loan sponsored by the export credit bank AKA and commercial banks, led by Deutsche Bank (KfW 1967a, 77). In 1969, KfW employed mixed financing worth DM 1705 million for the Argentinian nuclear power station Atucha I (KfW 1969, 95).

The utilization of mixed financing continued to grow throughout the ensuing decade—KfW was able to finance larger projects with diversified risk, and commercial banks found it profitable to invest in projects with responsible managers. In 1980, mixed financing generated DM 3.6 billion of KfW's investments, and through 1980, KfW had concluded nearly 1700 mixed financing agreements in 92 countries for a total of DM 35.3 billion (KfW 1980a, 30). Internal KfW documents revealed that management saw mixed financing as a way to expand opportunities for German commercial banks as well (KfW 1983). Mixed financing performed best in advanced developing countries and in sectors that produced consistent revenue streams. In 1984, this was concentrated in energy (70% of total) and transportation and communication (26%), and investments in Turkey, India, and Pakistan (KfW 1984, 74). By the late 1980s, mixed financing had grown in scope. In 1988, DM 1.5 billion of loans were administered, of which DM 0.7 billion was "Financial Cooperation" funds and DM 0.5 billion was KfW's own funds. The industrial and energy sectors absorbed the most mixed financing—33 and 27%, respectively, of the total—and they were used for major projects in Egypt, India, Indonesia, Cameroon, Pakistan, Syria, and Turkey (KfW 1988, 46). However, these mixed funds did not mobilize substantial amounts of additional private capital. Moreover, they served as the primary form of tied aid, and as the international development community moved away from these policies in the early 1980s, mixed financing lost its importance (Development Practitioner #34 2016).

An additional boost to KfW's efforts came with the deepening of global capital markets. Deriving experience from its export financing credits, KfW became more active in global currency markets and international bond markets to meet the demands of foreign borrowers. In 1985, KfW engaged with the US bond market for the first time and became one of the first German institutions to be rated by Standard and Poor's and Moody's, as well as registered with the Securities and Exchange Commission (SEC). The institution received a AAA credit rating. In January 1987, KfW issued its first US dollar-denominated bond of USD 200 million on the Euro-market. While actions did not directly impact KfW's operations in development finance, it did lay important groundwork for future innovations by giving KfW experience. In order to better access the American market, in 1988 KfW established a subsidiary, KfW International Finance, to facilitate funding; in 1989, KfW had issued DM 2.4 billion in foreign currencies (KfW 1989, 14). During this period, KfW also developed in-house financial capacities to operate on global financial markets. Most of the efforts were directed toward improving the efficacy of export credits (cf. Harries 1998), but they would later have important spillover effects when KfW began to implement more complicated financial instruments for development purposes. New financial instruments developed during this period included interest rate and currency swaps, variable interest rate bonds, and zero-coupon bonds for refinancing activities.

Early Support for Private Entrepreneurs and DFCs

KfW's latent support for private entrepreneurs and financial institutions was also based upon its own domestic experiences. Following reconstruction, KfW shifted its attention to SMEs since basic industries were able to raise capital on the domestic bond market, but SMEs struggled to find financing. As the backbone of the German economy, as well as an important CDU constituency, KfW implemented its first program for SMEs in 1956 with an initial amount of DM 52.4 million, all sourced from the ERP Special Fund (KfW 1957, 42). KfW's oldest external program was the export financing credits that were designed to assist German SME's to gain market access in developing countries. German political support for private enterprise inevitably spilled over into perspectives on international assistance. Even though West Germany heeded the call of the United States to increase its international aid funding, Chancellor Ludwig Erhard had also openly rejected the American proposal for development assistance to be centered on state aid. Rather, he thought that the viable successes of the German market economy should be exported to developing countries through private industry (Harries 1998, 77). As such, export financing programs were designed to have a dual function—support SME exports and promote the creation of a vibrant SME network abroad.

Domestically, KfW had also expanded its SMEs programs with great success. In 1971, after pressure from Bonn, KfW announced its M Programme. This program set out to provide long-term credit to the *Mittelstand* with money raised exclusively on capital markets. KfW's policy was to ameliorate market failures and provide financing to SMEs, which suffered a comparative disadvantage in the market for credit. In order to adhere to market principles, KfW on-lent through Germany's extensive network of savings banks (as well as larger commercial banks), but the bank also had to assume liability for the loans. The M Programme exploded in size from DM 500 million in 1971 to DM 6 billion by 1989 (Harries 1998, 122). By 1980, the M Programme had also been extended to SMEs. Loan repayment conditions were made flexible to compensate for oscillating interest rates, and, in an early bid to promote environmental protection, the loans could also be used for energy efficiency upgrades (KfW 1980a, 56–60).

The penchant for private enterprise was reflected in KfW's development strategy as well, even though its options were circumscribed in the first two decades. Prior to 1980, in addition to the support of German

SMEs via export credits, KfW further supported the World Bank in its mission to support private entrepreneurs. KfW approved joint examinations of capital assistance projects with the World Bank in 1971 (KfW 1971b) and reaffirmed its commitment to joint financing projects in 1972 (KfW 1972) and 1980 (KfW 1980c). DFCs were seen as a way to access SMEs in countries without a fully functioning banking sector. As of 1967, the Germans supported 24 development banks in 19 countries with 54 capital assistance loans amounting to a total value of DM 700 million, the majority of which supported SME projects (Lamby 1967, G6). By the institution's own assessment, KfW had supported over 50,000 individual loans to SMEs and agricultural enterprises via these development banks by 1975 (KfW 1975a, 87). Within KfW, Willi Engel provided the most ardent support, and he noted that this DFC support accorded with the German government's perspective that private sector and market-oriented industrialization via SMEs was the best strategy (Harries 1998, 89). Much like the World Bank, however, DFCs needed to be utilized because KfW was unable to directly reach SMEs.

Yet KfW was suspicious of the efficacy of DFCs. As early as 1973, KfW had requested BMZ for the permission to divest in twelve DFCs (KfW 1973d). Limited oversight capacities and little budget for technical assistance and staff training meant that the institutional capacity of DFCs was underdeveloped, as the 1980 assessments of development banks highlighted (Schmidt 2016). However, as internal documents demonstrate, KfW disagreed with the DFC Department of the World Bank on how DFCs should be evaluated, particularly as Germany's own development ministries had different reporting requirements (KfW 1976b). The trouble with project loans by the late 1970s similarly worried KfW. Sectoral programs were added in 1983 and made some improvements to aid, but not to the promotion of private enterprises or financial institutions within the recipient country. Reflecting the long-standing conviction of self-help, some individuals within KfW pressed for development assistance to only be administered to countries that had adequately implemented macroeconomic reforms. One KfW member "above all demanded that capital aid should be concentrated on countries that were undertaking strenuous efforts of their own in their economic and fiscal policies, including education and training, and hence showed chances of developing autonomously" (Harries 1998, 85).

The concept of self-help in cooperation gained traction in the 1980s as development practitioners sought to complement large-scale infrastructure and industrial project funding with local initiatives. The premise of self-help programs was that they relied on the initiative of individuals in poor regions without adequate public facilities "to improve their living conditions through their own resources and with their own means" (KfW 1990, 67). KfW determined that sectors that utilized entrepreneurs were good candidates for projects. From 1984 to 1990, KfW committed approximately DM 1 billion to projects with a self-help approach, half of which were located in sub-Saharan Africa (KfW 1990, 67–70). In essence, these self-help programs sought to decentralize assistance and empower individuals—often through micro or small enterprises—to complement international development assistance. Even if these programs only received between 6 and 9% of total KfW financial cooperation funds, they nevertheless demonstrated the commitment of KfW to provoke private entrepreneurship. The increase in technical assistance was another component of this strategy, and in 1985, KfW provided DM 86 million for planning and implementation (KfW 1985a, 57).

In order to tackle the systemic problems, KfW followed the World Bank and IMF to address the macroeconomic conditions of developing countries via structural adjustment loans. Developing countries in the 1980s faced a number of economic crises, ranging from currency devaluations to balance of payment inequities. Through a reduction in the public bureaucracy, market-setting of prices, and privatization—or at the very least increased competition—of state-owned enterprises, economic development could accelerate. In conjunction with the World Bank, KfW created new programs in 1983 to engage in the stabilization of economies of developing countries through stricter fiscal requirements. KfW's own annual report was direct in the intentions: "The main aim is to improve or restore the efficiency of the markets. The reforms are therefore in particular aimed at external and internal liberalisation, deregulation and institutional reorganisation. With the help of the donors a gradual change is now taking place in the developmental model in many developing countries: less state and more market" (KfW 1988, 50). In 1987, KfW granted its first loan for economic policy reform measures in Tunisia, and four other countries (Ghana, Malawi, Niger, and Togo) were under review for similar loans worth a combined DM 72.5 million (KfW 1988, 3). In 1989, KfW contributed a single loan of DM 1.7 billion to the Enhanced Structural Adjustment Facility Trust (ESAF) of the IMF (KfW 1989, 51).

These structural adjustment loans were meant to liberalize the economies and to encourage the emergence of domestic entrepreneurs to attract FDI.

Taken together, KfW was inclined to support private investment. Capacity building via technical assistance and structural adjustment loans was meant to help the broader macroeconomic environment to make smaller entrepreneurs succeed. However, KfW was still limited in its ability to directly engage with the private sector. Money distributed via DFCs to support SMEs was often misused and market distorting. Private investment in projects was still lagging, leaving governments and development aid agencies to try and bridge the funding gaps. Deepening capital markets only provided limited relief, as there was still no way of combining development assistance with private investment.

1989–1992: The Nexus of Political Crises and Economic Development in Germany

The end of the 1980s brought uncertainty for KfW as an institution. The near militant line of the World Bank and IMF during structural adjustment challenged the notion of state-owned banks. If developed countries were promoting privatization in their development policy, then privatization should also occur in the developed countries' own economies. Sensing that its purpose may be under strain, KfW reemphasized the importance it played within the German economy (Development Practitioner #8 2016). Export financing was expanded, as were programs designed to extend credit lines to SMEs. More than half—or DM 6.3 billion—of domestic financing in 1988 was directed to SMEs. KfW also became involved in the structural transformation of the German economy. By 1988, more than one-fifth of KfW's domestic investments went to support localities and municipalities to support environmental protection, ranging from forest renewal to updated sewer systems. The increase in project financing necessitated a tantamount quantity of fundraising; in 1988, KfW raised a record DM 15.5 billion in long-term capital market funds (KfW 1988, 1).

KfW also sought to counter the trend of privatization through increased international partnerships. Cooperation with other development banks would allow greater opportunities for co-investment projects and help create a redefinition of the role of national development banking. In response to the growing clout of financial markets in the global economy,

KfW sought a transformation of its business model. In one notable project, KfW and the Development Bank of Japan (DBJ) arranged a series of bilateral workshops to meet the changing demands of their respective home governments. The first workshop occurred in October 1987 and focused on the shared experiences in SMEs, environmental protection, research and development, and applications of new technologies and innovations. It concluded that KfW had an important role in promoting structural change and SME financing within the German economy, and that its future viability rested on facilitating this transformation (DBJ and KfW 1987, 38).

The following year, in 1988, KfW and the DBJ held their second meeting. The revealing title of the conference—"New Role of Policy Financing"—provided a platform for two aspects. First, the agreement was designed to spur investments of both banks in each other's country, in conjunction with a private enterprise. The DBJ was also interested in using Germany as an investment entry point into the forthcoming European common market. Second, the conference also sought to extend the process of revitalizing policy financing to ensure its survival. In the inauguration address to conference participants, Yusuke Harada of the DBJ elucidated the motivation for this partnership. Specifically, impetus for the conference arose from the push for ever-greater privatization in the developed world:

> Now in the world's advanced countries, a movement aimed at "small government" can be detected, with the US and England at its core. Progress in this area is evidenced by the movement toward deregulation, the privatization of public industries, and redirection in the role of public financing. Even in Japan, under the label of administrative reform, discussions are underway concerning the conduct of public regulations. In Europe also, prior to the completion of the 1992 EC internal market, continued domestic debate concerning the future conduct of policy financing in each country can be expected. With this in mind, we must earnestly consider and discuss the new role of policy financing in the future. Personally, I believe that the role of policy financing at present is to function as a catalyst for the smooth incorporation of a new phase of economic life. Through this process, it will be possible for each country to more smoothly resolve its economic problems. (DBJ 1988, 12–13)

As state-owned financial institutions that could lose influence with increased privatization, both KfW and the DBJ had incentives to bolster their relevance. The new directions of policy financing included an effort to leverage the market via capital markets, better account for project risk along commercial standards, and find importance in the promotion of economic structural reform in their respective domestic economies.

The reorientation of KfW's domestic role had implications for its international operations as well, albeit more indirectly. Throughout the conference proceedings, KfW was preoccupied with reinventing how a state intervened in private financial markets, and this revised strategy relied heavily on markets to facilitate state involvement to enable—rather than replace—private actors. Financing would be conducted through on-lending via private financial institutions, as KfW had traditionally done, but additional funding would be raised on capital markets through bond issuances and other more complex capital market interactions. Industries that favored private enterprises would be expanded as primary recipients of market-rate financing; SMEs formed the backbone of this strategy, but areas in environmental protection and innovation provided new investment opportunities. The breadth and complexity of development assistance meant that marketized instruments could not immediately replace decades of procedures, but the experience KfW gained was important for deploying new projects and strategies in nearby countries and beyond. What was needed, however, was an opportunity.

German Reunification and the Expansion of KfW's Role

The collapse of the East German government in October 1989 stunned the German political establishment. Decades of political and economic separation between the two countries was disintegrated in a matter of weeks, and the quick announcement in February 1990 by West German Chancellor Helmut Kohl demanded an economic and monetary union between East and West Germany after Soviet attempts to prop up the GDR failed. These high-level political objectives necessitated a quick solution. For one, the prospect of a reunification process gave KfW a renewed purpose, particularly as it struggled to find meaning in era of privatization. Even prior to the announcements by Kohl, KfW had been approached by West German industrial companies that wanted to form joint ventures with East German counterparts, though these initial plans were scuttled by rapid political shifts (Harries 1998, 164). Nevertheless, it became quickly evident that the West German government needed to facilitate the rapid economic development of the former East Germany to smooth the process for reunification. By spring 1990, KfW's Board of Directors was preparing to play an important role in reunification, yet the precise details were still unknown.

The political economy of the West German government eventually dominated the priorities of KfW in two ways. First, enterprises in the GDR were intimately intertwined with supply chains and distribution networks in the Eastern bloc. Eventual economic integration with the richer and more developed West German economy put these businesses at a competitive disadvantage. Fearing that the former GDR's economy would be cratered out by the sudden integration with West Germany, KfW quickly expanded its export credit lines, offered at generous terms, to continue the flow of exports to the GDR's former communist neighbors. Priority was given to modernize East German businesses.[6] For example, in June 1990, KfW began the Start-Up Programme, which was aimed at facilitating already planned investments in state-owned enterprises in co-financing arrangements with West German commercial banks. This particular program encountered difficulties as a consequence of currency reforms and the poor fiscal health of East German enterprises, but reflected the conviction that GDR state-owned industries should be reformed and rescued rather than immediately disbanded (Harries 1998, 164). Second, the German government was concerned about maintaining levels of employment out of fear that the massive dislocation of workers in the former GDR would lead to political unrest. As such, extensive funding was made available for loans from housing to infrastructure to small-scale entrepreneurs. KfW estimates that in 1990 alone, its investments created or saved 200,000 jobs via more than 20,000 individual loans in East Germany (KfW 1990, 26).

While politicians provided the guidelines, KfW was left responsible for the details of implementation. KfW therefore focused on the programs that it was most familiar with and in sectors that accorded with its perspectives on proper policy financing. Support for SMEs was given the highest priority as it had formed the backbone of KfW's operations for decades.

[6] The East German shipbuilding industry provided one clear example. Shipbuilding employed thousands of workers in Mecklenburg-Vorpommern, which relied on exports to the COMECON regions. However, the former GDR shipbuilding industry was at a competitive disadvantage vis-à-vis the West German shipbuilding firms. KfW commissioned a study and found that capacity needed to be rationalized and infrastructure modernized, but also that the elimination of unprofitable production would also be necessary. See KfW (1990, 48) for more details.

For instance, on 14 February 1990, KfW used the ERP special funds to launch a modernization program for SMEs as well as expand the federal guarantee program (ERP Liability Fund) for SMEs to obtain commercial-rate loans. KfW also extended its existing programs on environmental protection to the new GDR states as well as other public investments via the Communal Lending Program. The Communal Lending Program was generous in its terms—interest rates were set at 6.5%, which were below market rate—and given for a term of 30 years, with a grace of 5 years. In the first year alone, KfW issued DM 2.6 billion in ERP funds within the GDR (KfW 1990, 12). Like its own domestic promotional credit lines, KfW followed the practice of on-lending through local commercial banks, however, given that the private commercial banking sector was underdeveloped in the former GDR, KfW also provided significant financial and technical assistance. In an effort to inject economic efficiency, KfW also provided consulting services for local authorities on financial best-practices and lent staff to the *Treuhandanstalt* to advise on the privatization of *Volkseigene Betriebe* (VEBs) (KfW 1990, 20).

In the ensuing years, KfW greatly expanded its operations in the former East German states, most commonly on behalf of the Federal German government. The *Aufbau Ost* program modernized East German housing blocks, and by 1997, nearly half of the existing stock had been renovated with KfW-backed loans. Municipal credits were given to improve the dilapidated infrastructure and attract additional private investment. So-called implementation aid was also granted to provide advisory services to local authorities with technical and financial solutions for these infrastructure projects. Efforts to reach SMEs also expanded with additional credit lines. In 1987, KfW had issued approximately 20,000 loan re-financings; by 1997, the annual total nearly tripled to just under 60,000 (Harries 1998, 169). The vast majority of its new funding liabilities came via capital market operations. By 1997, DM 100 billion out of a total of DM 120 billion had been raised on capital markets, with only DM 19 billion coming from ERP funds. This proved to KfW and global investors alike that capital market operations could become a viable avenue for raising funds, provided that a capable institution and political support were present. In order to further expand KfW's operations, the former GDR *Staatsbank* was integrated into KfW in 1994, giving KfW a greater capital base to allow it to issue more bonds and grow its investment portfolio. Additional credit lines such as the Participation Fund for East

Germany provided tax incentives to refinance venture capital donors who wanted to invest in SMEs in the former GDR.

The crisis of reunification offered KfW two important opportunities—first, a political mandate to carry out market-oriented reforms and, second, increased latitude to fund and scale-up projects and existing KfW credit lines. Relying on its experience in the domestic reconstruction of West Germany, KfW quickly employed its market-based strategy in the former GDR and hewed closely to markets principles. Full-throated support for the privatization of state-owned enterprises (VEBs) was conducted with a massive project through the *Treuhandanstalt*. Within two years, the *Treuhandanstalt* had privatized nearly 85% of the formerly state-owned enterprises and provided training for everything from sales to marketing to education (DBJ 1992). Privatization efforts were complemented with broad support for SMEs, environmental protection, and housing retrofit. Technical assistance for businesses and governments alike supplemented the endeavors, with particular attention focused on developing the internal financial sector (KfW 1994a, 20). In the process, KfW also achieved a reorientation of its purpose within the German economy. Rather than serving as a pure reconstruction agency, KfW would act more forcefully as a policy bank to implement political priorities. Government support for industry should be selectively protected, but KfW administered the aid in non-market distorting mechanisms (DBJ 1992). In short, KfW's reorientation toward market-based mechanisms blunted criticisms that it interfered with free markets, and gave KfW a new lease on life.

The implications for the international development assistance paradigm were substantial. On the funding side, KfW's reliance on capital markets boosted its experience with financial markets (Development Practitioner #40 2016). On the impact side, the shock therapy-like reintegration of East Germany into West Germany also fully illustrated the power of structural adjustment policy when coordinated with funding, training, and macroeconomic stabilization. While KfW was not interested in replicating these policies, it did highlight the importance of being able to better manage—and even control—financial intermediaries, particularly if influencing macroeconomic conditions was not possible (Development Practitioner #7 2016). In addition, the relative successes of the raft of SME credit lines demonstrated to both KfW and the German government that these sectors could be supported abroad with government-backed funding, with at least some private participation. Consequently, KfW's experiences in East Germany provided early lessons for how to shape a development policy based on market forces and, in time, marketized development financial instruments.

The Collapse of the Eastern Bloc and Financial Assistance

The ensuing collapse of the USSR in 1991 exacerbated the already delicate situation for the German government. Within a matter of months, a political vacuum emerged that created uncertainty for the regional economy. Moreover, the newly independent states of Poland and Czechoslovakia bordered Germany, and political instability raised the prospect for extensive social unrest and dislocation. In particular, German politicians were concerned about how such a monumental change could threaten the tenuous process of reunification with the collapse of the GDR's Eastern European export markets. In addition, the prospect for a flood of immigration incentivized German politicians to invest in the newly independent states in an effort to bolster their flagging economies. Concurrently, West German industry saw huge opportunities for investment and new export markets, and politicians saw avenues to bring Eastern Europe into the political fold of the EU (cf. DBJ 1992). For its part, KfW had already significantly expanded its services via export finance credits and programs in the former GDR. The prospect for even greater demand necessitated an increase in staff, credit lines, and capital market operations. Moreover, unlike reunification, KfW would have to operate internationally without the ability to directly influence government operations.

Prior to the fall of the Eastern Bloc, KfW attempted to shore up the former GDR's external economic relations via an expansion of export finance credits. The GDR was compelled to export to Eastern Europe prior to reunification, but incorporation with West Germany opened opportunities to export to new markets. Existing commitments with the CIS countries were denominated in rubles and weighed upon the balance sheets as savvy businessmen could exploit arbitrage opportunities between currencies (Harries 1998, 193). Immediately following the Soviet Union's disintegration, KfW needed to shore up the GDR's economic relations with the newly independent states. In 1991 and 1992, KfW rescheduled existing financing debts on generous terms and provided new credit lines while the transition to market rates continued. Extensive export guarantees, supported in conjunction with the Federal German government's Hermes credit coverage, to Eastern Europe were supported with additional KfW financing from ERP funds. For exports to the Soviet Union from the states of East Germany, Hermes guaranteed 100% of the loan when normally there was a maximum rate of 85% (DBJ 1992, 39). In 1992, KfW issued a record-breaking DM 2.6 billion in loans for exports from the former GDR states; this accounted for 30% of total KfW export financing volume. However, these remained heavily concentrated in the CIS states; of the DM 530 million in export credits from KfW in 1996, only DM 17 million went to countries outside the former Soviet Union and its allies (Harries 1998, 194). It was quickly apparent that both the former GDR and the newly independent Eastern European states were not competitive on the global market, and economic transition concomitantly made these new states poor markets for exports. As such, export credits did not prove to be a good strategy to shore up the economies of any of the countries (KfW 1993, 37–38).

In addition to propping up existing economic relations, German politicians were concerned about what a destabilized Eastern Europe would have on Germany itself. Top of the list of concerns was that Germany would receive an influx of immigrants. KfW's Wolfgang Siegel, Senior Vice President of the Sectoral Credit Department, tersely noted that West Germany and the West had to cooperate with the newly independent Eastern European states to encourage economic development as this would prevent large-scale immigration to Germany: "We cannot allow the people of these countries to remain in their existing state, but must make some effort to help. If no progress is made in developing these economies, people will emigrate to Germany en masse, creating another disastrous situation" (DBJ 1992, 76). KfW was quick to emphasize, however, that export financing policies aided the newly independent nations in Eastern Europe: "[Export finance] assists the importing countries, which would not otherwise have been able, due to their lack of foreign exchange, to import urgently required modern investment goods or equipment" (DBJ 1992, 40). Ideally, these would at the very least maintain economic stability until deeper market-oriented reforms could be implemented.

In order to achieve domestic stability, KfW followed a dual strategy of private enterprise promotion and technical assistance. This mirrored the market-oriented and private investment mobilization strategy pursued in the GDR, albeit with less overall financing. First, KfW targeted SMEs with credit lines and technical assistance. For instance, a loan facility for DM 100 million was established for direct investment in Eastern Europe, DM 37 million of which was issued in its first year. In a bid to attract more commercial banks to the endeavor, KfW offered to exempt 50% of liability to these banks (KfW 1992, 15). However, KfW found it difficult to fund SMEs in Eastern Europe in the same manner as it had done in West Germany. Commercial banks for on-lending were nonexistent and, unlike the GDR, KfW was not able to immediately employ West German commercial banks to administer the loans. There was also hesitance—if not outright hostility—to working with the state-owned financial institutions.

As such, KfW began to experiment with financial instruments that adhered to market principles, but that were ultimately backed by the German government. First, KfW established so-called Basic Agreements with commercial banks to specifically promote the promotion of SME exports. Under these agreements, the "stipulations that reoccur in all agreements are laid down, essential legal provisions are made, so that the individual loan agreements can be concluded rapidly and unbureaucratically" (DBJ 1992, 39). By 1992, KfW had concluded more than 60 Basic Agreements, including with 11 banks in Eastern Europe and the CIS countries. Second, KfW created special funds to administer financing to the Eastern European region. Two of the earliest ventures of KfW were to promote the development of SMEs in Russia. In coordination with the newly established European Bank for Reconstruction and Development (EBRD), KfW, on behalf of the Federal German government, established two regional venture funds to invest in equity in SMEs (KfW 1994a, 15). In 1995, KfW cooperated with the EBRD to establish a second regional venture fund. In September 1996, KfW established the German-Ukraine loan fund for SMEs with an initial capitalization of DM 10 million (KfW 1996a, 19). These funds were groundbreaking in that they provided loans at market rates, but had been organized and guaranteed by the German government (Development Practitioner #40 2016).

Second, as part of an effort to produce better macroeconomic stability, KfW was entrusted with implementing much of the Federal government's policies. First, KfW argued that, much like its policies in East Germany, a version of "shock therapy" would be required if the economic transition was to succeed. KfW's perspective on policy in Eastern Europe was to privatize enterprises, shore up the legal and financial systems, and liberalize currency and investment flows. For example, Dr. Günther Wolf, the Senior Vice President of KfW's Planning and Coordination Department, noted that "effecting a transition from such a planned economic system to a market economy is an extremely important political measure" and that it is necessary to "carry out the privatization of enterprises quickly and smoothly," much like KfW had coordinated in East Germany (DBJ 1992, 73). In the absence of these privatization policies, Dr. Günther Wolf was not sanguine about a country's future prospects: "Even if other countries spend one or two years trying to incorporate the principles of a market economy without adopting the shock therapy method, they will probably not succeed. It is more likely that the old structure will remain in place, privatization will not advance and the inefficient administration will continue to exist" (DBJ 1992, 78).

These measures also consisted of consultancy programs in the so-called TRANSFORM program in 1992. This program was designed to provide technical and advisory services to local authorities in an effort to transform them into market-oriented economies. In its 1992 Annual Report, KfW stated that the objective of this assistance was to help "the countries of central and eastern Europe and the CIS develop their democracies and social market economies by offering consultancy in the economic sphere" (KfW 1992, 15). KfW did indeed have extensive experience, but this time had to extend its reach across a region. For the first time, KfW began to establish a network of local offices attached to official German diplomatic missions, and by 1994, had 8 missions in Eastern Europe.[7] As the program matured, KfW expanded the scope of assistance. For instance, in 1993, KfW cooperated with the German government to also draw up concepts for economic consultancy projects. That year, KfW committed "DM 17.5 million for 40 consultancy projects to create market economy structures and 33 projects for restructuring in the enterprise sector" (KfW 1993, 16). Concurrently, KfW also began to intensively implement projects in conjunction with the Federal Ministry of Finance that supported and funded activities in the development of the banking sector, stock exchange, and insurance industry. All of these institutions had been deemed necessary to provide the appropriate environment for private enterprises to flourish. Between 1991 and 1997, KfW provided more than DM 1.6 billion for German consultants and advisory services across Eastern Europe (Harries 1998, 204).

[7] By 1994, KfW had personnel staffed at German embassies in Belarus, Hungary, Bulgaria, Latvia, Poland, Slovakia, Ukraine, and the Russian Federation. KfW had provided consultancy on behalf of the Federal Ministry of Economics, the Federal Ministry of Finance, and the Federal Ministry of Transport (KfW 1994a).

However, at times KfW's role in Eastern Europe verged on proselytization as it endeavored to demonstrate to the newly independent states the benefits of the German political economy. As Heinrich Harries, a former member of the KfW Board of management, recalled:

> The German package of consultancy services was intended to impart to the partner countries involved the particular experiences and strengths of the Federal Republic: the model of a social market economy with functioning competition as the first basic pillar and a broadly spanned social security network as the other basic pillar; the expertise and insights which it had gained in reconstruction in the post-war years and during the process of German reunification in the recent past; and the benefits of a federal political structure. (Harries 1998, 205)

Some criticized the government and KfW of attempting to recreate the German economic system via a thinly-veiled structural adjustment policy. However, it should be noted that the German government and KfW were not necessarily successful in their endeavor.

In conjunction with the consultancy services, KfW increased the quantity of training sessions it offered for DFCs as well. While DFCs had been dismissed in the mid-1980s on account of widespread corruption and inefficiency, KfW did recognize the role that a state-backed financial institution could play in structural transformation and the promotion of the private sector. For this, KfW pursued a policy that recreated its own successes. Rather than serving as a public bank, KfW sought to make them operate as private banks with a public mission. In the early stages, these banks served mainly as on-lending facilities for KfW lines of credit to SMEs. KfW also provided extensive consultation services on everything from loan appraisal to institutional organization to the legal framework of incorporation. By 1993, KfW had intensified its efforts in 9 Central and Eastern European countries, and banks in Estonia, Croatia, and Poland were cleared for operations; this expanded to 14 institutions in 1997. By this time, KfW had jointly enacted programs to refinance investments issued by banks in Hungary, Croatia, Estonia, and Lithuania, mainly for the purposes of SME financing (KfW 1997, 66). KfW also promoted guarantee banks. In 1996, KfW organized a conference for NDBs in Central and Eastern Europe to discuss financing opportunities and share experiences. It was the first meeting of long-term development banks in Europe and the basis for the IDFC (KfW 1996b).

West German business also had incentives to push for a stabilization of the Eastern Bloc. The quick integration into the European market opened up new opportunities for business. KfW's regional network of offices not only provided badly needed technical assistance, but it also served to coordinate KfW's rapidly growing investment portfolio and encourage German private investment. Wolfgang Siegal, a Senior Vice President at KfW, tersely pointed out that the former Soviet states provided a huge market potential for German firms (DBJ 1992). This was also enabled through KfW's efforts to encourage the development of cross-national business interactions. New banks in Bulgaria and Russia emerged, which were specifically targeted at the promotion of SMEs. For instance, the German-Polish Business Promotion Agency was established with assistance from KfW to connect private businesses in a fruitful exchange (KfW 1993, 17).

Yet despite the desire to replicate KfW's operations within East Germany, there were numerous barriers to a full transposition. Most importantly, many independent Eastern European states lacked a full-time privatization agency like the *Treuhandanstalt*. There was also much less possibility that SOE privatization could be implemented via acquisition by West German companies. Moreover, the administrative system and macroeconomic policy had not advanced to modern standards, and there was still a lack of transportation, financial depth, and human resources. The commercial banking sector was virtually nonexistent. Or, as Dr. Wolf succinctly explained, these Eastern European countries were "in some chaos" (DBJ 1992, 79). There was therefore significant pressure on KfW—provide the same transformative services to Eastern Europe as they had done with East Germany, but also without the advantages of direct access to government policymakers.

In many ways, KfW's operations in the newly independent countries of Eastern Europe provided an initial foray into applying the strategies deployed in the former GDR in an international context. Unlike KfW's intensive operations in East Germany, KfW lacked the political mandate to take control of privatization, advise on economic governance, and directly engage with known commercial banks. As such, KfW compensated through the provision of consulting services in newly-established offices, the channeling of SME funding via funds in coordination with other international development agencies, and even supporting the conversion of existing financial institutions into modern promotional banks. On top of this was KfW's adamant adherence to the promotion of private enterprise, particularly through the support of SMEs, and was able to capitalize on German politicians' fears to obtain risk-sharing arrangements. As such, KfW's operations during these two crises demonstrated that private investment mobilization was possible, and development assistance could be administered in ways that abided with market discipline. The stage was set for KfW's international development operations to shift to marketized development financial instruments.

The Growth of a Market-Based Development Model

Reunification with East Germany and the collapse of the Soviet Union had a profound impact on how KfW administered development assistance. Breaking from the problems that had stymied the World Bank to reform, the extensive political support for a new strategy allowed KfW to reorient development policy toward one that adhered to financial markets. This provided an important step in KfW's evolution to support new marketized development financial instruments in two ways. First, KfW was granted more latitude to experiment with new mechanisms, such as composite finance and SME finance. In particular, KfW gained important abilities to better control the investment decisions for these new instruments. Second, the experience with applying market-based mechanisms for the purposes of economic development validated to both KfW and the German government that such a regime was possible, and encouraged them to pursue ways to apply these instruments in a broader development policy.

These experiences impacted Germany's international aid regime in a few tangible ways. For one, it provided evidence that financial instruments could be the basis of a development strategy. Market rates and revolving funds could be used to engender development while minimizing the German government's annual ODA outlays (Development Practitioner #40 2016). Moreover, it encouraged the promotion of macroeconomic reforms. The appointment of Carl-Dieter Spranger as the new head of BMZ emphasized this perspective, as he demanded that developing countries institute reforms within the domestic economy. In a speech at the 1991 World Bank Annual Spring Meeting, Spranger reiterated that a developing country can only prosper when political, economic, and social conditions are conductive, and that the German government would prioritize assistance to such countries (GTZ 1991). In 1992, structural adjustment loans from KfW increased from DM 100 million in 1991 to DM 400 million in the following year (KfW 1992, 13).

By the mid-1990s, German development policy had drifted more forcefully into the promotion of democracy and free-market economics. BMZ had announced a policy that would tether foreign assistance to a developing country's progress toward democratization, a strong rule of law, a market economy, and a protection for human rights (cf. Rüland and Werz 2002). Its development institutions further promoted German-style savings banks, SMEs, and even decentralization of government structures to reflect Germany's own political organization (OECD 1998, 37). This encouraged the attachment of implicit conditionality on its loans. However, other MDBs were restricted in how much they could demand from recipient countries. By-laws forbade multilateral institutions from directly interfering in the domestic affairs, greatly limiting the ability to engender necessary reforms. In this way, KfW was uniquely positioned because of its complete ownership by the German government: "The Federal Republic of Germany was not constrained by the same limitations in its development policy. This meant that Spranger could require more from the developing countries. He demanded respect for human rights, the population's participation in political decision-making, the rule of law and order and legal certainty, a social market economy, and a government policy in the recipient countries that was clearly geared to the development of the country" (Harries 1998, 199). The status of KfW as a bilateral development bank—rather than a multilateral one—presented flexibility in ensuring that financial intermediaries abided by the objectives. Consequently, KfW often had more stringent requirements on projects (Development Practitioner #32 2016).

What KfW would do with this flexibility, however, was neither preordained nor premeditated, but given the tectonic shifts both within KfW and in the global economy, there was a distinct trend toward marketized development finance instruments. This can be viewed from three different aspects. First, KfW's own business model within Germany had shifted profoundly to market operations, and these schemes were slowly influencing KfW's international operations as well (Development Practitioner #7 2016). Second, the global economy had developed such that financial markets and private capital flows were becoming the standard rather than outlier, and KfW was uniquely positioned to leverage these shifts. Finally, changes to the international development agenda incentivized the use of increasingly advanced financial instruments. When these trends were combined with the political support of the German government to absorb risk, as well as the evolving but deeply-rooted conviction of KfW in support of market rates for private investment promotion, significant innovations began to take shape.

First, the growing reliance on new financial instruments reflected the shifts KfW was undergoing in its domestic business. KfW had expanded its credit lines to promote environmental investments, as well as created new ones to promote innovation and provide venture capital to SMEs in 1994. These were all administered using KfW's own capital resources. The explosion in investment not only in the former GDR and Eastern Europe, but also within West Germany, meant that KfW needed to rely more heavily on financial markets and composite financing (OECD 1998, 40). The growing export financing credit portfolio necessitated greater operations in foreign currencies, and in 1996, KfW introduced the Debt Issuance Programme to issue bonds in foreign currencies with standard documentation. To meet the growing needs of domestic programs, KfW supplemented its fixed-rate bonds with additional structured products that included callable loans and dual currency bonds. By 1997, KfW had raised DM 8.5 billion in foreign currencies and had expanded the amount of derivative instruments used (KfW 1997, 21). The successes on the domestic front created a reputation that KfW investments accorded to market principles, and private investors began to seek KfW debt, as evidenced by the declining interest rate spread between KfW bonds and the German bund. These had positive spillovers into KfW's existing mixed and composite financing programs and encouraged the greater application of domestic programs to the international context (Development Practitioner #8 2016).

Second, private investment flows started to expand exponentially as official flows decreased in both nominal and proportional terms. In 1991, for the first time, more than half of the total financial flows to developing countries were via the private sector, and, in 1993, fully 58% of the total net transfer was via private investment, with only 42% arising from official sources. Improvements in the investment conditions of East Asia, and China in particular, provided the attraction (KfW 1993, 47). By 1996, approximately 85%, or USD 243.8 billion out of USD 284.6 billion, of the net capital flows to developing countries was via the private sector. FDI constituted the plurality (44.7%) of these private flows, with debt instruments constituting 36.3%, and equity participations trailing with 18.7% (World Bank 1997, 5). The quantity of private flows indicated a growing interest on part of the private sector to seek investments in the developing world. However, these flows were concentrated in the more developed emerging market economies; fully half of FDI in 1997 went to Brazil, Mexico, and China (KfW 1997, 56).

Finally, changes in the international aid regime also further pushed KfW to seek new types of financing arrangements. Mixed financing—which had combined the use of government and the bank's own funds—had been used since the 1960s, but these had often been tied to both direct government outlays and contracts to purchase German products. Also in the 1960s, the KfW Board of Management had largely opposed using commercial financing for capital assistance. By the 1980s, these mixed financing projects suffered from a declining real amount of ODA, but, on account of the market operations, had provided more than USD 700 million by 1994. International changes added a complication to this strategy. In 1993, the OECD altered the calculation for ODA in according with the "Helsinki Agreement," and, in order for mixed financing to be ODA, it would need to be used only in projects that were unprofitable. Aid could not be tied to donor country procurement contracts. German mixed financing fell to USD 100 million by 1996 (OECD 1998, 44).

In order to continue to have this funding count as ODA, KfW created another financial innovation called composite financing in 1995. Similar to mixed financing, low-interest German government financing was combined with KfW's own capital market resources. They were recognized as ODA because it was not mandatorily tied to procurement agreements, and the guarantees for market funds were shared between KfW (10%) and BMZ (90%), rather than the Federal government's Hermes export credits. In exchange for the risk assumption, the German government set the conditions by which composite financing could be administered. For instance, composite financing was restricted only to eligible countries in order to ensure that loan default risk was minimized (Development Practitioner #34 2016). Moreover, concessional funding had to account for at least 35% of the total composite financing agreement, and any default could be considered as an ODA grant rather than a loan in arrears. In 1996, the German budget law allowed a ceiling of USD 900 million for the official guarantees for the capital market portion of KfW's composite financing (OECD 1998, 44). Later, KfW also innovated integrated composite financing, which did not detail the breakdown of

KfW and government funds, but implementation was deemed too difficult to be successful (Development Practitioner #34 2016).

Given that composite financing relied on financial markets, it was initially restricted to middle-income countries. More easily bankable projects also formed the initial investments and were concentrated in the energy and transportation sectors (Development Practitioner #32 2016). One of the first composite financing projects was issued in 1995 for an extension of the Tunis urban railway. In 1996, the total credit volume for the Tunisian project reached DM 1.16 billion, with DM 449 million provided via capital market resources. In 1996, five projects in the energy and transportation sector with DM 709 million committed through Federal budget funds and DM 450 million via KfW market funds (KfW 1996a, 60). Impressively, by 1997, four composite finance projects were able to be funded primarily through mobilized private capital; in this year, DM 272 million was committed via Federal government budget funds and DM 357 million from the market (KfW 1997, 60). These early experiments were also "critical to convince the German government that this was feasible risk-wise and that it provided good development outcomes" (Development Practitioner #34 2016).

While composite finance was successful, KfW further innovated interest rate subsidization. Rather than directly combining funds to provide financing, interest rate subsidization provided a discount on the interest rate of the loans. Since this arrangement was riskier to the German government, they only agreed to cover 80% (Development Practitioner #36 2016). Later, this type of arrangement became known as blended finance, another form of marketized development financial instruments. Yet the ability of KfW to negotiate with the German government to assume its risk provided the foundation for interest rate subsidization. As one development practitioner remarked: "That is one of the big advantages of KfW—that it can push 80–90% of the risk to the German government" (Development Practitioner #34 2016).

The impact of these pressures on KfW's development policies began to become apparent. On the funding side, KfW began to obtain an increasing proportion of its development assistance budget via the capital market, though total amounts remained at around DM 65 million by 1998 (KfW 1998, 59). The realities of a declining German budget for ODA commitments hastened this trend, as KfW endeavored to maintain levels of development finance. Scarcer public funds for ODA also meant that KfW sought ways to reduce administrative costs (Development

Practitioner #32 2016). By the end of the 1990s, KfW had accumulated considerable experience in the privatization of East German enterprises and, as a result, had "begun to enlist more private participation in the administration of its projects in developing and transitional countries." As the OECD assessment continues, this was because KfW considered that "the sharing of risks, the supervision of the private company, the right regulatory system and the necessary infrastructure are important issues in public-private partnership" (OECD 1998, 37). The successes of private administration, however, were often less spectacular than envisioned.

With regard to sectoral promotion, SME funding continued to serve as the centerpiece of promotion, yet the advocacy of domestic financial sectors began to rise to prominence. KfW had long contended that a functioning domestic financial sector would be critical to the self-sufficiency of a country, and agreed with the groundbreaking 1989 World Development Report that highlighted the important role of the financial sector. However, for the ensuing years, funding had been limited. But by 1998, 12%, or DM 300 million, of KfW's development obligations was committed to improving the financial system, primarily to encourage the development of the SME sector (KfW 1998, 60). Relatedly, in 1998, KfW's renewed successes with promotional banks were expanded to Thailand and Indonesia. KfW, in conjunction with domestic banks, developed investment loan programs for SMEs and provided a credit line of DM 50 million to each newly-reformed state bank. Renewed interest in development banks grew out of the shift to promote social infrastructure via smaller loans; this inevitably required a local banking partner that KfW could invest through. Additional SME promotion credit lines worth a total of DM 180 million were provided to promotion banks in Estonia, Croatia, Slovakia, and Ukraine (KfW 1998, 66).

KfW's market-promoting activities expanded as well. The TRANSFORM program continued to receive German government grants of DM 177 million in 1997 (KfW 1997, 66). In January 1998, KfW established a revolving fund as part of the Housing Construction Loan Programme in Bosnia-Herzegovina. This was the first mandate agreement between KfW and the EC, and it was designed to fix the housing shortage for refugees. Like many of its other credit lines, this one was distributed as low-interest rate loans via the commercial banking sector, and was attached with technical and supervisory services from KfW's program office (KfW 1997, 68). In autumn of the following year, a credit line for SMEs was added to significant demand (KfW 1998, 49).

Finally, as part of the shift toward more marketized development finance instruments, KfW bolstered the way that it evaluated the projects. The institution's first comprehensive evaluation project was administered in 1991 and, while acknowledging deficiencies in implementation, found that its actions had been beneficial (KfW 1991). Most importantly, KfW decided to better define the project prior to implementation so that an assessment could later be made to determine whether or not the project achieved its intended goals. The second comprehensive evaluation report codified the role that free markets should play in selecting projects. For instance, two recommendations were that projects should be given to governments that "allow the markets to perform their distribution and steering function" and "allow the private initiative the necessary latitude for action through the rule of law and with legal security" (KfW 1994b, 32). More broadly, and particularly critical for any project that involved private financial investment, KfW highlighted the importance of better risk assessment along commercial banking guidelines. Higher risk projects would therefore require more comprehensive documentation. While this practice was intended to increase the developmental impact, it also better aligned procedures with the requirements from commercial banks (KfW 1992, 52).

Conclusion

The roots of KfW's support for marketized development finance instruments stretched back to the postwar reconstruction. KfW's interaction with SMEs and domestic bond markets solidified the perspective that private investment was beneficial, but transferring these processes to a developing country context were not initially obvious. Negative experiences with project loans and DFCs provided important lessons about the need to maintain market discipline. Early experiments provided the contours of a new marketized policy, but initially KfW faced the same constraints that had stymied the World Bank. Critically, two political crises—German reunification and the collapse of the Soviet Union—enabled KfW to garner political support from the German government to overcome the hurdles. First, political support granted KfW significant latitude to experiment with new types of financial instruments that redeployed development assistance as risk buffers for private investors. By shifting the risk away from recipient countries, KfW aimed to bolster the quality of the investment and attract private interest through guarantees.

Efforts with composite financing and SME funding in Eastern Europe, for instance, provided experience and validated to policymakers that these were viable avenues. Second, KfW began to convince the German government that, in order to maintain proper incentives on the part of recipients, KfW needed to exert greater control over the financial instruments. While changes to allow KfW to hold equity stakes and make investment decisions were not immediate, these critical years laid the foundation for the full shift to marketized development financial instruments.

While KfW's experiences with reunification and the collapse of the Soviet Union created a perfect storm of political support for a revised development strategy, lessons can be drawn to other cases. KfW was not unique among development institutions in either its conviction that private investment was superior or that close integration with financial markets was important. In this regard, other development institutions were equally well-suited to receive the same political support. However, KfW did uniquely benefit from its strong political backing, extensive domestic experience in investments, and a particularly flexible institutional design, enabling it to better navigate a pathway toward marketized development financial instruments. Though a full maturation of the instruments was still a few years away, these shifts in the late 1980s and early 1990s provided the necessary impetus to jump-start a new set of marketized development financial instruments.

References

BMZ. 1982. Finanzielle Zusammenarbeit Mit Nicaragua.

DBJ. 1988. *New Role of Policy Financing in the Federal Republic of Germany and in Japan: In Tokyo, October 24–28, 1988*. Tokyo: Development Bank of Japan.

———. 1992. *New Roles of Policy-Based Finance in Tackling Global Issues: In Tokyo, October 11–18, 1992*. Tokyo: Development Bank of Japan.

DBJ, and KfW. 1987. *Aspects of Structural and Environmental Policy in Japan and in the Federal Republic of Germany: Working Papers, Materials, and Protocols of Discussions of a Workshop in Frankfurt Am Main from October 12 to 19 1987*. Frankfurt am Main: Kreditanstalt für Wiederaufbau.

DSE. 1986. *Armutsbekämpfung Durch Selbsthilfe II*. Berlin: Deutsche Stiftung für Internationale Entwicklung.

Grünbacher, Armin. 2001. The Early Years of a German Institution: The Kreditanstalt Für Wiederaufbau in the 1950s. *Business History* 43 (4): 68–86.

———. 2005. *Reconstruction and Cold War in Germany: The Kreditanstalt Für Wiederaufbau (1948–1961)*. Aldershot, UK: Ashgate Publishing.
GTZ. 1991. Development Aid Concerns Society as a Whole. *GTZ Gate*.
Harries, Heinrich. 1998. *Wiederaufbau, Welt und Wende: Die KfW–Eine Bank mit öffentlichem Auftrag*. Frankfurt am Main: Knapp.
IBRD, IDA, and KfW. 1961. *Administration Agreement (Roseires Irrigation Project) between the Republic of the Sudan and Kreditanstalt Für Wiederaufbau and International Development Association and International Bank for Reconstruction and Development, Dated as of June 14, 1961*. Washington, DC: International Bank for Reconstruction and Development.
KfW. 1957. *Ninth Annual Report Covering the Year 1957*. Frankfurt am Main: Kreditanstalt für Wiederaufbau.
———. 1960. *Twelfth Annual Report Covering the Year 1960*. Frankfurt am Main: Kreditanstalt für Wiederaufbau.
———. 1967a. *Annual Report for the Year 1967*. Frankfurt am Main: Kreditanstalt für Wiederaufbau.
———. 1967b. Kreditanstalt as Development Bank.
———. 1969. *Annual Report for the Year 1969*. Frankfurt am Main: Kreditanstalt für Wiederaufbau.
———. 1970. *Annual Report for the Year 1970*. Frankfurt am Main: Kreditanstalt für Wiederaufbau.
———. 1971a. *Annual Report for the Year 1971*. Frankfurt am Main: Kreditanstalt für Wiederaufbau.
———. 1971b. Länderdirektorium, 8. Sitzung Am 15. Mai 1971.
———. 1972. Länderdirektorium, 29. Sitzung Am 17. April 1972.
———. 1973a. Arbeitsgruppe Zur Besprechung von Grundsatzfragen Im Rahmen Der Kapitalhilfe.
———. 1973b. Ergebnisvermerk Über Die Diskussionsveranstaltung 'Entwicklungsbankenfinanzierung'.
———. 1973c. Gemeinschaftsfinanzierung Mit Der Weltbank Oder Anderen Internationalen Finanzierungsinstitutionen.
———. 1973d. Vermerk: Gemeinschaftsfinanzierung Mit Der Weltbank Oder Anderen Internationalen Finanzierungsinstitutionen.
———. 1974. *Annual Report for the Year 1974*. Frankfurt am Main: Kreditanstalt für Wiederaufbau.
———. 1975a. *Annual Report for the Year 1975*. Frankfurt am Main: Kreditanstalt für Wiederaufbau.
———. 1975b. Arbeitsgruppe Zur Besprechung von Grundsatzfragen Im Rahmen Der Kapitalhilfe.
———. 1976a. *Annual Report for the Year 1976*. Frankfurt am Main: Kreditanstalt für Wiederaufbau.
———. 1976b. Entwicklungsbanken - Berichtssystem Der Weltbank.

———. 1977. Prüfungsleitfaden Entwicklungsbanken.
———. 1980a. *Annual Report for the Year 1980*. Frankfurt am Main: Kreditanstalt für Wiederaufbau.
———. 1980b. Ergebnisvermerk Der Sonderarbeitsgruppe Über 'Arbeitsweise Der KfW Bei Der Abwicklung von Entwicklungsbankendarlehen'.
———. 1980c. Grundsätze Für Gemeinsame Finanzierungen Mit Anderen Bi- Oder Multilateralen Geberinstitutionen.
———. 1982. *Projektfinanzierung in Entwicklundsländern*. Frankfurt am Main: Kreditanstalt für Wiederaufbau.
———. 1983. Länderdirektorium, 168. Sitzung Am 24. März 1983.
———. 1984. *Annual Report for the Year 1984*. Frankfurt am Main: Kreditanstalt für Wiederaufbau.
———. 1985a. *Annual Report for the Year 1985*. Frankfurt am Main: Kreditanstalt für Wiederaufbau.
———. 1985b. Gliederung Und Inhalt Der KfW-Berichte Über Die Prüfung von Entwicklungsbanken.
———. 1988. *Annual Report for the Year 1988*. Frankfurt am Main: Kreditanstalt für Wiederaufbau.
———. 1989. *Annual Report for the Year 1989*. Frankfurt am Main: Kreditanstalt für Wiederaufbau.
———. 1990. *Annual Report for the Year 1990*. Frankfurt am Main: Kreditanstalt für Wiederaufbau.
———. 1991. *Ergebnisse Der Projektarbeit: Aus Der Praxis Der Finanziellen Zusammenarbeit Mit Entwicklungsládern*. Frankfurt am Main: Kreditanstalt für Wiederaufbau.
———. 1992. *Annual Report for the Year 1992*. Frankfurt am Main: Kreditanstalt für Wiederaufbau.
———. 1993. *Annual Report for the Year 1993*. Frankfurt am Main: Kreditanstalt für Wiederaufbau.
———. 1994a. *Annual Report for the Year 1994*. Frankfurt am Main: Kreditanstalt für Wiederaufbau.
———. 1994b. *Results of Financial Cooperation with Developing Countries: Second Evaluation Report 1994*. Frankfurt am Main: KfW.
———. 1996a. *Annual Report for the Year 1996*. Frankfurt am Main: Kreditanstalt für Wiederaufbau.
———. 1996b. KfW Organisiert Treffen von Förderbanken Aus Mittel- Und Osteuropa Sowie Der Europäischen Union. *KfW Aktuell*.
———. 1997. *Annual Report for the Year 1997*. Frankfurt am Main: Kreditanstalt für Wiederaufbau.
———. 1998. *Annual Report for the Year 1998*. Frankfurt am Main: Kreditanstalt für Wiederaufbau.
Krahnen, Jan Pieter. 2016. Interview.

Lamby, Werner. 1967. The Role of Regional Development Banks. In *The Role of Development Banks in Economic and Social Development*. Berlin: German Foundation for Developing Countries.

Mathéy, Kosta. 1982. *Literaturübersicht: Selbsthilfe als Instrument zur Bewältigung der Wohnungsnot in Entwicklungsländern: Tagungsbeitrag am DSE Wissenschaftsbörse Bonn am 7.,8. Dezember 1982*. Darmstadt: Technische Hochschule Darmstadt Fachgebiet Planen und Bauen in Entwicklungsländern.

Nitsch, Manfred. 1970. *Entwicklungsfinanzierung in Lateinamerika-Dargestellt Am Beispiel Columbiens*. Stuttgart: Enst Klett Verlag.

———. 1973. *Ergebnisvermerk Über Die Diskussionsveranstaltung "Entwicklungsbankenfinanzierung" Am 22. Und 23. Januar 1973 in Der Kreditanstalt Für Wiederaufbau*. Frankfurt am Main: KfW.

Nitsch, Manfred, Reinhardt Schmidt, and Claus-Peter Zeitinger. 1981a. *Berichtsentwurf: Inspektion Der "Förderung von Entwicklungsbanken" in Lateinamerika*. Unpublished manuscript.

———. 1981b. *Sozio-Ökonomische Auswirkungen Der Bisherigen Deutschen Entwicklungsbankenförderung in Ekuador Und Kolumbien*. Berlin: BMZ.

OECD. 1998. *Development Co-Operation Reviews: Germany 1998*. Paris: OECD.

Rüland, Jürgen, and Nikolaus Werz. 2002. Germany's Hesitant Role in Promoting Democracy. In *Exporting Democracy: Rhetoric vs. Reality*, ed. Peter J. Schraeder. Boulder, CO: Lynne Rienner Publishers.

Schmidt, Reinhardt. 2016. Interview.

Ullrich, Gabriele J., and DSE, eds. 1982. *Report/DSE FAO Seminar on Promotion of Self-Help Organizations of the Rural Poor in Africa: Problems of Implementation, Monitoring and Evaluation: Berlin, West, 8 to 13 November 1982*. Feldafing.

Voigt, Heinz. 1967. Quantitative Measures and Criteria in Development Finance. In *The Role of Development Banks in Economic and Social Development*. Berlin: German Foundation for Developing Countries.

Wabnitz, Wolfdieter. 1967. Appraisal and Promotion of Industrial Projects by Development Finance Institutions. In *The Role of Development Banks in Economic and Social Development*. Berlin: German Foundation for Developing Countries.

World Bank. 1997. *Global Development Finance*. Washington, DC: World Bank.

CHAPTER 5

The Maturation of Marketized Development Financial Instruments: Microfinance and Structured Funds

While reunification and the collapse of the Soviet Union provided the initial impetus for KfW to shift towards marketized development financial instruments, the ensuing decade would see their maturation. The Balkan crisis in the mid-1990s was another political juncture that the German government wanted to expeditiously solve. KfW was able to overcome the barriers to marketized development financial instruments because of strong political backing and new institutional advantages. In particular, KfW had the ability to (1) invest in a country without the recipient government guarantee, (2) create a new institution within a developing country, and (3) possess more than 50% of governing shares in any financial instrument. These three factors distinguished KfW from other development institutions, as no other institution possessed the ability to directly create and administer financial instruments. Critically, these allowed KfW to better control the investment decision-making process through direct management, a fact that reassured the German government that its money would not be squandered. Consequently, KfW was able to better leverage financial markets for development purposes because KfW's control over financial instruments boosted private investor confidence. During this period, KfW's efforts transformed marketized development financial instruments into a tool for development policy.

Two instruments were particularly important innovations. First, KfW became one of the earliest, staunchest, and most active supporters of

P. Volberding, *Leveraging Financial Markets for Development*,
Executive Politics and Governance,
https://doi.org/10.1007/978-3-030-55008-0_5

microfinance. In partnership with a private consultancy group, KfW established a network of microfinance banks in Southeast Europe that served as on-lending institutions for donor country credit lines. In order to maintain proper incentives, loans were distributed at market rates, and KfW maintained top management positions in the financial intermediaries. Second, KfW became the first development institution to use structured finance for development objectives (Development Practitioner #27 2016). The crisis in the Balkans allowed KfW to combine a myriad of credit lines into the European Fund for Southeast Europe (EFSE), which would serve to finance private entrepreneurs and mobilize international capital. Most importantly, both the microfinance institutions and structured funds relied heavily on donor government risk assumption, a hallmark for marketized development financial instruments, and the consequence of German government trust following reunification and the fall of the USSR.

While KfW did not create entirely new financial instruments, it was revolutionary in deploying them in a development context. Critical was KfW's ability to control the means of distribution of the financial instrument, a step that the World Bank was unable to do. Since KfW raised the funding, trained the on-lending institution, and managed the institutions, these new instruments avoided the traditional principle-agent problems. The impact of these two financial instruments was wide-reaching. First, both demonstrated that development assistance could be distributed with market mechanisms, so long as financial intermediaries were managed. Second, these instruments required donor country risk assumption in order to attract private investors. Finally, the successes within the European context provided an important example of how financial markets could be leveraged for development objectives abroad. KfW and other development institutions sought to replicate these instruments in a broader set of countries that, in the ensuing years, became mainstays of the development paradigm.

The Microfinance Revolution

Beginning in the 1950s with church groups, and accelerating in the 1970s and 1980s, NGOs began to support the use of rotating funds for on-lending to local organizations for the provision of microcredits. They were driven by the notion that repressive government regimes did little to help the poorest, and microcredits could help empower these people to lift themselves out of poverty. Experiments with small grants occurred predominantly in Latin America and South Asia—most famously via Acción and the Grameen Bank, respectively—but small-scale initiatives were quite widespread. India's regional rural banks, Indonesia's self-help groups, and China's rural credit cooperatives were other manifestations (cf. Harper 2016; Morduch 1999). In short time, microfinance was in vogue, and development institutions scrambled to secure funding to expand operations. As before, subsidized credits from donor countries dominated the fledgling microfinance industry. Yet this old-style method of scaling-up microfinance institutions suffered from a debilitating set of deficiencies: "The programs often did not reach low-income farmers, repayment was frequently low, and losses were high. In addition, because the loans are subsidized and therefore rationed, they encourage corruption and often reach better-off rather than poorer villagers" (Robinson 2001, 72). Moreover, in order for the institution to survive, donor countries also needed to routinely inject new capital, a politically unpalatable proposition over the long run.

Despite these headwinds, the early 1990s witnessed an explosion of microfinance. By 1995, a World Bank survey on microfinance institutions found that microfinance institutions more than 7 USD billion in outstanding loans and more than 19 USD billion in savings deposits across 46 million accounts (World Bank 1996, 8). Microfinance was heralded as an important innovation that could be used to mitigate—if not entirely eradicate—poverty via financial inclusion (Helms 2006). Yet even though the new microfinance paradigm endeavored to adhere to commercial banking principles, results varied. Success stories of the Bank Rakyat Indonesia (BRI) and the BancoSol in Bolivia affirmed that large-scale microcredits could be provided at nominally commercial rates (Robinson 2001, 58–71). However, examples of poor performance from Bolivia to Cambodia demonstrated that without proper economic incentives or technical assistance, microfinance lacked transformative power (cf. Bateman 2010; Buckley 1997).

Regardless of the efficacy, development institutions struggled to find ways to support these new microfinance institutions. Ideally, funds to these banks should be distributed on a rotating basis—even if subsidized—as that obviated the need for additional grants. In order to avoid the problems that plagued DFCs, technical assistance and realistic assessments of the recipient institution were needed in conjunction (cf. Zeitinger and Schmidt 1984). However, the strategy specifically performed worse in an environment of economic instability and institutional uncertainty. In countries with no legal protections for borrowers, minimal information on end-users, or economic stability to provide opportunities for entrepreneurs, the provision of financing would accomplish little. Consequently, microfinance institutions exploded in regions such as India and Latin America, but faltered across the most underdeveloped regions in Africa (cf. David and Mosley 1996). Separately, NGOs, which had originally sponsored the promotion of microfinance institutions, began to observe that increasing debt burdens, the growing power of commercial banks, and the so-called privatization of poverty cast doubt on whether microfinance was a desirable strategy (cf. Mader 2015; Roy 2010). Finally, there was the critical problem that there was very little quantitative evidence to demonstrate that microfinance was actually effective (cf. Morduch 2000).[1]

It was only following the Balkan crisis that KfW leadership began to view microfinance as a viable development strategy. Earlier efforts to have KfW fund microfinance had been rebuffed. For instance, Muhammad Yunus of the Grameen Bank had approached KfW in the mid-1980s to seek funding for his fledgling bank in Bangladesh; KfW declined the offer because of the enormous uncertainty (Development Practitioner #40 2016). However, KfW was still searching for ways to better administer its development assistance, and the Balkan crisis presented an opportunity to test microfinance in ways that maintained the incentives of financial intermediaries (Development Practitioner #26 2016; Development Practitioner #27 2016). One way to avoid these hazards was to establish or control the financial intermediary within the recipient country, but for most MDBs, extensive regulations prevented them from doing so. In addition, the World Bank was prohibited from holding any equity stake in financial intermediaries, while the IFC was prohibited from holding a majority stake (Development Practitioner #29 2016).

KfW was not bound by such rules. While KfW had always had the legal ability to do so, the lack of political support meant that previous to these set of crises, BMZ had been skeptical to approve any such project. The Balkan crisis, however, had convinced members of the German government that allowing KfW more flexibility in the direct creation and management of microfinance institutions was beneficial, particularly

[1] For a more recent survey of microfinance, see Hermes and Lensink (2011).

considering that German bureaucrats were wary of joint investments with Balkan governments (Development Practitioner #48 2016). As such, KfW possessed a wider range of tools to administer development assistance in ways that allowed greater control over how financial intermediaries behaved and, consequently, overcame the creation of moral hazards. To implement this strategy, KfW enlisted the support of the consultants at IPC to create a network of financial institutions in Southeast Europe that would serve two purposes. First, these institutions would be leveraged as local on-lending institutions for the credit lines of international development institutions. Second, these institutions could form the backbone of a new domestic financial sector that could be transferred back to local ownership (Development Practitioner #40 2016). Therefore, in exchange for greater funding and risk assumption for microfinance projects, the German government permitted KfW greater latitude in controlling the financial intermediaries.

Even though KfW had been hesitant to support microfinance, it was approached by the IFC and the newly-founded EBRD to begin a co-investment project for a new microfinance bank in Southeast Europe (Development Practitioner #9 2016). At the time, this was seen as a triple win. The recipient country could receive much needed international investment, international development institutions could affect profound change, and local entrepreneurs could receive the financing they sorely lacked. In many ways, this microfinance paradigm had solved the problems plaguing development institutions by harmonizing project funding and disbursement. Since KfW was able to create, operate, and monitor the on-lending microfinance institution, investment decisions could be controlled. This boosted the confidence of private investors and governments, who were assured that their development assistance would be used properly. With the financial backing of the German government and the use of its own credit lines, KfW helped in the establishment of entirely new microfinance institutions within the recipient countries. In no short time, KfW had sponsored a network of two dozen microfinance institutions by 2005 in partnership with IPC (and later ProCredit).

The Growth of IPC and Support for Microfinance

In order to understand how KfW came to embrace microfinance, it is necessary to understand how the German aid regime interacted with earlier forms of microfinance. The German technical assistance agency

GTZ and BMZ had provided the earliest support for microcredits via numerous projects in Colombia, Bolivia, Peru, and El Salvador. Like the global microfinance industry, these were predominantly administered via grants for NGO-sponsored programs. Other German institutions, such as the German Savings Bank and Giro Association (DSGV), were also interested in microfinance because of the opportunity to replicate the German savings bank model in the developing world (Schmidt 2004, 6). However, critical to KfW's eventual embrace of microfinance was its interaction with the consulting firm Interdisziplinäre Projekt Consult (IPC).

Incidentally, the history of IPC had its roots in the negative experiences of KfW's DFC promotional strategy in 1980. Claus-Peter Zeitinger, who would later become founder of IPC and its later institutional forms of IMI and ProCredit Holding, was first exposed to development when he served on the assessment mission sponsored by BMZ and headed by Prof. Nitsch to inspect financial institutions in Latin America. His experience in witnessing the failures of the existing development paradigm led to a determination to implement a new strategy that avoided the pitfalls of the existing regime; or, more specifically, to implement development policy "differently, and doing it right" (Schmidt 2004, 6). After returning from the mission, Zeitinger and three of his colleagues established the consulting firm IPC in 1981, which was dedicated to supplying development finance in a way that created sustainable economic growth. Their experiences in assessing existing development banking projects in Latin America led them to believe that assistance should adhere to market logic (von Pischke 2003, Chapter 4).

The fledgling firm had just one problem—its Latin American report harshly critiquing KfW and BMZ made them persona non grata, and they had been blacklisted from receiving any further consulting contracts from those institutions. Therefore, their earliest reports were commissioned by GTZ. Their two publications were on the use of alternative sources of fuel in developing countries (Heber et al. 1982) and Germany's proposed aid project on the Special Energy Programme (SEP) that promoted renewable energy sources in Latin America and Africa (Zeitinger et al. 1982). Additional consultancy projects in both regions continued until 1989 (Lepp, n.d.).

Later that year, in November 1982, IPC received an opportunity to implement a larger project that better accorded with its ambitions. A master's student in Piura, Peru, had written a thesis that contained a proposal to convert a local pawn institution into a savings bank along the lines of the German *sparkassen*. A 1979 constitutional change decentralized the administrative system, and a new 1981 municipal law extended the autonomy of local governments, allowing the local Piura government greater control over the local banking sector (von Pischke 2003, Chapter 1). However, with high national inflation rates (officially 73% in 1982) and low savings rates (5.8% in 1979), the local banking sector faced numerous headwinds. Mobilizing additional savings for the use of capital investment was almost impossible, particularly for small borrowers. To assist in the endeavor, the local mayor had passed along the thesis to his superiors and eventually the proposal arrived at the German embassy. At the time, there had been interest on the part of the German banking sector to reach out to developing countries out of a conviction that the German financial model was successful and that there was a material interest in a global network of savings banks. Ultimately, the project was organized by the German Savings Bank Fund for International Cooperation (*Sparkassenstiftung für internationale Kooperation*) and GTZ, with funding provided by BMZ. IPC was tasked with assessing and implementing the proposal. Claus-Peter Zeitinger, Heinz-Günter Geis, and Manfred Nitsch—all of whom participated in the 1980 BMZ-sponsored assessment missions—performed the first assessment of the local economy to determine demand from SMEs and the viability of converting the local institution into a savings bank. The report also made clear that this was just the first step—it explicitly noted that it sought to make generalizable statements regarding the "value, survivability, and the chances of municipal savings banks in Peru" (IPC 1983, I).[2] It made further recommendations that this style of publicly-backed financial institutions could compensate for shortfalls of the private sector.

The savings bank, or the Caja Municipal de Ahorro y Crédito (CMAC), had the official objective to promote small-scale loans that had been underprovided by the commercial banking sector. Since 1981, CMAC had already provided loans as a pawn institution, with jewelry and gold serving as collateral, and by the end of its second year operations were nominally profitable (IPC 1983, 57–58). Yet most of the loans had been provided via an informal banking sector, and predatory lenders frequently charged exorbitant interest rates, sometimes in excess

[2] Translated by author from German: "Darüber hinaus gilt es, zu verallgemeinerbaren Aussagen über den Stellenwert, die Überlebensfähigkeit und die Chancen von kommunalen Sparkassen in Peru zu gelangen und mögliche Perspektiven aufzuzeigen."

of 400% per annum. IPC hoped that by formalizing this segment of the financial sector through the transformation of an existing bank, small entrepreneurs would be more willing and able to take out loans for capital improvements that would ultimately generate economic growth. Depending on the relative success of the CMAC, the report noted that the provision of financing to small businesses should be expanded throughout Peru (IPC 1983, 97).

In the following years, CMAC managed to continue to grow its balance sheet, and the model was replicated in numerous other cities in Peru. Critical to this success of this project was to create a national network of savings banks within Peru, a goal which necessitated the rewriting of the Peruvian banking laws. In the mid-1980s, IPC consulted with German development agencies and the Peruvian government to draft a national law that would regulate the governance of these savings banks. Of particular concern to IPC was to maintain proper incentives. For one, this meant that equity capital of the savings bank needed to be provided by the recipient institution—either through municipal funding or the accumulation of savings deposits—and that no international funding could be provided. In addition, the law required that bank boards were composed of seven members, four of which could not be government employees (Lepp 2017). This was meant to guard against political interference in the institution. This profound engagement with the political process, however, would later form part of GTZ's sharp criticism that IPC was too interventionist in its policies as a mere consulting company. Opposition also sprung from Peruvian financial institutions that saw IPC as replicating "Teutonic" values in the banking sector, but they had limited ability to counteract these forces (Schmidt 2004, 9).

Despite the optimism, the CMAC savings banks encountered similar problems to those of the DFCs. The largest obstacle was the cost of business. Individually administering small-value loans was expensive as the overhead cost of finding a project, assessing the borrower's creditworthiness without a history of credit, and monitoring were all high. Repayment rates of the loans were good, but the interest generated was insufficient to cover the high cost of implementation. The savings bank also had difficulties in mobilizing savings that could be used to capitalize the small institution. An ingenious lottery scheme was designed to encourage citizens to put their savings into the bank (and still continues to this day), but the quantities proved not enough to make the inexperienced institution financially self-sufficient. As such, IPC approached the Inter-American Development Bank (IDB) for additional working capital. The IDB already had a program in place—the *Programa de Pequeños Projectos*, or the Program for Small Projects—which consisted of USD 500,000 to on-lending projects and USD 50,000 in technical assistance to existing financial institutions. Zeitinger applied and received the grant, which was subsequently distributed via the national CMAC federation rather than the individual savings banks as a precaution against corruption (Schmidt 2004).

In 1987, GTZ sponsored another IPC-led consultancy program on the potential to transform more Peruvian financial institutions into German-like communal savings banks. The objective was to continue the formalization of the financial sector, but the authors noted that limitations by the national development banks stymied a full commercialization of the institutions. Through an investigation of the CMAC, they recommended that international institutions strengthen their financial commitments to shore up the finances of the institutions, but also allow that these communal banks to make business decisions about their loans at the local level (Krahnen and Nitsch 1987, 5–6). However, one instance of embezzlement by a manager in Arequipa and the subsequent inaction on part of the Peruvian banking regulatory authority eroded confidence in the endeavor, and GTZ pulled IPC from the project (Schmidt 2016).

Despite the setback in Piura, IPC's connections with the IDB opened another opportunity in Bolivia. Like Piura, IPC received starter funding from the IDB to upgrade the Banco Caja Los Andes into a full-fledged microfinance institution, and the institution received German development assistance via GTZ and BMZ as well. In order to maintain a local credit partner, IPC also arranged a small association of ProCrédito to be founded (Schmidt 2004). To be certain, this was not the only attempt at creating a proto-microfinance bank in Latin America. Acción Bank, which was under the direction of siblings Pancho and Maria Otero, had established BancoSol in 1984. While they purported to be involved in group lending along the lines of the Grameen Bank in Bangladesh, the business model was strikingly similar—Acción used its own funds to compensate private actors to invest in small entrepreneurs. Friendly competition between Caja Los Andes and Banco Sol engendered positive results (Schmidt 2016). However, the success of Caja Los Andes solidified IPC's reputation as an institution-builder. Its banks were performing well financially and developmentally. Caja Los Andes received a prize by the

IDB in 2000 entitled "Excellence in Microfinance Award for Regulated Institutions."[3]

IPC's third trajectory-changing event arrived in the autumn of 1986. During that month, the CDU German Minister of Labor Norbert Blüm had controversially visited Pinochet's Chile, which human rights activists decried as lending credibility to a repressive regime and had generated a substantial negative press.[4] In order to initiate positive press coverage of the trip, the minister flew last-minute to El Salvador, where a large earthquake had recently devastated the region. Once there, he promised millions of DM not just to be used for reconstruction as "helicopter money," but also in the promotion of SMEs (Schmidt 2016). At the time, BMZ tasked GTZ with the project, who then contracted out with IPC to design a strategy to upgrade an existing bank with an initial grant of DM 100 million. Zeitinger flew to El Salvador to discuss the proposal with the national association, but in the course of the meeting, realized that three businessmen had siphoned previous grant money for their purposes, leaving the 97 remaining smaller institutions with nothing. Zeitinger recommended that the remaining members move to the meeting hall next door where a new institution was drafted. Zeitinger successfully convinced BMZ to redirect the money to the new association, and Crédito Servicio Ampes was created officially in 1988 (Lepp, n.d.). Ampes acted much in the same way as the other early microfinance institutions. Only a few years later, Ampes was converted into a fully functioning bank named Calpiá, a reference to a sturdy local flower that persevered in difficult conditions.

As the first decade of Latin American experimentation drew to a close, the fall of the Berlin Wall and subsequent dissolution of the Soviet Union provided the established consultancy firm new opportunities. At an EBRD workshop in 1993, Elizabeth Wallace had begun a project called the Russia Small Business Fund (RSBF) that sought to provide microcredits to SMEs in Russia. She solicited recommendations for a reputable consulting firm, and the IDB recommended Zeitinger's IPC. After a brief joint assessment, Wallace and Zeitinger decided that microloans at commercial rates were the best strategy, and in 1994 a pilot credit program worth USD 10 million was implemented with successful results.

[3] "Inter-American Development Bank awards microenterprise prizes," *Inter-American Development Bank,* 19 October 2000. See http://www.iadb.org/en/news/news-releases/2000-10-19/inter-american-development-bank-awards-microenterprise-prizes,722.html.

[4] "Kein Zentimeter wird zurückmarschiert," *Der Spiegel*, 3 August 1987.

Shortly thereafter, the RSBF gained an additional round of capitalization and engaged in downscaling Russian banks. Maximum loan values were set at USD 30,000 per enterprise, and while the EBRD would not guarantee the individual loans, they would guarantee the intermediary institution in the case of failure (von Pischke 2003, Chapter 13). This structure had made use of contemporary financial innovations, including the prevention of Russian government participation and limited amounts of financial intermediaries; by 1998, the RSBF had a USD 100 million portfolio across 13 Russian banks and over 10,000 microloans.

Unfortunately, the ensuing Russian financial crisis and devaluation of the ruble bankrupted many of these institutions. The EBRD and other donor institutions then sought to reclaim their assets on the defaulted loans. The RSBF seized collateral and recovered a majority of its funds. The main lesson drawn from this experience was that while the underlying SME loans were unaffected, the banks through which the funding had been channeled were unreliable. This made IPC and the other participating development institutions realize that a donor government-backed institution was necessary (von Pischke 2003, Chapter 13). In 1998, the Russian Small Project Bank was transformed, under IPC guidance, to the Small Business Credit Bank (KMB-Bank) (Schmidt 2004, 9). DEG, part of KfW, took a 22% stake. Ultimately, the KMB-Bank became a viable retail bank and saved the RSBF. Even though the Russia projects were beset with concerns, this validated to IPC and other development institutions that downscaling could work, provided that donor governments took time to improve the quality of the financial intermediary. Additional downscaling projects were launched in Paraguay, Ukraine, Kazakhstan, Kyrgyzstan, Romania, Bulgaria, and Armenia between 1994 and 1999 (Lepp, n.d.).

The experiments in Latin America and Eastern Europe impacted the broader trajectory of development finance. Peru demonstrated that small loans were possible with effective financial institutions and a commercial orientation. IPC was able to affect institutional change throughout its Latin American endeavors via two mechanisms. First, since IPC was the responsible consultancy institution for the disbursement of development funds, it had leverage over the domestic financial institutions that needed its technical assistance and working capital. Second, IPC's close connection with the German development agencies gave it influence over the politics of important factors such as the Peruvian savings bank law.

These factors helped IPC affect the incentives of financial intermediaries. In Eastern Europe, the varying degrees of success held important lessons about governance and cooperation with development partners. Nevertheless, IPC had a long-standing desire to expand beyond advisory services. The added frustrations of politicized development bureaucracies, haphazard interests on the part of NGOs, and domestic political restrictions had limited IPC (Schmidt 2004).

Expansion of Microfinance in Southeastern Europe: KfW's Regional Initiatives

The restructuring of the existing banking sector in Eastern Europe was decidedly mixed. Oftentimes the banks remained de facto departments of the new government, and even privatization failed to bring transparency and efficiency because of the close political connections of the new owners. International efforts for downscaling existing banks and NGO efforts to upgrade microcredits into financial institutions were met with disappointing results. It was during this time that an alternative approach emerged—establish new financial institutions. Globally, microfinance was expanding rapidly. On 4 February 1997, James Wolfensohn, the President of the World Bank, gave the closing speech to the Microfinance Summit where he announced that his institution would whole-heartedly support microfinance institutions as a means for poverty relief (Wolfensohn 1997). With the global acceptance for microfinance accelerating, KfW saw the opportunity to shift their strategy.

KfW's extensive consulting via German embassies in Eastern Europe provided opportunities for technical assistance and credit lines, but KfW was still unsatisfied by what it saw as incapable financial intermediaries. As one banker remarked, the "situation with no financial partner was entirely novel—before you may have had the wrong partners, but now you did not have any" (Development Practitioner #42 2016). Existing efforts by the EU, which had provided a credit line to Albania, suffered a 94% loss of equity (Development Practitioner #38 2016). In 1995, an opportunity arose in Albania to create a new bank that would lend to microenterprises. KfW, with the blessing of the German government, founded the Foundation for Enterprise Finance and Development (FEFAD) in Tirana. KfW provided DM 3 million in equity investment in 1995, with additional credit lines in 1998 and 2001 worth a combined EUR 7.1 million in credit (KfW 2001). FEFAD was the first time that a development institution had founded a financial intermediary abroad, though technically FEFAD remained a foundation, not a microfinance bank at the beginning (Development Practitioner #38 2016). The distrust of the available staff in Albania—most of which had worked for state-owned banks during the communist era—prevented them from being hired; instead, KfW and IPC thought that new staff trained by IPC's managers from the Bolivian Caja Los Andes would be the best way forward (Development Practitioner #40 2016). The technical assistance greatly strengthened the microfinance institution, which allowed it to weather a series of economic and political crises in 1997. The major lesson for KfW was that governance structure was important in ensuring success than the methodology of how credit was distributed (von Pischke 2003, Chapters 6 and 16). In order to maintain control over the foundation, KfW had two board member seats. Later, the other microfinance banks would be based on the model that KfW pioneered with FEFAD (Matthäus-Maier and von Pischke 2004a, 6).

Yet the most transformative opportunity for KfW arrived in 1996. Following the bloody war in the former Yugoslavia, the Dayton Peace Accords were signed in December 1995 and politicians endeavored to return Croatia, Serbia, and Bosnia-Herzegovina to economic prosperity (UN 1995). To most observers, the Dayton Accords closely adhered to the principles of the Washington Consensus—the standard mixture of international capital and exchange rate liberalization, SOE privatization, capital market development, and central bank independence were codified in the agreement (Drezgic et al. 2011). During the negotiations, there were also early proposals to establish a microfinance institution to facilitate the revival of the financial sector and provide a funding conduit for both housing reconstruction and small and microcredits for industry. As part of this effort, the World Bank was the first to invest in microfinance. In 1996, the institution provided grants and loans for the Local Initiatives Project (LIP), which was dedicated to capacity building and project management as well, and by 2000 had disbursed some USD 67 million via 50,000 microloans (World Bank 2000). Concurrently, a separate group of investors—namely the IFC, EBRD, and KfW—wanted to establish their own greenfield microfinance institution via IFC to promote private enterprise in Bosnia-Herzegovina. IFC was selected because of its early commitment to the promotion of microfinance in the Balkans. However, the IFC was limited in its ability to do such a task as its articles of confederation explicitly restrict both the creation of a new financial institution (particularly one without the backing of the government) as well as ownership in a controlling stake of an investment. This ultimately prevented IFC from founding the institution (Development Practitioner #29 2016).

As such, the IFC approached KfW to begin a new microfinance institution since KfW had no restrictions on owning and creating new institutions. The IFC only required that the microfinance institution be based on private markets (Development Practitioner #9 2016). However, since KfW's experience in Eastern European modernization was limited to technical assistance and credit lines, and not creating microfinance institutions, the Board of Governors was not initially enthusiastic (Development Practitioner #40 2016). KfW's interactions with IPC in various projects in Eastern Europe provided a potential avenue forward, as the ambitions of IPC were coterminous with KfW's. The initial proposal involved bringing IPC as a consultant on the microfinance project, with international development institutions providing the initial equity and technical assistance. However, the IFC was reluctant to hire a consultancy institution to establish a new bank because of a belief that the consultants would have no vested interest in the long-term viability of the project. Consequently, a new solution was proposed—IPC would have to take an initial equity stake in the Bosnian microfinance bank. After negotiations, KfW required that IPC take a 30% equity share in the new financial institution. This solution was revolutionary because, at the time, there was no precedent for an equity stake by a private consultancy group in any microfinance project (Development Practitioner #40 2016). As Aftab Ahmed of the IFC remarked regarding the ownership structure, "in terms of its development impact, I rate this innovation as one of the most exciting in development finance in recent years" (Ahmed 2004, 76).

Zeitinger, whose long-term desire had been to establish institutions, was pleasantly surprised by the invitation of the "consultant as shareholder" model. However, IPC was unable to provide enough equity for the Bosnian bank, as well as the large pipeline of new projects in other Eastern European countries. Therefore, in order to formalize the process of investing in equity stakes, Zeitinger founded the Internationale Micro Investitionen AG (IMI, International Micro Investments) in 1998. It was founded as a joint-stock company under German law with an initial capitalization of EUR 700,000 (Schmidt 2004). Its advisory board initially consisted of academics, such as Prof. Manfred Nitsch and Prof. Reinhardt Schmidt, both of whom had previously worked for IPC and in consultancy services with KfW (Development Practitioner #56 2017; Schmidt 2016). Finally, since IMI only took up to 30% of the equity in any given project, it relied on development agencies. Aside from KfW and IFC, other investors included the Dutch FMO and DOEN Foundation, the EBRD, and the Belgian development agency BIO.

KfW's involvement in the process can be starkly seen in the first two microfinance banks in Bosnia-Herzegovina and Kosovo. In 1999, the new microfinance bank of Micro Enterprise Bank Bosnia (MEB Bosnia)[5] was established in Bosnia-Herzegovina in a joint partnership between IMI, IFC, DOEN, and KfW. KfW was the legal signatory because of its ability to establish the bank and had invested its own equity directly into the microfinance bank as well. Complementing this new bank were two other programs. First, on behalf of several European donors, KfW established its first refinancing fund in Bosnia in 1998 to channel financing to commercial banks, including KfW's own microfinance bank. Under this fund structure, the donors appointed KfW as the lending agent that KfW itself vetted for institutional quality, which, following the model in Germany, would be on-lent to local banks that assume the credit risk themselves. Additionally, KfW provided technical assistance to the banks and endeavored to supply credit lines in order to foster domestic financial competition (Glaubitt and Schütte 2004). Moreover, KfW established its own two credit programs—the Housing Construction Loan Programme and the SME Loan Programme—to channel KfW-raised funding to Bosnian projects (Matthäus-Maier and von Pischke 2004a). These programs were further attached with ODA funds to provide staff training, management consultancy, and the installation of new banking software. For example, the SME Loan Programme distributed more than EUR 20 million, half of which had come from KfW's own funds and capital market financing, with nearly EUR 1 million provided in technical assistance grants (KfW 2013). Nevertheless, one development practitioner noted that FEFAD and MEB Bosnia were "in the global trend to promote sustainable financial development, it was a small but important step" (Development Practitioner #38 2016).

Shortly thereafter, the Micro Enterprise Bank of Kosovo (MEB Kosovo) was established in 2000 with the same founding partners, with KfW serving as the lead institution once more. This time, MEB Kosovo

[5] This bank would later become ProCredit Bank BiH.

garnered the participation of Commerzbank, the first time that a private commercial bank had taken an equity stake in a new microfinance bank (Nitsch 2002). Unlike in Bosnia, MEB Kosovo served for the first three years as the territory's only bank. As in Bosnia, KfW created the European Fund for Kosovo (EFK) in 2000, which by 2002 had some EUR 9.2 million committed by donors, and grew substantially in 2003 with the addition of a new SME program and housing loan program, both of which on-lent through MEB Kosovo (Glaubitt and Schütte 2004, 63). Two additional credit lines in 2000 were earmarked for SMEs and farming enterprises, worth a total of EUR 2.5 million with EUR 0.5 million for technical assistance, and were intended to contribute to the continuing deepening of the Kosovar financial system (KfW 2003). Its successes extended beyond the provision of loans. MEB Kosovo was the only functioning commercial bank within country and, as a KfW-backed institution, attracted local deposits (Zeitinger 2004). At times, MEB Kosovo also served as a make-shift central bank, and the German government used it to distribute payment and pension to local soldiers working on behalf of international peacekeepers (Development Practitioner #40 2016).

Quickly following the successful establishment of the Bosnian and Kosovar microfinance institution, IMI grew precipitously and new equity stakes in recently founded microfinance institutions proceeded in rapid succession. By 2000, IMI had equity stakes in microfinance banks in Haiti (MCN Haiti; 2000), Albania (ProCredit Bank Albania; 2000), Moldova (ProCredit Moldova; 2000), Nicaragua (ProCredit Nicaragua; 2000), Mozambique (NovoBanco Mozambique; 2000), and Ukraine (ProCredit Ukraine; 2000) (Lepp, n.d.). By 2004, IMI had taken equity stakes in 18 various banks and microfinance companies, ten of which were located in Eastern Europe. IMI's combined portfolio reached EUR 1 billion, with a growth rate of over 50% per year in the first five years of operations. True to IMI's goal of providing credit on commercial terms, IMI was also reasonably profitable, with a return on equity of approximately 10% per annum. These high rates of return were also rewarded with the addition of two Swiss investment funds in 2004, IMI's first private investors (Schmidt 2004).

KfW's stakes grew as well. By 2000, KfW had made equity investments in six microfinance institutions in the region: the Microfinance Bank of Georgia (Georgia), MEB-Banka (Bosnia-Herzegovina), MEB Kosovo (Kosovo), Microenterprise Credit (Romania), Micro Enterprise Credit (Moldova), and FEFAD-Bank (Albania). In all six cases, the IFC and KfW had taken an equity investment, and, in all but Georgia, the EBRD had invested as well (Nitsch 2002). Between 2000 and 2002, KfW concluded agreements with other donors worth EUR 70 million with the financial sector accounting for a bulk of the projects (Matthäus-Maier and von Pischke 2004a, 4). In addition, by the end of 2003, KfW had downscaled 34 banks in nine countries with combined total assets of EUR 8.6 billion, a move that further expanded its influence and managerial control of other microfinance institutions. For KfW, "the financial innovations developed and employed in Southeast Europe could also benefit other volatile countries and regions. Examples include the introduction of new financial products, the provision of credit lines, the opening of economies formerly closed to foreign investment in the financial sector, and the launching of private banks specialized in serving the small end of the market" (Matthäus-Maier and von Pischke 2004b, 226). The successes had also received plaudits from BMZ, who argued that these should be used as a model for the future: "In Kosovo, for instance, Micro Enterprise Bank—which we were instrumental in setting up and have subsequently supported—is just one success story...Revolving funds were also set up to increase the effectiveness of resources deployed. We are exploring how this mode of operation can be made permanent" (Bohnet 2004, viii). Building on these successes, KfW held a series of conferences beginning in 2002 aimed at developing more innovative approaches to development finance, particularly in volatile environments (cf. Matthäus-Maier and von Pischke 2005).

The reasons for the self-ordained success were multifaceted. According to Nitsch, the reason for the success was that they provided small, short-term loans at market-rate to microbusinesses that could grow. Institutions were created with appropriate incentives and strong governance. Conversely, IMI avoided numerous other characteristics, including interest rate subsidization, group credits, loans to found a new microenterprise, and loans to finance the entire working capital of a microenterprise (2002, 207). To KfW, another explanation was working within a coordinated framework for market reforms. Together, this created KfW's multifaceted strategy in Southeast Europe as the creator of European Funds, equity stakes in microfinance banks, credit guarantee facilities (CGF), and the capitalization of deposit insurance agencies (Köhn and Erhardt 2004). The successes of microfinance institutions validated the "effectiveness of KfW's perspective and strategies that work with and through the financial sectors" (Matthäus-Maier and von Pischke 2004b,

225). Kloppenburg, KfW's Senior Vice President, posited that "public sector support has enabled some [microfinance institutions] to become sufficiently seasoned to engage capital markets and the rigorous discipline that these markets impose in order to function efficiently" (Kloppenburg 2006, 4). In short, the regulations of these new banks endeavored to keep the incentives of entrepreneurs aligned with market discipline and were successful because they eliminated distortions and empowered entrepreneurs. This sentiment of empowerment via financial institutions was reiterated by countless other sources (Development Practitioner #38 2016; Lepp 2017; Neuschütz 2004; von Pischke 2003; Schmidt 2016).

In addition, these microfinance banks did attract private participation, which hitherto had been interested but unable to invest in Southeast Europe. KfW had approached Commerzbank and Deutsche Bank in the late 1990s to establish a joint venture with up to 50% risk mitigation in the event of an institutional collapse, but both rebuffed KfW because of the still high level of uncertainty (Development Practitioner #40 2016). Zeitinger noted that the first few years of expansion had brought tremendous portfolio growth, but that, despite intentions of becoming fully private, were still heavily reliant on credit. In nine of the joint KfW-IPC microfinance banks, 68% of the on-lending funds came from either KfW or the EBRD, and still by the end of 2002, "it was still virtually impossible to obtain on-lending funds from commercial banks" because of high risk (Zeitinger 2004, 132). The exit of development institutions from equity stakes had also been slower than envisioned (Neuschütz 2004). Yet the continued stability of the microfinance banks slowly began to attract participation from the commercial banking sector. Commerzbank's pioneering investment in MEB Kosovo in 2000 marked the first equity investment by a commercial institution, and by 2004, Commerzbank had participated in the equity capital in seven different microfinance institutions. Why this occurred, however, was because of the opportunities for portfolio diversification and risk reduction on the part of German government protection. As Jan Baechle, a former Senior Vice President of Commerzbank, remarked, "KfW's guarantee enables us to make longer-term loans available, which we would be unable to do at our own risk" (2004, 137).

Yet the positive results were also a consequence of how development institutions interacted with financial intermediaries. By maintaining commercial rates, moral hazards on the part of the new institutions were minimized. The extensive amount of technical assistance also was crucial in building up in-house capacity. KfW's ability to directly create and manage the institutions, particularly during their fledgling years, was critical to growing them into mature, commercially viable financial institutions. As KfW noted, its control over operations was essential: "Donors have been instrumental in improving the regulation and supervision of banks in Southeast Europe…Donor intervention has led to a significantly improved ownership structure in the region's banks, both through equity investments and indirectly through 'picking winners.' This in turn has attracted investments and, through restructuring, led to acquisitions by private foreign banks" (Matthäus-Maier and von Pischke 2004b, 232).

Key to KfW's achievements was that donor governments strongly backed the marketized development financial instruments through four mechanisms. First, development institutions provided the necessary working capital. These contributions accounted for at least 70% of the initial capitalization, and additional credit lines, mainly from KfW and the EBRD, were often channeled through these microfinance banks in the subsequent years. Moreover, this provided the financial stability to increase the trust of these new institutions, an advantage that they leveraged when seeking deposits from bank-wary consumers. Second, while IMI brought in the commercial logic, the development institutions could bring the necessary technical assistance. Yet this burden largely fell on KfW, as the IFC had no budget for technical assistance (Development Practitioner #40 2016). Third, KfW's flexibility in being able to create new microfinance institutions and keep controlling stakes in them enabled KfW to circumvent the principle-agent problem of bad financial intermediaries. Finally, direct risk assumption by donor governments was essential. The approach is "based on the realization that a public-sector investment institution can take risks and pursue strategies which may be considered too risky by private investors, while at the same time being accountable for the responsible use of taxpayers' funds." In fact, the authors continued that KfW's greatest innovation was "the refinement of the valuation processes"; that is, by leveraging donor country guarantees, credit lines, and managerial control, KfW could transfer the risk to encourage private investors (Matthäus-Maier and von Pischke 2004b, 226). These experiences of KfW in microfinance in Southeast Europe demonstrated one of the first fully operationalizations of a marketized development financial instrument.

The European Fund for Southeast Europe (EFSE)

While KfW's push to establish microfinance banks was designed to bolster the domestic economy of these fledgling states, they were also accompanied by a growing desire on the part of the European Union (EU) and other MDBs that greater financing also needed to be provided. Microfinance banks presented themselves as a viable alternative to the newly privatized commercial banks that had better training and more insulation from politics. Moreover, the support for these banks was widely seen as a means to bolster the nascent financial sector, a prerequisite for these countries to eventually accede to the EU (cf. Matthäus-Maier 2005). However, given the paucity of domestic savings and tepid private international interest in financing projects, donor governments also sought to supplement the newly established microfinance institutions with additional credit lines. In order to facilitate this integration, there was a recognition that the various sources of EU development assistance should be coordinated. It was during this period that proposals for harmonized European credit lines to Eastern Europe and the Balkans first emerged.

While calls for coordination were easy, implementation was more difficult. Despite the impressive amount of funding through multilateral institutions, all were unable to create these new financial intermediaries. As with the microcredit institutions, the World Bank's Articles of Agreement restricted it from establishing new institutions and recipient government guarantees. However, in the unstable political and economic conditions of Eastern Europe and the Balkans, the use of local commercial banks was neither advisable nor possible, and KfW, which possessed the financing capability and legal ability to found new financial institutions, established these banks (cf. Köhn and Erhardt 2004). Similarly, this flexibility allowed KfW to serve as the founding institution for a variety of European credit lines. As such, KfW became an important conduit through which EU funds were distributed, initially through four European revolving credit lines for four countries in Southeast Europe. Moreover, KfW's institutional agility and experience with domestic credit lines in Germany enabled creative applications of market instruments to development practice. Despite the success, these credit lines were only partially coordinated, and a growing reserve of repaid loans was accumulating in the accounts of development institutions. In 2005, KfW arrived at the creative solution to create the European Fund for Southeast Europe (EFSE), a structure that would combine the various credit lines into a centralized European fund. EFSE was KfW's most important contribution in establishing a marketized development financial instrument, as it was the first time that a structured fund had been utilized by a development institution to promote international development assistance. As with other instruments, the German and European governments bore the majority of risk.

The Balkan Crisis and European Assistance Initiatives

Central to the German strategy in Eastern Europe was the provision of government-subsidized credit lines for on-lending activities. These financing schemes would also be accompanied by significant technical assistance for the newly-established commercial banks, in order to raise their standards, as well as macroeconomic policy advice administered through KfW's TRANSFORM program or other consultancy service. A revived interest in establishing or rehabilitating national development banks became important to serve as on-lending institutions, and, by 1998, KfW had issued DM 450 million in credits via Eastern European development banks (Winkler 1999, 65). The Croatian Bank for Reconstruction and Development (HBOR) demonstrated the most promise in the early years, and KfW had supplied DM 110 million in credit lines for SMEs, infrastructure, and housing projects by 1998. HBOR also secured credit lines from the World Bank and EBRD and became the first Eastern European promotional bank to issue a bond in the Euromarket (Winkler 1999, 65). Other successful KfW-sponsored banks included those in Hungary, Slovakia, Lithuania, Estonia, and Ukraine.

Despite the apparent successes, development banks did not serve as a panacea to KfW's operations in Eastern Europe. Like their predecessor institutions, NDBs proved to be inefficient and politically captured, and debates were fierce within KfW as to whether or not this strategy should be revitalized (Development Practitioner #7 2016). In one particularly bad effort, the Business Development Bank of Russia failed to fully transform into a commercial-oriented bank, and KfW's DM 50 million credit line for SMEs in 1996 was never disbursed. While KfW maintained that its own experiences served as the model, there were significant differences in the operational environment. Rather than SMEs, the new credit lines in Eastern Europe were newly formed with no experience in a market-based economy. The financial system was also recently founded with little knowledge of Western banking standards. Finally, these reformed banks operated in a political economy often inimical to their operations (Development Practitioner #35 2016). These differences made KfW's strategy in Eastern Europe inapplicable to Southeast Europe. Persistent political instability meant that there was never enough political support to transform an existing institution into a development bank. When a development bank was proposed, such as in Macedonia, it was torpedoed by political dealings (Development Practitioner #40 2016). A similar proposal by the Bulgarian government in 1999 was rebuffed by KfW (Development Practitioner #27 2016).

While prior to the fall of the Eastern Bloc Yugoslavia was relatively wealthy, the civil war and ethnic strife that followed in the mid-1990s devastated the region. By the end of the 1990s, the economies of the Western Balkan states had shrunk by 70% (Ziller 2006, 194). The financial sector theoretically existed, but proved to be unsustainable. Credit institutions were effectively bankrupt and no new private investors were willing to recapitalize the banks, particularly when there were widespread fears that they would not adhere to international standards. The new microfinance banks provided a workaround for this problem, but, at this time, they were too small and undercapitalized to provide a full range of retail banking services (Lepp 2017). Under these conditions, KfW was unwilling to sponsor any credit lines to these newly independent Balkan countries as it had done a few years earlier in Eastern Europe (Development Practitioner #40 2016).

European governments and their attendant institutions took the initiative to stabilize the region via economic aid packages, with the IMF and World Bank providing support as well. These were principally targeted at bolstering the domestic financial sector. In order to fund the reconstruction and integration of the war-torn Balkan countries, and at the German government's initiative, the international community created the Stability Pact for Southeast Europe on 10 July 1999 (Bohnet 2004, i–ii). The pact called for international donors to harmonize their efforts to create political and economic stability centered around three essential pillars. First, basic goods and infrastructure would need to be quickly rehabilitated. Second, these emerging countries would need to attract domestic and foreign investors. This would be done by creating "an economic system functioning along the lines of the Central European model of a social market economy, and to do so as quickly as possible" (Ziller 2006, 196). Policies included the privatization of SOEs and the creation of a stable and transparent legal system, with significant amounts of technical assistance from the EU and bilateral agencies. Finally, the pact called for the promotion of the local economy. While foreign investment was crucial, it could not replace the engine of growth of SMEs and microenterprises. This would insulate the economies from becoming too dependent on developed countries and create employment at the local level. In order to fund such an ambitious endeavor, European governments provided hundreds of millions of euros; in the first five years, the German government made available EUR 615 million, in addition to BMZ and KfW-related funds worth over EUR 1.6 billion (Bohnet 2004, vii).

Critically, the Stability Pact exempted KfW from needing to receive a recipient government guarantee for its investment. KfW had already circumvented some of the equity stake restrictions with a creative redeployment of grants via foundations (Development Practitioner #57 2018). Yet the changes were also rooted in the German government's distrust of recipient governments. In order to facilitate this, the German government distributed the money via Title 23 rather than Title 60, which governed traditional aid. Title 23 was much more flexible, and KfW could disburse money without an intergovernmental agreement, an untested practice until then. According to one development practitioner, "the German government was willing to do that step because Eastern Europe was so close to home, and they wanted to show presence and wanted to do something significant, fast" (Development Practitioner #34 2016). Yet it was up to KfW how to administer the funds. KfW could have distributed the funds as project grants but, reasoning that its own successes had been based upon the idea of revolving credit, decided to administer it as loans (Development Practitioner #38 2016).

This flexibility meant that KfW and its microfinance banks could compensate for an uncertain commercial banking sector. The earliest approach consisted of a dual mandate. First, microfinance banks would need to be established in order to provide reliable financial partners within these countries. Few private banks existed and, even so, development practitioners and donor governments alike were hesitant to work with them because of the communist legacy (Development Practitioner #41 2016). Given KfW's unique ability to both invest in controlling stakes, as well as create new financial institutions without the guarantee of the recipient government, it took the lead in founding a new network of microfinance banks. This attracted other development institutions, namely the IFC, FMO, and EBRD, to become equity participants or channel credit lines via these banks. Additionally, the IPC consulting group and Commerzbank were early participants.

Second, and in parallel with the creation of the microfinance banks, four "funds" would be established for micro-, small-, and medium-sized enterprises (MSMEs). These were designed to alleviate the difficulties that SMEs faced in raising long-term finance in Southeast Europe by providing rotating credit lines (Glaubitt and Schütte 2004, 62). One "European Fund" was created each for Bosnia and Herzegovina, Kosovo, Montenegro, and Serbia from 1998 to 2001, and initial capitalization would largely come from the EU and bilateral aid from Germany, Switzerland, Austria, and the Netherlands. At the outset, this collectively amounted to approximately EUR 130 million. Like the microfinance banks, however, most of the European institutions neither had the legal ability nor the experience with market-rate credit lines to establish and administer these funds; KfW was the only institution that could. Consequently, the structure of these four European Funds was similar: "Donors appointed KfW as their agent to lend funds to local financial institutions carefully selected by KfW" (Glaubitt and Schütte 2004, 61–62). Once again, KfW served as the link between the donors, the recipient, and the financial markets. However, it is important to note that while these were initially called funds, "these vehicles were technically not real funds, but rather similarly-designed parallel credit lines for microfinance, SME and housing modernization" (Ziller 2006, 197).

The ultimate objective of these European Funds was to bolster the domestic financial sector and increase financing for local entrepreneurs. This was based on the experiences of KfW during the process of reunification and financing the newly independent states of Eastern Europe, as well as the predominant thinking of development practitioners since the late 1980s. As such, it was important that they were administered along commercial lines. Credit lines were issued at or near market rates to any qualified financial institution so that they may on-lend to microenterprises, SMEs, and individual households. Technical assistance was provided via consulting firms to increase their technical capacity, though this was done with grant contributions from donor governments. In order to foster domestic competition, each of the funds provided refinancing to a number of domestic on-lending institutions (Development Practitioner #40 2016). One particular innovation for development assistance within the European context was the rotating nature of these credit lines.

As repayment of the small loans came back to the credit line, new loans to financial intermediaries would be distributed.

The first was the European Fund for Bosnia and Herzegovina (EFBH), which was established in 1998. After four years of operation, the EFBH had loaned to six commercial banks and six microfinance banks for SME, housing, and rural business loans. By 2002, the EFBH had 32.2 million in outstanding loans with an additional EUR 24 million pledged from donor countries in 2003. The second project was the European Fund for Kosovo (EFK), which was established in 2000. EFK had an initial commitment of EUR 9.2 million, through which it on-lent through the Bank for Private Business for SMEs and the KfW-sponsored MEB Kosovo for housing retrofit. The third was the European Fund for Montenegro (EFM), established at the end of 2002, which had EUR 8 million in outstanding loans after its first quarter in operation. Finally, there was the European Fund for Serbia (EFS), which also started in 2002. Refinancing loans and technical assistance were provided to the Microfinance Bank of Serbia, and by the end of 2002, a total of 163 loans worth EUR 5.6 million had been disbursed (Glaubitt and Schütte 2004, 64). By the end of 2004, they collectively issued more than 45,000 loans amounting to more than EUR 250 million in total financing (Ziller 2006, 198).

Nevertheless, the early endeavors with the four European Funds were not always a success. As Dominik Ziller, the Deputy Head of BMZ, elucidated, there were three limitations. First, since these European Funds were actually a collection of approximately thirty different lending lines, projects were often selected based on political objectives rather than economic benefits. Moreover, the investment decisions among the various lending lines were uncoordinated and, as such, did not achieve economies of scale or network benefits. The administration of thirty lines of credit required onerous reporting and accounting practices as each one had to be independently maintained; as a consequence, the overhead administrative cost was quite high. Second, other donors and international financial institutions had expressed their interest in participating, but the lack of a coordinated strategy and common policies worried investors, particularly if they wanted to divest from the fund. Third, the credit lines were implemented with an end date between 2006 and 2012, meaning that they could not be indefinitely administered. This raised questions of financial sustainability and of ownership, since donor countries were exclusively responsible for the funding and project selection (Ziller 2006, 198–99).

For its part, KfW was concerned about the contractual basis of each fund, which limited the flexibility of KfW from proactively tackling problems. The absence of local involvement—partner banks aside—further limited the ability to consult with local politicians and central banks to achieve policy synergy. The reporting standards required for assessing each stage of the credit lines were also burdensome. Looking towards the future, KfW was concerned that the ineffectiveness of local financial institutions would not be able to successfully replace the four European Funds when the terms expired. The broad distrust of banks in the region not only meant that locals would not deposit in the bank, but also that foreign investors would not invest capital (Glaubitt and Schütte 2004, 67).

Transitioning to a Structured Fund

By 2003, European governments and MDBs had invested billions in various loans, investments, and funds to finance projects in Eastern Europe, the majority of which were given via the European Funds. These credit lines, while overseen and managed by KfW, were largely left to the individual donors to select which projects would be financed. Ironically, in implementing this strategy, the development agencies encountered an unexpected problem—the vast majority of loans were beginning to be repaid with interest, yet the money did not officially belong to anyone. Since KfW had received an exemption from administering loans with a recipient government guarantee in the Stability Pact, the retuned money did not belong the recipient government. From the perspective of the donor governments, they had already disbursed the money and, more importantly, did not want to be seen as profiting from development assistance to the newly democratized countries (Development Practitioner #34 2016). Moreover, according to ODA regulations, funding that was already counted as ODA could not be returned to donor governments without the amount being removed from their current ODA figures as negative flows (OECD 2008, 3). The relevant ministries refused to reaccept the funds. For KfW and other development institutions, even though they provided the funds on a revolving basis, in reality they were mere distributors of the money and had no legal claim to reinvest it. The result was that development institutions had accumulated the returned assistance but could do nothing with the proceeds; by 2004, KfW alone had millions in returned assets (Development Practitioner #27 2016).

Donor countries were loath to see their ODA repatriated to the various finance ministries of recipient countries. Throughout the 1990s, there was widespread suspicion that reform efforts had not been able to reverse the corruption of the government. At an impasse over what to do, KfW began to float ideas. Dr. Klaus Glaubitt of KfW spearheaded a working group that created proposals for a possible solution. One option was to place the existing funds into a foundation with a codified mission; the benefits of this would be that misappropriation would be difficult and that administration could be quickly devolved back to the developing countries. However, this option would not be able to attract new donors and could not adapt to the changing needs of the domestic financial sector. A second option was to create a regional development bank that could distribute funds to various projects. This proposal faced difficulties in the ability to gain tax-exempt status or effectively issue bonds; moreover, the EIB and EBRD were also vehemently opposed since it had the possibility to create a competing institution (Ziller 2006, 200–201).

Nevertheless, Dr. Glaubitt and his team recommended that the best solution would be to institutionalize these credit lines into a single European structured fund. Structured funds are powerful instruments because they pool money from multiple investors and provide loans or equity to recipients. This can be done at or near to market conditions, and attractive because of the possibility for risk diversification, financial discipline, and wide applicability (Goodman 2006). Specifically, they noted that this would have enormous benefits for the flexibility of distributing funds: "The major benefit of institutionalisation would be to facilitate long-term finance by providing a legal structure for pooling funds, for obtaining new funds, and for improving the efficiency of re-flows across donor and sector lines" (Glaubitt and Schütte 2004, 68). A fund would also have the added benefit of eliminating competition among development agencies, a welcome departure from previous policies (Development Practitioner #41 2016). In short, an institutionalized investment structure could effectively combine the various credit lines into a single, flexible legal entity. By leveraging public funds, additional private funds could be attracted. Yet they also noted that this would have benefits for the recipient countries as well, particularly in fixing the lack of long-term finance: "Institutionalised European Funds could lengthen maturities and reduce mismatches by providing long-term refinancing, helping broaden the banks' outreach to yet unserved clients, and by promoting financial sector innovations through the co-financing of development and risk costs" (Glaubitt and

Schütte 2004, 67). To KfW, this seemed like a win-win strategy, as donors obtained economies of scale and flexibility, and recipient countries were able to retain a steady source of international financing.

The real question was how to structure an institutionalized fund. Structured funds had existed for private investors, but KfW's efforts to use this method within a developing country context were unprecedented. There were some early agreements on how this could be done. First, the new entity would need to have legal flexibility and should be administered by donor countries until the recipient countries were ready to make the investments independently. This also needed to allow for investors to maintain oversight through the legal foundation while being able to dispense with the tedious process of selecting and monitoring individual projects. Second, there was the advantage that the fund could be separated into different risk tranches. The existing money in the four European Funds would be transferred into the fund to help form the capital base. In order to expand the lending capacity, donor governments could provide additional ODA funds that could occupy the highest-risk tranche, with additional credit lines provided at the mezzanine tranche from KfW or other development institutions. Third, this structured fund could better attract private investors. Southeast Europe had struggled to gain private investors because of the political and economic risk; with a structured fund, donor governments and development institutions could cushion risk for private actors (cf. Glaubitt et al. 2008; Maurer 2011).

Other details of the program, however, ran into more difficulties. For instance, should the fund be located on-shore within the recipient countries or should it be located offshore? On-shore institutionalization potentially provides more local influence, but the requirement of greenfield institutions and tax and legal complications were seen as too difficult. Additionally, there was discussion as to whether the fund should be combined at the country or regional level. If continued at the country level, this could provide more local autonomy, but a fund with a regional focus could facilitate a better deployment of reflow funds and achieve economies of scale in fund management (Glaubitt and Schütte 2004, 61). Even within KfW, there was widespread apprehension about the feasibility of using a structured fund for on-lending purposes. There had been the initial 1998 fund for microfinance, but this was limited in size, scope, and ability; the proposed fund would be significantly larger, and it would be structured more on commercial terms. First, there was no precedent for establishing a structured fund for the purposes of development. Structured funds were used as an investment diversification and a risk-sharing mechanism for private investment, and, as such, both the German government and KfW management were cautious. Second, the KfW management worried about the quality of the financial intermediaries that would be necessary. Finally, there was uncertainty over how a structured fund would alter the risk profile of KfW (Development Practitioner #40 2016).

Additionally, resistance arose from other donor countries as well as recipient countries. Many of the donor countries were similarly hesitant to invest in an untested development fund, particularly one that would rely so heavily on marketized development finance instruments. The European Commission and EBRD were so skeptical that they refused to invest in the structure at the beginning. For its part, BMZ did not like the plan because it would divert its influence of the distribution of development assistance (Development Practitioner #27 2016). However, KfW employees explained that since the money from the funds could not be returned to the respective donor governments, the funds would eventually need to be distributed to the governments of the developing countries. For instance, in trying to convince the Swedish delegation, one practitioner recalled asking whether they wanted the money to be used for SMEs or given back to the Serbian government for the purchase of tanks; the Swedish promptly signed onto the fund (Development Practitioner #40 2016). Additionally, the Serbian government was particularly against the reformed fund because it would involve sharing resources with countries it had previously been at war with, and it preferred that the earnings on loans in its own country were not redistributed to its neighbors. To placate these demands, KfW prevented the retroactive regionalization of any of the funds that had been earmarked for a specific country (ibid). KfW ultimately convinced the Serbian government that using this fund would, in the end, attract private and government investment greater than any redistribution.

Nevertheless, the combined fund was determined to have a regional focus and was to be set up offshore in Luxembourg. In December 2005, EFSE was founded by combining the four existing European funds. Under Luxembourg law, a promoter—or main advisor—needed to be selected, and the donor countries agreed that KfW should serve that role. Funds were transferred from the four credit lines, and the German, Swiss, and Austrian governments added additional equity shares to EFSE

(Development Practitioner #27 2016). In addition to coordinating the foundation and providing additional capital, KfW took a further administrative role in EFSE. Dr. Klaus Glaubitt served as the first chair of the Board of Directors, along with two other KfW employees on the Board. In 2009, all fund management responsibilities were transferred to Finance in Motion, a Frankfurt-based fund manager that was created by KfW and staffed with numerous former KfW employees. KfW's dominance was also extended unofficially, as a member or former member of the institution was present on every investment committee.

The purpose of EFSE was to create economies of scale that could more effectively leverage European development assistance. The mission of EFSE was therefore dual. First, it would provide affordable financial services to poor households and SMEs in Eastern Europe. Private entrepreneurship was key. Second, EFSE promoted the model of a public-private partnership (PPP). More specifically, the PPP model enabled "EFSE to mobilise funding from private institutional investors to top up international public donor funding for development finance."[6] European governments were eager to impact economic development, but were often unable to entirely fund projects in Southeast Europe. Initially, the fund was incorporated for the use in the four original European fund countries—Bosnia and Herzegovina, Kosovo, Montenegro, and Serbia—but at EFSE's creation in 2005, Albania, Bulgaria, Macedonia, Moldova, and Romania were added.

Key to EFSE's operations was a tranched risk structure (EFSE 2016a, 56). When KfW structured the new financial instrument, the institution provided three tranches, each with a different risk profile. The first-loss tranche, or C-Shares, would be assumed by governments; the mezzanine, or B-Shares, would be subscribed to by international development agencies; and the senior or A-Shares would be sold to private investors. The C-Shares would face the highest risk by absorbing the initial 15% loss of any investment and the B-Shares an additional 5%. This would leave private investors relatively well-positioned against any sudden loss to the fund, as the total investment portfolio could lose 20% before the senior tranche was impacted at all. In theory, this innovative idea was designed to attract private investors to countries and industries that would otherwise be deemed too risky. At the creation of EFSE, the fund consisted of

[6] https://www.efse.lu/about-the-fund/mission/.

EUR 380 million. The C-Shares, or first-loss tranche, contained EUR 128 million (34%) and were subscribed by public investors. This was mainly the EC and the German government via BMZ, with smaller portions from the Swiss and Austrian governments. The B-Shares, or mezzanine tranche, accounted for an additional EUR 80 million (21%) and were financed nearly exclusively by MDBs. KfW held the majority, with FMO and IFC with smaller shares. The EBRD and EU participated with purchases of B-Shares in 2007 after they were convinced that the fund structure was viable (Development Practitioner #27 2016). Finally, the A-Shares comprised the senior tranche, and contained EUR 172 million (45%), and also included Notes aimed for private investors (EFSE 2006, 34). By 2016, the percentages had changed slightly, but the operating logic remained the same (EFSE 2016a, 55–56) (Table 5.1).

By reorienting development assistance to the first-loss tranche, governments were gaining a multiplicative impact on their initial investment as this mobilized private investment. Since these investments from EFSE would also be on-lent through pre-approved institutions (selected and assessed by KfW) and supplied with technical assistance, the likelihood of a bad investment decision was minimized. In 2012, EFSE mobilized an additional EUR 115 million in private investment (EFSE 2012, 4). As Erich Stather, the State Secretary for BMZ, explained: "EFSE is a trailblasing example of the intelligent use of public budget funds available for development purposes. It leverages the impact of scarce budget funds, and at the same time opens the gateway for private capital investments to our neighbouring countries in Southeast Europe" (EFSE 2006, 34). EFSE has been successful at generating private investors who are seeking impact investments. This has included a number of high-profile investments by Crédit Coopératif, Tufts University, and Deutsche Bank. When the Good Growth Fund joined in 2008, it became the first private investor fund open to the public (EFSE 2016a, 56).

One year later, the EFSE Development Facility was established to provide technical assistance that either recipient institutions requested or that EFSE deemed as important partners. This facility provided technical assistance that had previously been distributed via an assortment of government grants and included a wide range of services ranging from core capacity building to internal auditing to marketing services. In line with the structured fund, the majority of the technical assistance has been targeted at facilitating microenterprises and SMEs. Yet after the first two years of operation, grant-based technical assistance was slowly

Table 5.1 Tranched risk structure for EFSE as of 2016

Tranche	Risk Profile	% of Total Assets	Select Investors
Notes	• Senior tranche • Lowest risk and only suffer loss after relevant A, B, and C Shares depleted • Target private investors • Maturities generally ~3 to 5 years	15.5%	Crédit Coopératif Deutsche Bank Steyler Bank
A Shares	• Senior tranche • Lower risk and only suffer loss after relevant B and C Shares depleted • Target DFIs or IFIs • Maturities ~3 to 10 years	36.5%	KfW (*Germany*) EBRD EIB FMO (*Netherlands*) OeEB (*Austria*) IFC
B Shares	• Mezzanine tranche • Medium risk and only suffer loss after relevant C shares depleted • Nearly exclusively DFIs or IFIs • Maturities ~5 to 15 years	9.7%	KfW (*Germany*) EBRD EIB FMO (*Netherlands*) OeEB (*Austria*) IFC
C Shares	• Junior tranche • Highest risk, first-loss • Nearly exclusively public investors • Maturities often 20+ years	38.3%	BMZ (*Germany*) ADA (*Austria*) DANIDA (*Denmark*) SDC (*Switzerland*) European Commission

Source EFSE (2016a)

replaced with two other sources of funding (Development Practitioner #27 2016). First, a share of EFSE's investment profits would be allocated on an annual basis by the Board of Governors. This accounted for approximately two-thirds of all technical assistance funding. Second, recipient institutions were also expected to share the cost of technical assistance; by 2016, recipient institutions funded on average 30% of the total amount of technical assistance that they received. Since the establishment of the Development Facility, 337 projects to over 60 independent financial institutions with a volume of over EUR 16 million have been provided, with donor governments only providing roughly 10% of total technical assistance funding (EFSE 2016a, 58–59).

The durability in EFSE was based upon two factors. First, EFSE was established on a revolving basis, allowing the fund to thrive until today. By 2017, more than EUR 2.5 billion of investments had been approved since its inception, with more than EUR 871 million currently outstanding to 67 partner institutions across 900,000 loans (EFSE 2016b, 2). The fund has maintained its commitment to SMEs (72% of its current investment portfolio), while housing accounts for the remainder (28%); these proportions have been largely unchanged since its founding. Moreover, the fund structure added an enormous amount of flexibility. Rather than needing the approval of a donor government or the EU for every investment or technical assistance project, EFSE had the ability to determine these projects with only the approval of its investment committee. This greatly reduced the disbursement time of funds, making EFSE competitive with other funding sources. It also enabled EFSE to fund much smaller investments and technical assistance programs. For example, the average size of a technical assistance project is only EUR 30,000 for EFSE, compared with the EBRD's EUR 1 or 2 million (Development Practitioner #27 2016).

Second, and much like its strategy with microfinance banks, KfW used its ability to control the management of the funds as a way to avoid moral hazards. By "establishing proper development policies, and adhering to them through direct monitoring by a supervisory board, donors can mitigate the risk they face," and therefore, KfW played a critical role in structuring, launching, and managing structured funds (Glaubitt et al. 2008, 363–364). Two KfW employees even argued that the institution's main risk reduction tool "has been its ability to influence individual investments. This is done by structuring its investments in funds and by its ability to control funds' investment policy. This resulted in an initial focus on equity funds and direct involvement in their governing structures" (Biallas and Schwiete 2006, 105). They continued that only when fund risk is reduced will KfW reduce its governance involvement.

Since its creation, EFSE has undergone a few changes. First, EFSE has grown in the number of countries it served; while Southeast Europe still receives most of the funding, fully one-third is now located in the European Neighbourhood Region (ENR). Second, the structure of investors has shifted slightly. The first-loss shares have increased to 38%, while the mezzanine tranche reduced to 10%; the A-Shares and senior notes tranche collectively account for 52%, representing a slight expansion of private investor interest (EFSE 2017, 1). Third, technical assistance was funded primarily from the profits of the investments. Private actors agreed for reduced profits because of the benefits that technical assistance has had in reducing bank failures; EFSE has never had a bank default (cf. Matthäus-Maier 2005). Finally, the earliest iteration of EFSE provided A-Shares, but private investors were not always willing to invest with equity-like instruments. In response, EFSE began issuing notes that behaved more like debt instruments with regular payments and shorter investment requirements. These changes increased the effectiveness of the fund to flexibly respond. Yet despite the expansion, the logic of market rates for private entrepreneurs has remained the same. KfW, as the lead investor and initiator of the fund, has remained the principal actor in managing EFSE and expanding its operations.

The successes of EFSE led to further replication and expansion. Structured funds were lauded by KfW as "the most appropriate vehicle for improving access to local and international capital markets" (Glaubitt et al. 2008, 353 and 367). According to the EC, these government-backed development funds were instrumental to the development of the financial sector, a prerequisite for EU accession (Franco 2005, 40). There were also experiments with how funds could be expanded for equity and refinancing funds, as well as for securitization (Glaubitt, Hagen, and Schütte 2006, 224). The increasing sophistication of these funds also encouraged KfW to explore opportunities for increasingly complex securitization schemes: "KfW's approach is centered on the principles of promoting securitisation of microfinance assets through risk taking" as an anchor investor, as well as a provider of experience, technical assistance, and liquidity (Hüttenrauch and Schneider 2008, 343). In short, EFSE's combination of donor government risk assumption with financial intermediary control was an important step to the creation of more marketized development financial instruments.

Conclusion

KfW's creation of microfinance banks and establishment of EFSE highlighted the versatility and power of marketized development financial instruments. Broadly speaking, these innovations brought to fruition decades of attempts by development institutions to foster private investment through financial instruments. KfW's breakthrough was that, in exchange for the ability to redirect German development aid to risk-sharing schemes, KfW could better control the financial instruments. With the ability to create new instruments, maintain equity stakes, and supervise investment decisions, KfW overcame the problems of moral hazard that had bedeviled the World Bank's DFCs. The insistence of adhering to commercial practices further elicited proper behavior on the part of recipients. Together, these factors allowed KfW to attract more private investment to development projects across Southeast Europe, a region that lacked a functioning financial sector and bureaucratic transparency. While neither microfinance banks nor structured funds were themselves an innovation to the field of finance, it was the first time either was used for the purposes of development on a large-scale.

KfW was uniquely situated to push forward marketized development financial instruments. Extensive German political support following the Balkan crisis translated into greater permissiveness, as well as greater financing for investments and technical assistance. KfW's institutional flexibility also permitted more experimentation with donor funds. The fact that the EU and other donor governments channeled resources via KfW only further highlighted how important KfW's contributions were to shifting the development paradigm. While other development institutions undoubtedly played important roles in the process, KfW's experience during the 1990s and 2000s underscored how important the institution was in the creation and propagation of two marketized development financial instruments.

References

Ahmed, Syed Aftab. 2004. Strengthening Financial Sectors in Transition Countries. In *The Development of the Financial Sector in Southeast Europe*, ed. Ingrid Matthäus-Maier and J.D. von Pischke, 71–77. Berlin: Springer.

Baechle, Jan. 2004. Equity Participation in Microfinance Banks in Southeast Europe and Georgia—A Strategic Option for a Large Private German Bank? In *The Development of the Financial Sector in Southeast Europe*, ed. Ingrid Matthäus-Maier and J.D. von Pischke, 135–139. Berlin: Springer.

Bateman, Milford. 2010. *Why Doesn't Microfinance Work? The Destructive Rise of Local Neoliberalism*. Milford: Zed Books.

Biallas, Margarete, and Mark Schwiete. 2006. Risk Perspectives of a Development Finance Institution. In *Microfinance Investment Funds: Leveraging Private Capital for Economic Growth and Poverty Reduction*, ed. Ingrid Matthäus-Maier and J.D. von Pischke. Berlin: Springer.

Bohnet, Michael. 2004. Foreword. In *The Development of the Financial Sector in Southeast Europe*, ed. Ingrid Matthäus-Maier and J.D. von Pischke, v–ix. Berlin: Springer.

Buckley, Graeme. 1997. Microfinance in Africa: Is It Either the Problem or the Solution? *World Development* 25 (7): 1081–1093.

David, Hulme, and Paul Mosley. 1996. *Finance Against Poverty Volume 1*, 1st ed. London: Routledge.

Drezgić, Saša, Zoran Pavlović, and Dragoljub Stoyanov. 2011. Microfinance Saturation in Bosnia and Herzegovina: What Has Really Been Achieved for the Poor?" *Confronting Microfinance: Undermining Sustainable Development*, ed. Milford Bateman. Sterling, VA: Kumarian Press.

EFSE. 2006. *Annual Report 2006: Building Bridges: Public-Private Partnership for Development Finance in Southeast Europe*. Frankfurt am Main: European Fund for Southeast Europe.

———. 2012. *Annual Report 2012: Strong Partners—Strong Impact*. Frankfurt am Main: European Fund for Southeast Europe.

———. 2016a. *Annual Report 2016: EFSE: Creating Opportunities*. Frankfurt am Main: European Fund for Southeast Europe.

———. 2016b. *At A Glance*. Luxembourg: European Fund for Southeast Europe.

———. 2017. *Q2 2017: Investment Portfolio and Funding Quarterly Fact Sheet*. Frankfurt am Main: European Fund for Southeast Europe.

Franco, Marc. 2005. The Scenario for EU Accession by Southeast European Countries. In *EU Accession—Financial Sector Opportunities and Challenges for Southeast Europe*, ed. Ingrid Matthäus-Maier and J.D. von Pischke, 39–42. Berlin: Springer.

Glaubitt, Klaus, Hanns Martin Hagen, Johannes Feist, and Monika Beck. 2008. Reducing Barriers to Microfinance: The Role of Structured Finance. In *New*

Partnerships for Innovation in Microfinance, ed. Ingrid Matthäus-Maier and J.D. von Pischke, 349–78. Berlin: Springer.

Glaubitt, Klaus, Hanns Martin Hagen, and Haje Schütte. 2006. Mainstreaming Microfinance—Quo Vadis Microfinance Investments. In *Microfinance Investment Funds: Leveraging Private Capital for Economic Growth and Poverty Reduction*, ed. Ingrid Matthäus-Maier and J.D. von Pischke. Berlin: Springer.

Glaubitt, Klaus, and Haje Schütte. 2004. Providing Long-Term Funds to Local Financial Institutions—The European Refinancing Funds in Southeast Europe. In *The Development of the Financial Sector in Southeast Europe*, ed. Ingrid Matthäus-Maier and J.D. von Pischke, 61–77. Berlin: Springer.

Goodman, Patrick. 2006. Microfinance Investment Funds: Objectives, Players, Potential. In *Microfinance Investment Funds: Leveraging Private Capital for Economic Growth and Poverty Reduction*, ed. Ingrid Matthäus-Maier and J.D. von Pischke. Berlin: Springer.

Harper, Malcolm. 2016. "Interview."

Heber, Gabriele, Witold Teplitz, and Claus-Peter Zeitinger. 1982. *Nutzungsmöglichkeiten alternativer Kraftstoffe in Entwicklungsländern*. Eschborn.

Helms, Brigit. 2006. *Access for All: Building Inclusive Financial Systems*. Washington DC: World Bank.

Hermes, Niels, and Robert Lensink. 2011. Microfinance: Its Impact, Outreach, and Sustainability. *World Development* 39 (6): 875–881.

Hüttenrauch, Harald, and Claudia Schneider. 2008. Securitisation: A Funding Alternative for Microfinance Institutions. In *New Partnerships for Innovation in Microfinance*, ed. Ingrid Matthäus-Maier and J.D. von Pischke, 299–347. Berlin: Springer.

IPC. 1983. *Errichtung Der Städtischen Sparkasse Piura/Peru*. Frankfurt am Main: Interdisziplinäre Projekt Consult.

KfW. 2001. *Albanien: Förderung von KMU Über Die Stiftungsbank FEFAD*. Frankfurt am Main: KfW.

———. 2003. *Kosovo: Förderung Des Kleinkreditprograms Der Kosovarischen MEB*. Frankfurt am Main: KfW.

———. 2013. *BOSNIA AND HERZEGOVINA: Credit Guarantee Fund for the Promotion of SMEs and Business Start-Ups*. Frankfurt am Main: KfW.

Kloppenburg, Norbert. 2006. Microfinance Investment Funds: Where Wealth Creation Meets Poverty Reduction. In *Microfinance Investment Funds: Leveraging Private Capital for Economic Growth and Poverty Reduction*, ed. Ingrid Matthäus-Maier and J.D. von Pischke, 1–6. Berlin: Springer.

Köhn, Doris, and Wolfram Erhardt. 2004. Competition and Complementarity: KfW's Approach to Financial Sector Development in Southeast Europe. In *The Development of the Financial Sector in Southeast Europe*, ed. Ingrid Matthäus-Maier and J.D. von Pischke, 51–59. Berlin: Springer.

Krahnen, Jan Pieter, and Manfred Nitsch. 1987. *Studie Der Interdisziplinären Projekt Consult GmbH Im Rahmen Des Projekts "Förderung Des Aufbaus von Kommunalen Sparkassen" (Cajas Municipales de Ahorro y Crédito) in Peru*. Frankfurt am Main: GTZ.

Lepp, Anja. 2017. Interview.

———. n.d. *30 Years of IPC and PCH Development*. Frankfurt am Main: ProCredit.

Mader, Philip. 2015. *The Political Economy of Microfinance: Financializing Poverty*, 1st ed. New York, NY: Palgrave Macmillan.

Matthäus-Maier, Ingrid. 2005. Opportunities and Challenges Facing Financial Sectors Moving Towards EU Accession. In *EU Accession–Financial Sector Opportunities and Challenges for Southeast Europe*, ed. Ingrid Matthäus-Maier and J.D. von Pischke, IX–XII. Berlin: Springer.

Matthäus-Maier, Ingrid, and J.D. von Pischke. 2004a. Introduction. In *The Development of the Financial Sector in Southeast Europe*, ed. Ingrid Matthäus-Maier and J.D. von Pischke, 1–6. Berlin: Springer.

———. 2004b. Summary and Conclusion. In *The Development of the Financial Sector in Southeast Europe*, ed. Ingrid Matthäus-Maier and J.D. von Pischke, 225–234. Berlin: Springer.

———. 2005. Foreword. In *EU Accession—Financial Sector Opportunities and Challenges for Southeast Europe*, ed. Ingrid Matthäus-Maier and J.D. von Pischke, V–VIII. Berlin: Springer.

Maurer, Klaus. 2011. Mobilising Capital for the Poor—How Does Structured Finance Fit in Emerging Markets? In *Mobilising Capital for Emerging Markets*, ed. Ingrid Matthäus-Maier and J.D. von Pischke, 13–27. Berlin: Springer.

Morduch, Jonathan. 1999. The Microfinance Promise. *Journal of Economic Literature* 37 (4): 1569–1614.

Morduch, Jonathan. 2000. The Microfinance Schism. *World Development* 28(4): 617–29.

Neuschütz, Volker. 2004. Institutional Development and Commercialisation—Optimal Exit for Equity Financiers. In *The Development of the Financial Sector in Southeast Europe*, ed. Ingrid Matthäus-Maier and J.D. von Pischke, 101–111. Berlin: Springer.

Nitsch, Manfred. 2002. Die Neuen Mikrofinanzinstitutionen in Osteuropa. *Glaspaläste Und Mikrofinanz: Beiträge Zur Entwicklungsfinanzierung*, 203–209. Frankfurt am Main: Peter Lang Verlag.

OECD. 2008. *Is It ODA?*. Paris: OECD.

Robinson, Marguerite S. 2001. *The Microfinance Revolution: Sustainable Finance for the Poor*. Washington, DC: World Bank.

Roy, Ananya. 2010. *Poverty Capital: Microfinance and the Making of Development*. New York: Routledge.

Schmidt, Reinhardt. 2004. *The Perspective of the Participant Observers: A Brief Account of the History of IPC and IMI from an Institutional Economics Perspective*. Frankfurt am Main: Unpublished manuscript.

———. 2016. Interview.

UN. 1995. *General Framework for Peace in Bosnia and Herzegovina*. New York: United Nations.

von Pischke, J.D. 2003. *Microfinance Institution Building: The IPC Story*. Unpublished book manuscript.

Winkler, Adalbert. 1999. Promotional Banks as an Instrument for Improving the Financing Situation of Small and Medium-Sized Enterprises in the Transition Economies of Central and Eastern Europe: Some Observations Based on the Development of the German Financial System. *Würzburg Economic Papers, No. 2e*.

Wolfensohn, James. 1997. *Address to the Closing Plenary Session of the Microcredit Summit*. Washington, DC: World Bank.

World Bank. 1996. *Worldwide Inventory of Microfinance Institutions*. Washington, DC: World Bank.

———. 2000. *Implementation Completion Report on an IDA Credit in the Amount of SDR4.9 Million to Bosnia and Herzegovina for the Local Initiatives Project*. Washington, DC: World Bank.

Zeitinger, Claus-Peter. 2004. Sustainable Microfinance Banks–Problems and Perspectives. In *The Development of the Financial Sector in Southeast Europe*, ed. Ingrid Matthäus-Maier and J.D. von Pischke, 125–134. Berlin: Springer.

Zeitinger, Claus-Peter, Eberhardt R. Biermann, and Gerhard Zieroth. 1982. *The Utilization of Renewable Energy Resources: A Programme of the Federal Republic of Germany for the Third World; Analysis of the Planning Phase of the Special Energy Programme (SEP)*. Eschborn, Germany: Deutsche Gesellschaft für Technische Zusammenarbeit (GTZ).

Zeitinger, Claus-Peter, and Reinhardt Schmidt. 1984. *Kreditgarantiefonds - Einige Überlegungen Zu Diesem Kreditfinanzierungsinstrument*. Frankfurt am Main: IPC Working Paper.

Ziller, Dominik. 2006. The European Fund for Southeast Europe: An Innovative Instrument for Political and Economic Stabilisation. In *Microfinance Investment Funds: Leveraging Private Capital for Economic Growth and Poverty Reduction*, ed. Ingrid Matthäus-Maier and J.D. von Pischke, 193–212. Berlin: Springer.

CHAPTER 6

The Scaling Up of Marketized Development Financial Instruments from 2005 to the Present

The achievements with microfinance banks and structured funds encouraged KfW to continue pursuing marketized development financial instruments. Building upon its existing network of microfinance institutions, KfW established new banks in Central Asia and the Caucuses and, by 2006, 43 microfinance investment funds existed with a collective microfinance portfolio of EUR 338 million (Goodman 2006, 19). The positive results from EFSE also prompted KfW to expand its activity for structured funds. Since then, KfW has created and participated in over 40 new structured funds with total investments in excess of EUR 1.4 billion. Structured funds proved to be popular among donor governments and private investors alike because of the tranche design, which leveraged development assistance as an absorber of investment risk. KfW's continued management position over the funds' investment decisions has ensured long-term stability. The tranched structure has proven so versatile that it has expanded to other contexts, including the EU's own European Fund for Strategic Investment (EFSI). Development institutions have also expanded their marketized development financial instruments offerings. In recent years, institutions have utilized donor funds to mitigate risk in green bonds, insurance funds for development, and even a renaissance of DFCs.

P. Volberding, *Leveraging Financial Markets for Development*,
Executive Politics and Governance,
https://doi.org/10.1007/978-3-030-55008-0_6

While KfW has remained an important actor since 2000—particularly in the continued promotion and expansion of new structured funds—its outsized role in innovating and propagating marketized development financial instruments has been reduced. Other development institutions ranging from the World Bank to the Nordic Investment Fund (NIF) have pioneered their own instruments as their relevant stakeholders have permitted them to redeploy development assistance to financial instruments. Moreover, the growing interest of private investors in developing country projects has incentivized private financial institutions to create new instruments, even without donor government guarantees. Outside of development policy, these instruments have also gained traction within developing country institutions. Nevertheless, all of these new financial instruments are based on the formula of government risk absorption with financing provided at market rates in order to attract private investors.

The Expansion of Structured Funds for Development

The successes of EFSE emboldened KfW to replicate this structured fund in a variety of new contexts. After only 18 months, the EC and the EBRD had been convinced that this strategy was fruitful, both for its developmental impact as well as for its cost effectiveness (Development Practitioner #27 2016), and were prepared to become equity partners in new funds. European regulatory familiarity for how these funds should be administered was also formed in a way that streamlined the creation of new funds. On the other side of the Atlantic, the IFC, content that it proved that microfinance investments could be commercially bankable, was similarly eager to replicate the development fund structure in new regions and partnered with KfW and the EU on new investments (Development Practitioner #9 2016). Following EFSE, the same contingent of development institutions—the IFC, EBRD, and FMO—relied on KfW's unique ability to establish these funds in partnership with first-loss equity shares from the German, Swiss, Austrian, Dutch, and EU governments. By 2016, KfW had created or taken equity shares in over 42 various funds around the globe in a variety of sectors, the commonality being that all have been conducted on market terms (Development Practitioner #42 2016).

The Influence of EFSE on Future Development Fund Instruments

As the first development fund of its kind, EFSE had an outsized role in how future funds were established. First, the institutional structure of EFSE, with its tiered risk structure and commercial orientation, was easy to replicate. Lessons from EFSE were also implemented, such as a reduced managerial role for private investors, recycled profits for use in technical assistance, and strong backing from donor governments in equity participations. Together, this cemented EFSE's structure as a durable, albeit flexible, strategy for establishing these development funds. The successes of EFSE further allayed fears within the German and European governments that a fund structure was an appropriate use of development assistance, as EFSE demonstrated that private entrepreneurs could be financed without large subsidies (Development Practitioner #27 2016).

Most importantly, EFSE created a legal and institutional model that could be replicated in various contexts. The flexibility of the model helped adapt the fund structure to new sectors and new countries. For instance, C-Shares absorbed by the government could be increased as a percentage of the total shares when the underlying investment was riskier. C-Shares could also be phased in or out at different rates, depending on the projected risk profile of the investment portfolio after a few years. Second, EFSE established a coherent set of standards for the investment. Reporting requirements were harmonized, risk assessment measures were established, and safeguards for labor, human rights, and environment were adapted, often from various existing regulations (Development Practitioner #40 2016). For instance, FMO provided the guidelines on human rights protections while BMZ rules on environmental stewardship were combined into the guiding document. The established set of guidelines further impacted the recipient governments as well, as these guidelines were often repurposed for other investment agreements with other donor states (Development Practitioner #27 2016). EFSE's standardization therefore had important network effects that reduced transaction costs and increased transparency, even in investments in which it had no direct participation.

The replication of the structured fund model was also driven by the fact that it was, to a certain extent, in the interest of the development agency, the donor government, and the recipient government. European donor countries found this flexibility beneficial for implementing development policy in underdeveloped regions. A senior development banker noted that, in many ways, the fund structure was a perfect substitute for the absence of national development banks or a domestic financial sector. Rather than lumber through the process of establishing a new government-owned development bank and creating the domestic regulatory framework, it proved to be significantly more flexible to simply use the fund structure to coordinate donor country investment (Development Practitioner #27 2016). Moreover, there was little need to utilize unreliable domestic commercial banks. EFSE familiarized both donor and recipient countries to the fund structure. At least within Southeast Europe, this facilitated the speed of investments from subsequent funds, such as the Green for Growth Fund (GGF), as there was already an infrastructure of known on-lending institutions, policy guidance, and technical support facilities. Incidentally, this also reduced the cost of technical assistance programs of the GGF as EFSE had already provided a substantial amount of training (Development Practitioner #23 2016).

For development practitioners, the fund structure streamlined the process of development disbursement and insulated the institutions from political interference. First, since projects were administered at market rates with the objective of being commercially bankable, there was less concern that foreign assistance would distort local financial markets. This was a key tenet of ensuring that market discipline prevailed and that recipient countries became self-sufficient in the provision of financing (Development Practitioner #40 2016). The structured funds' ability to recycle profits into technical assistance further dovetailed with the objective to bolster domestic capacity. However, the interest of development banks was also rooted in their desire to reduce interactions with the political system. The structured fund limited the ability of politicians or bureaucrats to interfere with the investment selection process because third-party managers were technically responsible for selecting projects. These third-party managers were more insulated from political pressures because of their non-governmental status, and the threat for governments to divest from the fund was difficult because of the long-term and diversified nature of the government investment (Development Practitioner #27 2016). Moreover, structured funds reduced the administrative costs to the development institution. As one expert remarked, channeling investment decisions via the fund required only a one-time approval from BMZ—for the fund's initial creation. Individual projects conducted by the fund did not require government approval, which not only increased the speed of disbursement, but also reduced the amount of interaction with the political structure (Development Practitioner #51 2017). This dovetailed with a change in 2011 to EU financial regulation that made it easier for a structured fund to disburse funds (Development Practitioner #24 2016).[1]

Concurrently, the model of structured funds also found support from budget-constrained donor governments. Following the 2008 Global Financial Crisis, structured funds were a budget-friendly way of providing ODA. These funds had proven themselves to be largely financially self-sufficient and required only limited additional capital injections. Since they effectively operated as financial instruments, donor governments could also divest from the fund if the government was not pleased with the target investments or domestic political considerations changed. In addition, they were also seen as "responsible" development, as the funds were less likely to generate financial dependency among recipient governments. Moreover, the success of recycling profits from the investments into technical assistance further enhanced the viability of the fund model and pleased donor governments that they were less responsible for grants for technical assistance (Development Practitioner #48 2016). To be certain, the shift toward structured funds was present within the European context as well. Begun in earnest with the Cohesion Policy during the early 2000s, the EU created and invested in a series of financial instruments that provided loans, guarantees, and equity for programs in regional renewal and SMEs. As in economic development, these were meant to divert public funding by combining them with private financial sources. By 2014, this had included 26 various financial instruments and funds (Ferrer and Infelise 2015, 6). Most famously, the EU created the European Fund for Strategic Investment (EFSI), more colloquially known as the Juncker Plan, in 2015.

Finally, recipient countries were also encouraged by the shift toward structured funds. First, the majority of developing countries have been eager to attract FDI, but have been unable to convince private investors to independently invest. By leveraging the German government guarantee, however, developing countries could signal increased trustworthiness.

[1] In 2011, the EU issued a directive entitled the Alternative Investment Fund Managers Directive (AIFMD) that issued new regulations on investment managers and investment funds. However, there was an exemption that if 75% of the decision-making bodies are from public institutions, then the regulations do not apply. This has meant that KfW and other development institution employees have dominated the boards of these structured funds, providing a legal reason as to why KfW should continue to wield decision-making power (Development Practitioner #24 2016). For the legal text, see EC (2011).

Participation also showed that the institution had been properly vetted and technical assistance provided to bring the level of the financial intermediary to international standards. Countries like Serbia, for instance, had specifically requested that KfW establish a fund to channel foreign direct investment to the country (Development Practitioner #40 2016). In addition, there were numerous potential benefits of structured funds for local on-lending financial institutions. Maurer (2011, 21–22) highlights three aspects. First, it could provide much greater access to refinancing facilities in international capital markets at rates that would be unattainable if pursued without an international development partner. Second, market access could allow the transfer of risk. Securitization in particular may allow local banks to move assets off of their balance sheets. Finally, structured funds could help overcome domestic regulatory restrictions, as local banking regulations and central bank policies can limit the flexibility of domestic financial institutions. Consequently, both recipient governments and the local on-lending financial institutions had an interest in partnering with these funds.

Structured funds are not applicable in every sector. As a high-ranking banker of EFSE noted, "the key is to have the underlying asset class profitable, and it can't operate in sectors that require too much subsidy" (Development Practitioner #27 2016). They noted that this has worked particularly well in supporting private enterprises that lack financing—namely SMEs and green technology. This is a consequence of the fund structure. While investors gain flexibility in the speed of disbursement and diversification of investments, the fixed cost of hiring a fund manager raises the overall cost of operations, particularly as a fund increases in sectoral and geographic scope. Since it is now commonly accepted that significant subsidization should be avoided, fund structures have primarily expanded into bankable services, though there remains variation in how the funds are structured, with a trade-off between profit retention and dividend distribution (Goodman 2008, 35–36). Nevertheless, KfW has pushed forward with funds in education and drought insurance, two sectors that were previously deemed unbankable.

Interestingly, all of these KfW-sponsored funds are still incorporated in Luxembourg. Despite periodic questions from German policymakers, KfW has steadfastly maintained that Luxembourg is the best location because the regulators have specialized knowledge of how these funds operate. Luxembourgish regulators are also more flexible than their German counterparts at BaFin. Moreover, Luxembourg has developed a rich network of secondary infrastructure to administer these funds, including fund managers, third-party assessors, and legal teams well-trained in development structured funds. Of course, the permissiveness of Luxembourg is also a benefit. KfW notes that tax purposes are not the reason for a Luxembourg, as the investment funds are taxed by country of investment and BMZ's funds are already tax-exempt.[2] As one person acknowledged, when the Luxembourg financial regulator threatened to change the rules that would permit the German government to have a vote on the Board of Directors,[3] KfW was one of many institutions that convinced the maintenance the status quo of the regulations (Development Practitioner #40 2016).

KfW's Expansion of Regional and Global Structured Funds for Development

For KfW, EFSE demonstrated the economic viability of structured funds for development and generated substantial support from partnering donor countries. The high degree of cost effectiveness also gained plaudits from BMZ and others in the German bureaucracy, who were initially suspicious of the endeavor. German government support arose from a mix of funding efficiency and, if for no other reason, these structured funds were also supportive of the exportation of SME financing. Consequently, structured funds for development transitioned from experiment to policy prescription.

The breadth of KfW's investment in development funds is impressive. As of December 2017, KfW has invested in more than 42 separate fund structures for the purposes of development, 24 of which KfW has served as a founding institution. This has amounted to a cumulative total of more than EUR 1.4 billion. The original EFSE fund was a multilateral development fund focused on microfinance in Southeast Europe, and KfW's immediate investments afterward focused on expanding microfinance funding. Only two years following the creation of EFSE, KfW spearheaded the establishment of a regional microfinance and SME

[2] "Response to the Report by the Süddeutsche Zeitung About KfW in Connection with the Paradise Papers," *KfW Press Release*, 8 November 2017.

[3] While the German government has equity participation via C-Shares, they are non-voting. KfW maintained that the German government already had acquiesced to KfW as the administrator, and that allowing a government shareholder on the Board of Directors would add political interference.

investment fund for Africa. In 2010, REGMIFA was born in a tranched structure with 33% of total shares as C-Shares held by donor governments, and foremost among them was Germany's BMZ (REGMIFA 2015, 14). Two years later, KfW created the Microfinance Initiative for Asia (MIFA) Debt Fund to refinance existing microfinance institutions in order to expand their funding capacity. By 2014, KfW expanded its contribution to MIFA to over EUR 34 million.[4]

Yet as KfW has attained more experience and private investors more comfortable with the idea of a government-backed development fund, there has been substantial diversification away from regional microfinance funds. This has included geographical diversity—as there are now both regional and global funds—as well as sectoral breadth—as new funds have been established in environmental protection, microfinance promotion, and SME support. In each of these, the institutional structure is similar, and KfW invests a combination of its own, market-raised funds and German government grants on behalf of BMZ. The precise mixture of market-raised and government grants varies on the business model of each.

Table 6.1 lists all of KfW's participations in structured funds for development as of November 2017. The breadth of new funds is substantial. For instance, there are now funds that promote a single-issue area throughout the globe. The Blue Action Fund (BAF) was established by KfW and BMZ in December 2016 with an initial funding for EUR 24 million. The BAF endeavors to promote protection and revitalization programs relating to the oceans and coastline, working with NGOs who need additional financing. New funds have also been established for narrow purposes. For instance, in 2014 the Fund for Agri-Finance in Nigeria (FAFIN) was established by KfW and BMZ as a private equity fund to promote SMEs and agricultural finance in Nigeria. The USD 100 million fund was designed to provide debt, equity, and mezzanine financing for small entrepreneurs, and in 2017 raised USD 65.9 million from the African Development Bank, CDC Group, and the Dutch Good Growth Fund.[5] Therefore, funds now support single- and multi-country

[4] "Erweiterung MIFA Asia Debt Fund," n.d., KfW.

[5] "Supporting the Formation of the Fund for Agricultural Finance in Nigeria," n.d., Dalberg Group.

Table 6.1 KfW investments in structured funds as of 2017

	Name	*Year*	*Amount (mil)*	*Region*	*Target investment*	*KfW Founded*	*Project partners*
1	Aavishkaar II-Fonds	2011	USD 25	India	Social Enterprises	No	IFC, CDC, FMO
2	Aavishkaar Frontier Fund (AFF)	2015	USD 20	South Asia, Asia	Social Enterprises	Yes	Proparco, DGGF, FMO
3	African Agriculture and Trade Investment Fund (AATIF)	2011	USD 100	Sub-Saharan Africa	Agriculture, Financial Services	Yes	OeEB, Deutsche Bank
4	African Local Currency Bond Fund (ALCB Fund)	2012	EUR 16.5	Africa	Local Currency Bond Markets	Yes	IFC, FMO, DFID
5	African Risk Capacity (ARC)	2014	EUR 50	Africa	Extreme Weather Insurance	No	DFID
6	AfricInvest Financial Sector MSME Fund (AFS)	2007	EUR 5	Africa	SMEs	No	
7	Balkan Financial Equity Fund (BT)	2005	...	Balkans	Financial Institutions, Microfinance	No	
8	Blue Action Fund (BAF)	2017	EUR 24	Global	Environmental Protection	Yes	
9	Caribbean Biodiversity Fund	2012	EUR 25	Caribbean	Environmental Protection	Yes	World Bank, UNDP
10	Caucasus Nature Fund (CNF)	2007	EUR 32.5	Caucasus	Environmental Protection	Yes	WWF
11	DWM Inclusive Finance Equity Fund	2013	EUR 7.356	Sub-Saharan Africa	Microfinance Institutions	No	
12	Eco Business Fund	2014	EUR 40	Latin America	SMEs, Environmental Protection	Yes	OeEB, EU, FMO

(continued)

Table 6.1 (continued)

	Name	*Year*	*Amount (mil)*	*Region*	*Target investment*	*KfW Founded*	*Project partners*
13	Emerging Africa Infrastructure Fund (EAIF)	2002	EUR 227.6	Sub-Saharan Africa	Infrastructure	No	FMO, UK Aid
14	Enterprise Expansion Fund (ENEF)	2014	EUR 8	Southeast Europe and Turkey	SMEs	Yes	EBRD, EIF, OeEB, EU
15	Enterprise Innovation Fund (ENIF)	2015	(Joint funding with ENEF)	Southeast Europe	Growth Capital	Yes	EBRD, EIF, OeEB, EU
16	European Fund for Southeast Europe (EFSE)	2005	EUR 100	Southeast Europe	SMEs, Housing	Yes	SDC, EU, OeEB
17	Fairtrade Access Fund		EUR 10.5	Global	Agriculture	No	
18	Global Climate Partnership Fund (GCPF)	2009	USD 25	Global	Renewable energy, environmental protection	Yes	OeEB, Danida, FMO, IFC
19	Global Health Investment Fund II (GHIF II)	2013	EUR 10	Global	Health	No	Sida, IFC
20	Goodwell West Africa Microfinance Development Company	2009	EUR 8	Nigeria, Ghana	Microfinance Institutions	No	
21	Green for Growth Fund (GGF)	2009	EUR 25	Southeast Europe, Middle East	Energy Efficiency, Renewable Energy	Yes	IFC, OeEB, FMO
22	GroFin SGB Fund	2015	EUR 10	Sub-Saharan Africa	SMEs	Yes	NIF, DGGF
23	Higher Education Finance Fund	2011	EUR 10	Latin America	Microfinance Institutions	Yes	

(continued)

Table 6.1 (continued)

	Name	*Year*	*Amount (mil)*	*Region*	*Target investment*	*KfW Founded*	*Project partners*
24	Infrastructure Crisis Facility	2009	USD 11	Global	Private Infrastructure Investment	No	IFC
25	InsuResilience Investment Fund (formerly Climate Insurance Fund, CIF)	2015	EUR 13.5	Global	Climate Risk Insurance	Yes	
26	Lending for African Farming (LAFCo)	2015	EUR 10.5	Sub-Saharan Africa	SMEs, Agriculture	Yes	UK Aid, USAID
27	LeapFrog Financial Inclusion Fund II	2009	...	Global	Small-Scale Insurance	No	FMO, Proparco, IFC
28	Microfinance Enhancement Facility (MEF)	2009	EUR 207	Global	Microfinance Institutions	Yes	IFC, EIB, FMO, OeEB, Sida
29	Microfinance Initiative for Asia (MIFA)	2012	EUR 24	Asia	Microfinance Institutions	No	IFC, EU
30	Municipal Infrastructure Development Fund (MIDF)	2012	EUR 16	Southeast Europe and Turkey	Infrastructure	Yes	EBRD
31	PME Croissance (PMEC)	2012	...	Morocco	SMEs	Yes	EIB, Proparco
32	Progression Eastern Africa Microfinance Equity Funds (PEAMEF)	2011	USD 10	East Africa	Microfinance Institutions	Yes	EIB, CDC

(continued)

Table 6.1 (continued)

	Name	*Year*	*Amount (mil)*	*Region*	*Target investment*	*KfW Founded*	*Project partners*
33	Regional Education Finance Fund for Africa (REFFA)	2012	EUR 25	Africa	Education for Microfinance	Yes	
34	Regional Investment Fund for SMEs in Africa (REGMIFA)	2010	EUR 12.5	Sub-Saharan Africa	SMEs	Yes	FMO, Proparco, ICO, IFC EIB
35	ResponsAbility Participations AG	2012	…	Global	Microfinance Institutions	No	
36	Rural Impulse Fund II	2010	…	Global	Microfinance Institutions	No	FMO, Proparco, ICO, IFC EIB
37	Sanad Fund for MSME	2011	EUR 158	Middle East, North Africa	SMEs	Yes	FMO, Seco, OeEB, EU
38	Sarva Capital LLC	2010	…	India	Microfinance Institutions	No	
39	ShoreCap II Limited	2009	…	Africa, Asia	Microfinance Institutions	No	AfDB, CDC, EIB, OeEB
40	The Currency Exchange Fund (TCX)	2009	EUR 137.3	Global	Currency	Yes	AfDB, EIB, EBRD, FMO, AFD, IFC
41	TunInvest Croissance	2013	EUR 2.5	Tunisia	SMEs	No	
42	Women's World Banking Capital Partners	2012	…	Global	Microfinance Institutions	No	

Source Author's calculations; various KfW annual reports

projects, as well as topics as disparate as climate change mitigation to industrial promotion.

In certain cases, KfW controls a significant amount of the equity share as well. Table 6.2 lists the structured funds in which KfW controls more than 10% of total assets at the end of 2016. At the top of the list is the Microfinance Enhancement Facility (MEF), a facility designed to provide bridge capital to microfinance institutions; KfW holds 19.8% of total assets.

KfW retains significant voting shares in the Global Climate Partnership Fund (GCPF), EFSE, and Green for Growth Fund (GGF), all of which featured KfW as the initiator. KfW has invested the largest total amount in the GCPF and EFSE, in both of which KfW has had carry over amounts in

Table 6.2 KfW structured fund investments, 2016

Fund	*KfW's share of total assets (%)*	*Carrying amounts (EUR, 000s)*	*Dividend payments (EUR, 000s)*
Microfinance Enhancement Facility SA (MEF)	19.8	105,777	3829
Global Climate Partnership Fund	18.1	55,498	1006
EFSE	17.9	153,074	6408
Green for Growth Fund (GGF)	17	56,162	1395
Rural Impulse Fund II	16.5	9177	2447
Sanad Fund for MSME	16.1	30,000	245
Advans	15	9358	0
MIFA Debt Fund	14.6	21,676	842
Africa Agriculture and Trade Investment Fund	14.4	21,552	556
2020 European Fund for Energy, Climate Change, and Infrastructure	14.1	54,650	0
DWM, incl. Finance Equity Fund II	10	2367	0

Note Only funds with a development objective and KfW shares >10% are included
Source KfW (2016b)

excess of EUR 100 million. It is also interesting to note that these funds have almost uniformly generated positive returns as well, with returns on equity at approximately 1–3%. While it may be surprising that KfW does not hold the majorities in the investments, it is critical to note two factors. First, one of the primary strengths of the structured fund design is that it diversifies ownership in order to diversify risk. In order to minimize KfW's risk burden, its internal risk management department limits exposure to any one fund. Second, KfW ensures that its objectives are achieved through a combination of influence over the third-party managing institution and partnering with other like-minded equity participants. KfW uses Finance in Motion (FiM), a private fund manager with historical ties to KfW, for four of its funds; it also uses responsAbility for a number of others. Equity partners regularly include the IFC, EBRD, FMO, and the Swiss and Austrian governments.

Of course, also essential to the success of these structured funds for development has been the growth of interest on the part of private investors. For instance, a series of microfinance investment funds grew concomitantly with the structured funds of KfW, allowing KfW to more easily access private investors. The first fund exclusively created by a private institution for the purposes of investment in microfinance was the Dexia Micro-Credit Fund, originally launched in Luxembourg in 1998, and after 2000 grew substantially as the number of partner on-lending institutions within developing countries became available. The next few years witnessed the establishment of dozens of additional microfinance investment funds (MIFs) and, by 2006, 43 MIFs had been established with total assets in excess of EUR 700 million (Goodman 2006, 19). These structured funds are normally not directly purchasable by individuals; rather, larger institutional investors are found by a commercial banking partner.

Despite the variations, there is a consistent strategy. For one, KfW has noted two preconditions for any expansion of structured funds; first, the recipient country must have at least a basic financial sector that is able to on-lend foreign financing, and second, the products provided must have a secure future revenue stream (Wälde 2012, 4). These ensure that the financial aspects function properly. In addition, KfW has learned that a particular constellation of institutional aspects is also necessary. KfW's strategy relies on being able to control the fund for an extended period of time. For instance, KfW has reduced investment risk by its ability to structure the investment fund, control its policy, and direct its governing structure. Governance is only ceded to local authorities when specific institutional targets have been achieved. Moreover, private investors remain relatively small providers of capital investment and, at early stages of the fund, invest no more than USD 1 million. This has meant that KfW still needs to be prepared to provide a majority of the mezzanine shares, while relying on donor governments to provide the first-loss tranche (Biallas and Schwiete 2006, 95).

To be certain, while KfW has principally moved toward creating and expanding structured funds, the institution does maintain equity stakes directly in institutions. Equity stakes were largely eliminated in the early 2000s as it concentrated too much risk, and KfW shifted toward funds to enable a similar supervisory role. Today, KfW's most significant holdings are in microfinance institutions. KfW holds equity shares in ProCredit Holding, AccessBank, and FINCA. ProCredit Holding comprises the largest amount—both in terms of percentage (14.5%) and total equity (EUR 603 million). This was the consequence of ProCredit's restructuring in 2006, when KfW's equity stakes in the network of microfinance banks in Southeast Europe were converted into equity shares of the holding group. This was designed to simplify the management process and diversify risk. Finally, even though KfW still maintains equity stakes, in four of these banks KfW provided investment capital via other funding mechanisms. EFSE and the GGF invest via the microfinance banks operated by ProCredit, AccessBank, and FINCA. This fact highlights the complex way in which KfW has invested in development.

Within all of these investments, five funds deserve particular attention as they highlight the flexibility of KfW's fund structure in a variety of geographical and sectoral contexts. There are numerous commonalities. All five were established with a tranched risk structure with government backing in the highest-risk equity shares, all but one share KfW as the lead initiator, and three of the five have been managed by KfW's spin-off fund manager FiM. The remaining two funds (FINCA and TCX), while not directly managed by KfW, demonstrate the ability of KfW to affect change. While slight variations have occurred in the proportion of A-Shares to C-Shares, as well as equity instruments, they represent the multifaceted aspects of structured funds for development. The penultimate example of FINCA demonstrates the ability of KfW and other investors to transform an already existing microfinance facility into one that is commercially viable. TCX highlights the adaptability of the fund structure to non-financing objectives, namely protections for currency fluctuations.

Green for Growth Fund (GGF)
The Green for Growth Fund (GGF) was established in 2009 as KfW's first development fund dedicated to the promotion of environmental protection in 13 countries in Southeast Europe and the Caucasus region. The objective was to promote energy efficiency and reduce CO_2 emissions to achieve the Europe-2020 initiative (cf. European Commission 2010). Much like EFSE, the GGF was established with a tranche design of A-, B-, and C-Shares, with the governments of Germany, Austria, and the Netherlands taking the highest-risk C-Shares (GGF 2013, 41). KfW, the EIB, OeEB, EBRD, and FMO all purchased A- and B-Shares, providing equity and liquidity to the fund. Private investors now include Deutsche Bank (EUR 30 million in notes) and the Church of Sweden (EUR 10 million in notes) (GGF 2016, 31). Reflecting the conviction that development assistance should be conducted according to market principles, KfW arranged for a three-pronged strategy. First, there are direct investments in renewable energy projects in the form of cooperation with commercial banks or with senior debt purchases. To maintain market operations, the GGF is limited to EUR 10 million in each project and interest rates are set at market prices. Second, the GGF operates via local financial institutions, much like EFSE's credit lines for SME financing. The GGF offers a broad range of instruments that include medium- to long-term senior loans, subordinated loans, syndicated loans, and mezzanine debt instruments, with the maximum sub-loan of EUR 10 million. By 2016, the GGF had invested in 43 partner financial institutions. Finally, the GGF makes investments in non-financial partners, which is aimed at increasing the local capacity to operate and maintain the investments.

By 2016, the GGF had committed EUR 411.7 million in funds across 19 countries, with an outstanding investment portfolio of EUR 363.2 million. Identical to EFSE, the GGF also has an accompanying technical assistance facility that provides support to financial and non-financial partner institutions. Not only does the GGF provide technical assistance financing (EUR 500,000 in 2016), but it also organizes informational conferences, identifies new market opportunities, and develops a range of new projects and instruments. The technical assistance facility also provides project assessment reports on the regional level, allowing for a better comparison of outcomes. Under certain conditions, technical assistance is mandated for the installation of emissions-emitting software (Development Practitioner #23 2016). However, one key difference of the GGF from EFSE was the much higher provision of A-Shares relative to C-Shares. As of December 2016, A-Shares and A-Notes accounted for 53.5 and 16.5% of total shares, respectively; C-Shares represented 21% (GGF 2016, 31). This represents two factors. First, private investors have become more willing to invest in these funds with risk-sharing schemes of donor governments, and second, the underlying investments in renewable energy and housing sector efficiency are more bankable.

Microfinance Enhancement Facility (MEF)

The Microfinance Enhancement Facility (MEF) was also established in 2009 to provide additional financing to microfinance institutions globally. Like EFSE, MEF relied on the creation of a new German government title to distribute the funds on a regional—rather than bilateral—basis (Development Practitioner #34 2016). MEF was designed to be a stabilizing force for the global microfinance industry. The MEF was created as a "facility to provide short and medium-term financing to microfinance institutions ('MFIs') facing difficulties in securing financing as a result of the global financial crisis and, in particular, the 2008/2009 liquidity crisis" (MEF 2016, 3). In addition to shorter-term financing, MEF is also designed to have a signaling role to private investors that the recipient microfinance institutions are stable and have received managerial guidance from international development institutions. Its ability to disburse funds quickly allows it to act as an effective lender of last resort. KfW heads both the Board of Directors and the Investment Committee, and was the initiating member of the facility along with the IFC. Unlike the other three funds, MEF is co-managed by three different investment managers.[6] This was to encourage better outcomes as the various fund managers would be required to compete against each other to meet pre-established effectiveness and price outcomes (Development Practitioner #40 2016).

By the end of 2016, MEF had invested nearly USD 1.4 billion across 140 microfinance institutions in 42 countries via 436 loans. These microfinance institutions have issued a further 544,000 loans to final customers, 56% of which are women and 55% of which are located in rural areas.

[6]These are BlueOrchard Finance S.A., Cyrano Management S.A. and responsibility AG. Symbiotics SA had been a fund manager for the first five years, but was removed in 2015.

However, the nature of the last-minute liquidity to distressed microfinance institutions has made MEF a riskier investment for private investors. As such, there is a much greater proportion of C-Shares and B-Shares relative to A-Shares. Of the USD 673 million in capital subscriptions, 18.3% is provided in high-risk C-Shares by the same mix of the German (BMZ), Austrian (OeEB), and Swedish (SIDA) funds. 49.6% is subscribed in B-Shares, mostly arising from KfW, OeEB, IFC, FMO, the EIB, and the OPEC Fund for International Development (MEF 2016, 23). Only 16.5% is in A-Notes and 15.5% in A-Shares, with private placements for A-Notes arranged principally by Deutsche Bank. Interestingly for MEF, KfW also holds a substantial portion of lower-risk, higher return A-Shares as an attempt to diversify its own portfolio holdings. USD 23 million of the C-Shares provided by BMZ is also exclusively earmarked for target investments, allowing a greater amount of discretion for the German government to influence the selection of microfinance projects (MEF 2017, 4).

Sanad Fund for MSMEs
Another FiM-managed fund is the Sanad Fund for MSMEs in the Middle East and North Africa. Founded in 2011, Sanad has three imperatives: to maintain and create employment by supporting SMEs, to reduce poverty by facilitating self-employment through microfinance, and to build an inclusive financial system via the creation of a network of financial institutions. Like many of the other SME funds, it targets financing for the "missing middle," those entrepreneurs that are too small to obtain loans from commercial banks and are too large for NGO-sponsored microcredits. The fund has a target region of 10 countries in the Middle East and North Africa and, as with the other funds, works with local commercial banks and financial institutions. The principle task for Sanad is the refinancing facility, which provides a wide range of financial services that include subordinated loans, term deposits, co-investments, guarantees, and equity participations. The Sanad technical assistance facility also provides a wide range of services for feasibility studies, project design, product development, and risk management. By 2017, Sanad's technical assistance facility had provided assistance worth USD 8.7 million to 112 projects (Sanad Fund 2017b, 1). The German government and European Commission provided the initial C-Share funding, with the Swiss government purchasing shares and donating to the technical assistance facility in 2014, and the Austrian government in 2015 (Sanad Fund 2016, 20–24).

By 2016, Sanad had facilitated a cumulative of USD 358.7 million via 130,000 loans to MSMEs. The average loan from Sanad has been quite small—around USD 2700 each (Sanad Fund 2017a, 1). Unique to the Fund was the ability to invest in equity shares, as well as an additional debt sub-fund that was launched in August 2011. First, Sanad was the first fund since EFSE that was permitted to take equity stakes in the recipient country financial institution. Yet while EFSE had the ability, Sanad was the first to use it as a strategy. This was permitted because of the overall higher risk of the target region, which necessitated additional investor protector mechanisms (Development Practitioner #24 2016). Second, donor governments purchased L-Shares, which absorb the impact of local currency fluctuations and protects recipients from a sudden currency devaluation. In October 2012, an equity sub-fund was launched that provided equity investments in programs that can act as catalysts for market innovations. The junior shares function as a risk buffer to the senior tranches. Moreover, Sanad's risk protections are also quite strong, as the senior A-Shares and A-Notes only suffers losses when the C-, L-, and B-Shares are fully depleted. Nevertheless, the relatively slower growth of the Sanad Fund and the absence of a large-scale commercial bank investor reflect the primary drawback of the fund structure. The underlying investments in countries perceived to be poor investment climates—which, for Sanad, includes Iraq, Syria, Egypt, and Yemen—cannot compensate sufficiently for private investor skittishness (Development Practitioner #23 2016).

Eco Business Fund

The most recent fund sponsored by KfW has been the Eco Business Fund (EBF), established in 2014 with the aim of promoting consumption and business practices that "contribute to biodiversity conservation, to the sustainable use of natural resources, and to mitigate climate change and adapt to its impacts" (Eco Business Fund 2017a, 1). The fund was created in collaboration with FiM, which saw an opportunity in the provision of funding for sustainable agricultural production, but has since expanded to include forestry, fisheries, and tourism (Development Practitioner #24 2016). The fund targets Latin America and the Caribbean, and served as KfW's first structured fund in that region. Like its sister funds, the EBF has been structured with the tranche design, with BMZ, the European Commission, and the Dutch and Austrian governments in the

C-Share tranche, with KfW, FMO, and OeEB as its development institution partners. The EBF also follows market rates via on-lending through commercial banks and microfinance institutions, as well as through businesses and other non-financial institutions. Under certain conditions, the EBF will take up to a 15% equity share of the investment. The financial instruments are similarly broad to the Sanad Fund and GGF. The EBF's technical assistance facility is identical in structure and scope to the other funds as well. Given its objective to promote green investments, the EBF requires that the final borrower holds a certification for organic, ecological, or bio-production, and uses a variety of NGOs to ensure compliance. Moreover, the borrowers must have a positive impact on the EBF's list of eligible measures, which include reducing pollution or preventing soil deterioration.

By June 2017, the fund has achieved USD 105.5 million in investor commitments, and has approved 12 investments via 9 local partner institutions. The current outstanding investment portfolio is USD 130.9 million (Eco Business Fund 2017a). Aggregate project volume approved for technical assistance programs reached USD 1.3 million in 2017, spread across 23 projects in 7 different institutions. Funding has been roughly equal between individual technical assistance programs, research and development, and impact assessment reports (Eco Business Fund 2017b). One notable difference of the EBF was that it was incorporated under an umbrella investment meaning that, in the future, KfW could add additional credit lines within the existing legal structure. This innovation has the benefit of not needing to gain approval from donor governments or Luxembourgish regulators. Currently, there have been proposals floated to expand the fund to cover Africa as well (Development Practitioner #24 2016).

Finca

The example of FINCA demonstrates how an already existing microfinance institution was transformed into a modern, commercially-oriented fund structure. FINCA International was established in 1984 by John Hatch, and pioneered the village banking model. At the time, FINCA was one of the first microfinance institutions. Its first investments were in Bolivia, where John Hatch convinced USAID to provide an initial grant of USD 1 million to serve as the collateral for small loans, and for the ensuing two decades FINCA operated as an NGO that provided technical assistance to villages. However, by the early 1990s, the NGO-led microfinance institution had encountered problems of financing and flexibility, and its breakneck pace of growth necessitated a more advanced financing regime. For one, FINCA sought more funding on international capital markets (FINCA 2017). Additionally, FINCA received funding from international development institutions. In 2005, KfW committed USD 15 million in capital funds for FINCA, and the following year an additional USD 15 million was released.[7]

At the behest of KfW and IFC, FINCA was upgraded to a modern microfinance holding structure (Development Practitioner #27 2016). In 2011, FINCA launched the subsidiary called FINCA Microfinance Holding Company (FMH) that created a new, commercial-oriented investment platform for funding microfinance projects. In particular, the new FMH allowed FINCA to provide new financial and client services such as savings accounts and insurance products, while additionally reducing financial overhead costs by centralizing and streamlining administration. FMH also raised new funds; in 2011, a USD 74 million capital investment greatly expanded its portfolio. The donors were representative of the same mix of market-oriented development investors. IFC took the largest share of USD 35 million, with KfW investing USD 15 million and FMO USD 14 million. The fund manager responsAbility was brought on to manage the investments. After the conclusion of the deal, Doris Köhn, the Director General of the KfW Development Bank, heralded the restructuring: "We are very happy to intensify our longstanding relationship with FINCA through this market-driven transaction, which will greatly benefit poor entrepreneurs throughout FINCA's network."[8]

Since the restructuring, FMH has been able to better tap financial markets to raise additional funding. Moreover, the conversion into a holding company and acquisition of banking licenses—a process known as upgrading—allowed FINCA to expand rapidly in the past decade. By 2016, FINCA operated in 23 countries around the globe and has established 14 deposit-taking financial institutions, and has served nearly 2 million individual savers and borrowers. The incorporation of international development institutions also enabled FINCA to become the first microfinance group with assets larger than USD 1 billion (FINCA 2016).

[7] "Finca Holding Förderbeteiligung II," n.d., KfW.

[8] "FINCA Launches Socially Responsible Investment Subsidiary," FINCA, 17 June 2011.

The cooperation with financial institutions has further spawned innovative, market-based investments. For instance, in 2016, KfW and the Central Bank of Armenia created the Financing the Agricultural Sector in Armenia (FASA), a technical assistance program that provides financing to agricultural activities, and this was distributed via FINCA's Armenian bank.

TCX (The Currency Exchange Fund)
The Currency Exchange Fund (TCX) was not initially created by KfW, but rather by FMO and the Dutch Ministry of Foreign Affairs in 2007. TCX was designed to solve a problem of currency risk. TCX formally implemented an IMF-created instrumented called the Forecasting and Policy Analysis System (FPAS) as a way to hedge local currencies, as well as to organize currency swaps and currency forward. Like the other structured funds mentioned here, critical to the success was donor government risk mitigation. The Dutch government and, in 2009, the German government via BMZ provided funding for a first-loss risk buffer. Consequently, TCX was able to provide long-term currency hedging instruments while also providing long-term local currency financing. Since TCX was designed to mitigate currency risk and not credit risk, it limits its activities to currency hedging and provides no direct investment in any project (TCX 2013). In order to further provide risk diversification, TCX, as of 2016, limits total portfolio exposure to 10% in any one currency, and currently holds 50 foreign currencies.

The currency hedging strategy has posted impressive results. In 2016, TCX realized USD 562 million in new primary portfolio volume. This brought gross outstanding investments (both long- and short-term) to USD 1.7 billion. Microfinance accounts for the largest amount—65%—and Latin America and sub-Saharan Africa with the largest shares—29 and 27%, respectively. In recent years, the original shareholding structure between FMO and KfW has been diluted; by 2016, FMO, KfW, and the EBRD all held equal portions of TCX's shares, at approximately 15% each. However, the German government (via BMZ and BMU) still controlled most of the first-loss subordinated convertible debt, with an outstanding amount of USD 90.8 million (TCX 2016). The most important contribution has been the ability to perform currency swaps in largely illiquid markets and has enabled investments in countries with challenging currencies, such as Sierra Leone, Myanmar, Madagascar, and Haiti (Stravens 2017).

A 2012 evaluation by KfW agrees that TCX has made an important contribution to the local financial sector: "TCX has significantly enhanced the availability of hedging instruments for illiquid country currencies, fostering local currency funding to developing countries, especially to the SSA [Sub-Saharan Africa] region and to the microfinance sector" (KfW 2012, 2). However, the KfW report also notes that, while TCX has assisted in shorter-term currency hedging and in supplying liquidity to microfinance institutions, it has been less effective at enabling long-term borrowing and investment, particularly in the SME sector. Since then, Ruurd Brouwer, the CEO of TCX, has endeavored to expand the scope of TCX beyond microfinance: "Nowadays a third of our activities go towards SME's infrastructure and renewable energy, that have a need for more and longer term hedging. In ten years' time, we expect 80 percent of our funds to support these sectors." In order to realize these gains, TCX currently has plans to increase the current portfolio from USD 1.5 billion to USD 5 billion by 2025 (Stravens 2017, 70). In short, TCX demonstrates the flexibility of these fund structures to solve challenges in development financing with market instruments.

Outside of the aforementioned structured funds in which it has invested directly in the institutional structure, KfW has also extended credit lines to a variety of existing programs. In 2010, KfW contributed an additional EUR 500 million to the World Bank-created Clean Technology Fund (CTF), which promotes low-carbon technology investments in the developing world. Most notable is KfW's participation in the Green Climate Fund (GCF), the world's largest climate fund founded by the UN in 2010. In 2015, KfW received approval to fund up to USD 80 million for climate protection in Bangladesh.[9]

Despite the successful replication of the structured fund model, numerous challenges persist. First, the international market has become saturated with funds. Outside of KfW, a raft of new funds for development have emerged, arising from both MDBs (namely the World Bank and ADB) and private investors. Incidentally, this has made it more difficult for KfW to find bankable investments in underserved markets (Development Practitioner #27 2016). Second, and particularly among older funds, there is a need to reduce the administrative costs. The growth in funds has inevitably increased the cost for fund managers,

[9] "First KfW Green Climate Fund Project Approved," *KfW Press Release*, 6 November 2015.

impact assessment reports, and technical assistance. Costs for securitization also increase with the number of loans and complexity of the financial instrument, a cost which can only be recovered with long-term commitments. While the positive but low rates of return may work in an era of low interest rates, there is a fear among fund managers that a gradual increase of returns in alternative private investments will create capital outflows from these structured funds (Development Practitioner #23 2016). Finally, it has become increasingly difficult for this type of structured fund to attract development banks as holders of B-Shares. Since the B-Shares act as quasi-equity, bank regulators require that development banks hold higher reserve ratios. Moreover, since most development banks are required to have returns on equity investments ranging from 10 to 20%—a rate that is impossible with B-Shares—new investments in B-Shares in all funds have slowed dramatically (Development Practitioner #24 2016). Development banks have lobbied international regulators (principally through the BIS) to exempt these investments, though this has not produced any results.

There also exist risks for recipient countries and their attendant financial institutions. Critics of structured funds have argued that even though these funds are designed to create self-sustaining financial institutions, in practice there is a risk that these funds undermine domestic savings mobilization. Since these institutions have the ability to access debt capital from the fund and, on occasion, their regulations prevent them from accepting deposits from clients, their long-term viability as a financial institution is not guaranteed. Second, if the recipient institutions borrow too much in foreign currency, they remain susceptible to currency fluctuations and a potential sudden increase in their real liabilities in the event of a currency devaluation. The volatility of international capital markets is also passed on to these institutions. Relatedly, the reliance on international banks may ultimately undermine the objective to bolster the first-tier banking sector domestically. If financial institutions are established, managed, and trained by international partners, local ownership is diminished, and the incentives to create in-country capacities in financial transactions reduced (Maurer 2011, 23–24).

Despite these potential headwinds, structured funds of all varieties have been generally viewed as important tools to channel financial resources and strengthen domestic financial capacity within recipient countries. In many ways, this reflects the earlier desires of development institutions to fortify domestic capacity to provide a sustainable, long-term solution to underdevelopment. However, while structured funds today are important innovations, development practitioners cautioned that they cannot be used for every investment. Like other financial tools, structured funds are unlikely to be successful without a broader strategy of a strengthened legal framework, improvements in technical capacity, and stable macroeconomic policies.

New Frontiers of Development Finance: National Promotional Banks, Insurance Funds, and Securitization

While structured funds for development have taken the majority of the headlines of KfW's strategy with marketized development financial instruments, KfW has also engaged in a wide range of financial products. Interestingly, KfW has renewed its support for national promotional banks only two decades after it halted the practice. Unlike previous iterations, however, KfW only provides financial support to promotional banks that have embraced commercial operations, that are operated independent from politicians, and that have adhered to international standards for banking. Second, KfW has experimented with insurance funds for development. Like structured funds, KfW creates insurance funds with a tranche structure with donor governments holding the highest-risk junior shares, development institutions the mezzanine shares, and private investors the senior shares. Finally, KfW has been a lead development institution in the promotion of securitization. Together, these form a broader, comprehensive strategy on the part of KfW to bolster economic development via additional marketized development financial instruments.

Renewed Support for National Promotional Banks

Part of KfW's revised strategy in developing countries has been to revive the idea of a DFC—or, as is it now referred to, national promotional banks—as an on-lending institution for credit lines. Despite the extensive challenges of the 1970s and 1980s, development banks have been given a new lease on life as potential partners once again, although the parameters of what are expected of them have changed substantially (cf. Griffith-Jones and Ocampo 2018; Moslener et al. 2018; Thiemann et al. 2021).

These include a much greater focus on commercial bankability and institutional independence from political actors. KfW has also actively guided domestic economic policy programs, participated in the management of other development banks, and supplied technical assistance and training sessions at its Frankfurt headquarters for delegations from around the globe.

There are numerous reasons for this revival. First, global financial markets have deepened sufficiently such that market discipline can play a much stronger role in constraining promotional banks from engaging in politically-charged investments. Credit-rating agencies and market-set interest rates have curtailed the ability of national promotional banks to fund unbankable projects without being punished by international investors. This has created market discipline, something that has boosted the confidence of private investors (Development Practitioner #42 2016). Second, the challenges of the 1980s effectively weeded out the most inefficient of the promotional banks, particularly in Latin America. The most debt-laden institutions either have closed or merged with healthier banks. What remained were leaner institutions that had already abided by commercial banking practices (Development Practitioner #54 2017). Finally, technical assistance for recipient country development banks has dramatically improved. Particularly as a result of the structured funds, more technical assistance funding is available to train personnel. This has greatly improved the internal capacity of the institution to find new investment projects, conduct risk assessments, and evaluate outcomes.

For KfW, two trends have occurred. First, within the past decade, KfW has supported the establishment of multiple new national promotional banks across the developing world. This has occurred through a variety of advisory services, technical assistance, and funding measures. For example, in 2015, KfW provided USD 200 million from its own funds for the newly-founded Development Bank of Nigeria (DBN). The institutional structure of the DBN was modeled on KfW, as was its business model—the DBN supported microfinance banks and leasing companies to provide loans to SMEs and agricultural producers. Unlike previous models, the DBN only supported commercially-viable businesses and public-private partnership models. In addition to the refinancing schemes, both KfW and BMZ supported the strengthening of the DBN's human resource and organizational capacities.[10] Within Europe, KfW helped to found new development banks in Ireland, Latvia, and the UK, though these were designed to mimic KfW's operations in the domestic promotional context.

Second, KfW has increasingly channeled its funds—both from project assistance and from its structured funds—via national promotional banks and regional development banks. Much like their predecessor loans to promotional banks, KfW's financing arrives as credit lines that are earmarked for particular sectors. In the past decade, these investments have been concentrated in SME financing, microfinance, and green technology. KfW's credit lines to promotional banks gained particular attention within Europe following the Global Financial Crisis, as KfW provided loans for SME financing to the promotional banks of Ireland (SBCI), the UK (GIB), Portugal (PDFI), Spain (ICO), Italy (CDP), Poland (BGK), and Greece (IfG). The credit lines for Italy, Greece, Spain, and Ireland were in excess of EUR 100 million each. In February 2015, KfW concluded an agreement for a 10-year loan to support the State Bank of Poland (BGK) in its support of SMEs.[11] KfW has also actively participated in the EIB's European Fund for Strategic Investments (EFSI) for SMEs, infrastructure, and innovation in 2016.[12] KfW's initial contribution was EUR 500 million.[13]

Within a developing country context, KfW's support for national and regional promotional banks has similarly expanded dramatically. For instance, nearly three-fourths of new projects by KfW in Latin America were channeled through national and regional promotional banks in 2016 (Development Practitioner #54 2017). This notably included an agreement with CAF for an additional credit line from KfW and BMZ of EUR 350 million, of which EUR 250 million was earmarked for geothermal projects and EUR 100 million for urban transportation (CAF 2016). This was in addition to the EUR 303 million provided since 2011 for environmental projects and energy efficiency programs, which CAF then

[10] "KfW as a Model: Nigeria Establishes Development Bank," KfW, 25 March 2015.

[11] "KfW and Polish State Development Bank BGK Conclude EUR 100 Million Global Loan Agreement to Support Polish SME Sector," *KfW Press Release*, 11 February 2015.

[12] "Commission and EIB Announce a Fund for Broadband Infrastructure Open to Participation of National Promotional Banks and Institutions and of Private Investors," *EIB Press Release*, 12 December 2016.

[13] "500 Mio. EUR für innovative Unternehmen in Deutschland," *KfW Press Release*, 15 January 2016.

on-lent to projects in the region. In January 2017, KfW provided a second promotional loan worth EUR 150 million for CAF, which was used for eleven projects in renewable energy and public transportation systems.[14] KfW's efforts have also been active in Asian promotional institutions. In October 2015, KfW provided a USD 300 million to the State Bank of India (SBI) for the construction of affordable housing.[15]

Finally, outside of pure financial support, KfW has supplemented its strategy with a wide range of programs designed to enhance promotional bank capacity. This includes standard programs for technical assistance financing, but also includes numerous avenues for staff training. For instance, KfW routinely hosts delegations from national and regional promotional banks in Frankfurt for seminars on financial topics, which include financial inclusion for SMEs, responsible investing, innovative finance, and risk and evaluation procedures. These training sessions can last anywhere from a few days to a few weeks (Development Practitioner #54 2017). Recent guests have been from CAF and the Association of African Development Finance Institutions (AADFI). Moreover, KfW has taken the helm of the global revival of national promotional banks. In September 2011, KfW initiated the International Development Finance Club (IDFC), an organization of 19 of the world's largest promotional banks.[16] While the mandate is wide-reaching, with programs ranging from social development to public infrastructure, the principle objective has been to coordinate on topics of climate change (cf. IDFC 2015). According to interviews, the IDFC, while institutionally not powerful, has provided an important forum for the advancement of marketized development financial instruments (Development Practitioner #8 2016; Development Practitioner #55 2017). KfW's role as permanent secretariat has solidified its influence within this community.

[14] "KfW Is Paving the Way for Climate-Friendly Technologies in Latin America," *KfW Press Release*, 11 January 2017.

[15] "German Development Bank KFW Signs Loans Worth USD 300 Million with State Bank of India," *State Bank of India Press Release*, 6 October 2015.

[16] By 2016, the IDFC had added four additional members. Combined, IDFC members held assets of over USD 4 trillion and annual financing commitments of over USD 400 billion.

Development Assistance as Insurance

One of the most innovative financial instruments that has arisen in the past few years has been insurance schemes. Much like their structured fund counterparts, the insurance instrument is designed to provide market-rate insurance coverage with a tranched institutional design that leverages donor government-provided assistance in a public-private partnership. Within the past few years, insurance programs have specifically mitigated against climate change-related natural disasters. This has included a much more sophisticated methodology for monitoring and quantifying risks (Syroka and Wilcox 2006) and developing a regulatory system to administer the insurance plans (CISL 2015). The principle advantages of an insurance fund are its flexibility of institutional design and the efficiency in disbursement. First, and much like its structured fund counterparts, development institutions are free to design an insurance fund with a variety of variables. This includes the amount of donor government support, the size of the first-loss risk tranche, and the policies of investment diversification. The ability to adjust the amount of government subsidy gives the fund flexibility to ensure that insurances policies are additional and do not crowd out existing insurance companies. Moreover, the flexibility in designing insurance policies allows the insurance pool to provide separate policies to each country that vary in coverage scope and premium costs. Second, with regard to disbursement, an insurance fund clarifies the policies of payment prior to any natural disaster. In this way, the stipulation of requirements and payment amounts expedites the disbursement procedure to a matter of weeks or months, significantly less than the current strategy of gaining approval for project loans. This allows critical funds to quickly flow to the recipient government or other pre-approved recipient organizations, and, at least theoretically, eliminates the possibility of political interference in the process. Moreover, it reduces the dependence on public emergency assistance, which eliminates the recipient country from incurring large amounts of debt in a short period of time (Development Practitioner #55 2017).

Both the German government via BMZ and KfW have become ardent supporters of insurance schemes, particularly as a means to mitigate the impact of climate-related risks and create resilience in developing countries. In the past few years, KfW has participated in numerous insurance schemes. This has included a contribution to the Caribbean and Central American Catastrophe Risk Insurance Facility (CCRIF), the innovative

AgroProtekt bad weather insurance program in Serbia, and the National Health Insurance Fund (NHIF) in Kenya. Collectively these total nearly EUR 100 million (KfW 2016a, 2). However, the two most prominent funds are the African Risk Capacity Insurance Company (ARC) and the InsuResilience Investment Fund and InsuResilience Solutions Fund (ISF). In ARC, KfW and BMZ provided the initial capitalization for the fund; for the ISF, KfW was the primary initiator. KfW has also been crucial in convincing other donors such as the UK and the UN to support commercialized forms of insurance schemes, favoring tranched equity stakes over grant elements (Development Practitioner #42 2016). Together, these two insurance funds have transformed the way that development institutions have interacted with the private insurance markets.

African Risk Capacity Insurance Company

The African Risk Capacity Insurance Company (ARC) was the brainchild of Nobel Laureate Robert Shiller. The ARC was designed to offer African countries insurance policies in the event of a drought. ARC was a revolutionary instrument in development finance because it was the first donor government-funded insurance policy for developing countries. Prior to its creation, insurance was seen as an expensive and underwhelming option for disaster assistance. However, the creation of ARC demonstrated the ability to leverage market-oriented policies to create climate resilience projects. Like a traditional insurance plan, the ARC would disburse payment according to the insurance policy. In theory, the ARC would provide immediately disbursable funding to African governments that could be quickly deployed to prevent famine and hedge against the high cost of last-minute emergency assistance. The African Union (AU) sponsored the initial project with implementation assistance from the World Food Programme (WFP). In 2013, KfW and the UK's Department for International Development (DFID) supplied the seed capital for the establishment of ARC. KfW, in conjunction with BMZ, provided EUR 50 million in funding; EUR 46 million was for equity capital and EUR 4 million in grants for consultancy and technical assistance services. Additional technical assistance was provided by the Swiss (DEZA) and the Swedish (SIDA) governments.[17]

[17] "KfW Support for Drought Insurance for Africa," *KfW Press Release*, 24 January 2014.

ARC is composed of two entities. First, the Specialized Agency operates like a technical assistance facility. It is a cooperative mechanism that supervises the development of ARC capacity and services, provides capacity building funding to recipient governments, approves ARC contingency plans, and monitors implementation. These services are provided on a grant basis. Second, the ARC Insurance Company is the financial affiliate that implements the commercial insurance function of pooling and transferring recipient government risk. It was established in 2014. Risk diversification in the ARC Insurance Company is maintained geographically via the agglomeration of multiple African countries. In order to maintain the incentives of recipient countries to adequately prepare for natural disasters, foreign assistance can only be used in conjunction with recipient government co-funding. The capital principally arises from the participating countries' annual insurance premiums, which is determined by an ARC framework based on risk and recipient countries' ability to pay. As with traditional insurance, recipient countries select an insurance plan that reflects the amount of risk protection and the drought effects covered. Donor countries pay a one-time subsidy at the beginning of the plan in order to reduce the initial cost of the premium payment. However, after the initial payment, donor governments do not provide any additional assistance to the country premiums, but rather the junior shares are used to protect the private insurance companies in the case of an unusually large number of insurance payouts. Under the ARC rules, any one country can receive up to USD 30 million in an insurance payout for the year, though it is not restricted how many countries can claim this payout (ARC 2017a, 3).

By 2017, the ARC Establishment Agreement had been signed by 32 AU members, and ARC had launched four separate drought risk pools with eight countries subscribing to the insurance program (ARC 2017a, 3). Insurance payouts had amounted to a cumulative total of USD 34.4 million to Senegal, Niger, Mauritania, and Malawi. However, Kenya and Malawi have not renewed their contracts for the 2016–2017 agricultural year (ARC 2017b, 1). In the future, the ARC intends to expand its coverage to other natural disasters.

InsuResilience Investment Fund and InsuResilience Solutions Fund (ISF)

Following the success of the ARC, KfW established the Climate Insurance Fund (CIF) in December 2015 to provide additional insurance facilities for the world's poorest. The impetus came from the German government following its 2015-led G7 initiative on InsuResilience, which sought specifically to expand existing insurance schemes by enlarging the number of people covered by climate risk mitigation instruments. In 2017, the CIF was rebranded as the InsuResilience Investment Fund in order to better accord with this G7 initiative. Specifically, the objective of the fund was to reduce the vulnerability of MSMEs and low-income households to climate change-related events, and was the first fund of its kind within development finance. The initial capital outlay of CIF was provided jointly by KFW and BMZ, with USD 60 million provided for financing activities and an additional EUR 11 million for technical assistance, split between a traditional technical assistance facility and a premium support facility (Blue Orchard 2017, 16). Following the reorganization of CIF, the InsuResilience Investment Fund was split into a private equity pool and a private debt vehicle, which has so far raised USD 30 million and USD 50 million, respectively. KfW's contribution in coordination with BMZ was increased to USD 35 million in junior funding for each sub-fund.

The KfW-financed portion covers the first-loss risk to shield private investors, thereby incentivizing greater private participation. The dual nature of the fund expands flexibility. First, the equity sub-fund invests in private insurers and brokers that will actively build the market for climate insurance. In order to ensure compliance, the fund will take "minority stakes with significant influence, board representation, and invests alongside like-minded investors." Second, the debt sub-fund lends to financial institutions in return for the distribution of climate insurance. The main mechanism is through the provision of senior secured, unsecured, and subordinated debt to intermediary financial institutions. This has been predominantly local microfinancing institutions and cooperatives. Ultimately, this fund is flexible in its ability to intervene in the insurance market as well, and can invest in a variety of ways, including minority shareholdings, preferred shares, convertible loans, subordinated debt, and senior debt. Furthermore, the fund has also established a reinsurance business partnership with Swiss Re, Hannover Re, and Munich Re to provide reinsurance-related products on a commercial basis for climate risk-related projects. Moreover, much like its structured fund cousins, the InsuResilience Investment Fund also provides technical assistance in the form of grants to promote product design and, for limited periods, reduce the premium payments for end-clients. The technical assistance is also managed by the private Swiss firm Celsius Pro (Blue Orchard 2017, 16).

In conjunction with the InsuResilience Investment Fund, the InsuResilience Solutions Fund (ISF) is meant to be an innovative public-private partnership solution to the risks of climate change. In particular, the ISF is designed to provide insurance coverage against climate-related risks for 400 million poor and vulnerable people across the developing world. In October 2017, KfW and BMZ announced the creation of the ISF with an initial endowment of EUR 15 million. The government-backed funding is envisioned to promote the creation of new climate risk products and expand the existing products offered to individuals across three focus areas: (1) the development of new climate risk insurance products, (2) the scaling up of existing insurance products, and (3) the investment in technology to scale-up insurance operations. The ISF will only fund projects that are a cooperative partnership between an NGO or another humanitarian organization and the private sector, with grants of up to EUR 2.5 million per project and up to 50% of the total cost of the project. This is meant to enable only commercially-viable projects with local institutions as stakeholders. Since it is only a grant program, it is exclusively meant to serve as a catalyzing agent (ISF 2017, 5).

Together, the InsuResilience Investment Fund and Solutions Fund further highlights the transformation of the perspectives of the German government on the ability of government development assistance to be used in innovative marketized development finance instruments. As Thomas Silberhorn, Parliamentary State Secretary of BMZ, acclaimed, "[t]he fund enables us to bring the private sector, the scientific community and developing countries together for the first time, in order to develop customised insurance and financing solutions."[18] Currently, KfW is investigating the possibility for additional climate risk-mitigation insurance funds.

Nevertheless, the insurance schemes for development have not been without challenges. An illustrative example is a drought in Malawi that struck for the second time during the 2015–2016 agricultural year. During this drought, the devastation on the short-cycle maize crop raised the prospect of widespread food shortages and, as such, the Malawian government sought payout from the ARC. In 2015, Malawi had provided an insurance payment of USD 4.7 million for drought protection. However, the pre-approved policy was only for long-cycle

[18] "Hurricanes, Flooding and Droughts: KfW Promotes the Development of Climate Risk Insurance," KfW, 11 October 2017.

maize and, according to the internal models of ARC, the crop failure was limited to the short-cycle maize, therefore not triggering the payment. Following a revision of the risk forecasting model, the ARC concluded that Malawi did deserve a payment because it had not factored into account that farmers had substituted the long-cycle maize for short-cycle maize. Nine months after the initial onset of the drought, and following the approval of the Final Implementation Plan of the Government of Malawi, a USD 8.1 million payout was disbursed.[19] The actions of the ARC were highly criticized by civil society actors, who argued that the insurance scheme had provided too little, too late and was a poor use of donor funds (ActionAid 2017, 3). Malawi did not renew its subscription to the ARC during the following year.

Moreover, the example of Malawi has demonstrated the shortcomings of using these insurance schemes. First, even though the insurance plan is meant to be programmatic, and therefore independent of politics, political pressure can still play a role in whether the insurance is paid out. The primary motivation was to prevent a political scandal for ARC and ensure that other countries continued to pay into the insurance program. However, this may have set a dangerous precedent as the insurance payment was an outcome of political pressure rather than a programmatic policy payment (Development Practitioner #55 2017). Second, insurance has the potential of redirecting donor government assistance to insurance plans rather than emergency aid. While no study has quantitatively demonstrated this to be the case, fund diversion has been highlighted by numerous watchdog groups (cf. ActionAid 2017). As such, while insurance programs for developing countries may be useful in lowering the high costs of emergency assistance, they should not be treated as a primary strategy for risk mitigation (Development Practitioner #55 2017). These conclusions were echoed by the ARC itself, which has sought to remind recipient countries that risk insurance is a long-term commitment and should not be viewed as a substitute for domestic capacity building in risk mitigation (ARC 2017c, 12). Nevertheless, insurance funds have become more pervasive and have recently expanded to educational services as well. The High Education Finance Fund for Latin America and the REFA fund in Africa are but two examples (Development Practitioner #42 2016).

[19] "Malawi to Receive USD 8M Insurance Payout to Support Drought-Affected Families," *ARC Press Release*, 14 November 2016.

Other Financial Instruments: Green Bonds and Securitization

Outside of the structured funds and insurance funds, KfW also has promoted a variety of other marketized development financial instruments for economic development. Two that deserve mention are KfW's initiatives with green bonds on behalf of developing countries and KfW's assistance to help developing countries securitize their financing programs, particularly for SMEs. While neither initiative has the scope nor the volume of the aforementioned funds, they continue to demonstrate how KfW continues to search for new avenues to promote financial sector development via marketized financial instruments. Moreover, these initiatives underscore the consistency of KfW's approach of government-backed initiatives to mobilize private investment. In both cases, the original impetus arose from KfW's experiences in the domestic German market, which were then applied to a developing country context.

First, KfW had supported green investments in the domestic sphere for decades. As early as the 1970s, KfW sponsored domestic credit lines for energy efficiency upgrades for housing and SMEs (Harries 1998, 124). By the 1990s, KfW had expanded decisively into the renewable energy market with the Renewable Energy Program, and KfW's critical engagement with the German government's *Energiewende* program to shift away from the use of renewables has led to billions in funding. Throughout, KfW demonstrated remarkable commitment to funding green investments and developed a series of important innovations, such as the setting of housing energy efficiency standards and a complex system of feed-in tariffs to promote small-scale solar panel installation (Development Practitioner #50 2017). However, KfW was less trailblazing with the use of financial instruments for the purposes of green investments.

The most notable innovation has been green bonds, whereby institutions issue bonds earmarked for green investments. In 2007, the EIB issued a EUR 600 million Climate Awareness Bond, the first green bond used for development purposes. The following year, the World Bank launched the first specifically-labeled green bond in conjunction with the Skandinaviska Enskilda Banken (SEB) for approximately USD 440 million. Together, these two bond issuances pioneered the green bond market and encouraged private institutional investors to support green projects in developing countries. Unlike its multilateral development bank partners, KfW did not issue its first green bond until 2014. KfW's initial green bond was valued at EUR 1.5 billion, the largest green bond to date, with targeted projects for the domestic German market.[20] While KfW was initially slow to engage in the green bond market, this commitment has become so entrenched in the philosophy of KfW that one interviewee, when asked, said that KfW delayed the issuance of green bonds because "all of our investments are already green" (Development Practitioner #50 2017). Since then, KfW has become one of leading institutions—public or private—to support the expansion of the green bond market, although, as with the promotion of national development banks, KfW's initial foray into international green sector investments was within Europe. Since 2014, KfW has issued fully 71% of Germany's total amount of green bonds, worth EUR 12.8 billion in 11 separate issuances (Climate Bonds Initiative 2017, 1). In the first nine months of 2017 alone, KfW issued five bonds with an aggregate total of EUR 2.7 billion; 87% of this total was invested in wind energy, and 78% went to Germany with the remaining 22% to its European neighbors.[21]

KfW has provided financial support for numerous programs with a mix of grants, preferred loans, and equity participations. However, the bulk has been credit lines extended to developing country financial institutions for the refinancing of energy efficiency programs or renewable energy projects. For instance, between 2005 and 2009 KfW extended EUR 500 million in low-interest loans to developing countries under the Special Facility for Renewable Energies and Energy Efficiency (KfW 2005, 1). Financing has also included funds and grants for environmental protection programs in the areas of forest conservation and, more recently, climate adaptation. The total volume has been impressive; KfW issued a combination of grants and loans worth EUR 3.9 billion in 2015 across the developing world. Of this, EUR 1.8 billion was earmarked for renewable energy projects. Outside of purely renewable energy projects, KfW also provided grants and loans for investments ranging from energy-efficient power lines in India to an ecologically sustainable EcoCasa housing program in Mexico (KfW 2015, 109). KfW's extensive contributions via funds like the Global Climate Partnership Fund (GCPF), Eco Business Fund (EBF), and the Blue Action Fund (BAF) have complemented these project grants and loans. In the future, potential innovative financing

[20] "'Green Bonds—Made by KfW' Convince Investors," *KfW Press Release*, 15 July 2014.

[21] "Reporting on KfW Green Bond Issuances," *KfW Press Release*, 30 September 2017.

for developing countries could include the underwriting of a developing country's green bond issuance, but, given the structural problems with directly assuming risk of a sovereign government, these programs have not been solidified. Instead, specialized funds for the environment have been favored (Development Practitioner #50 2017).

Second, KfW's approach in the promotion of securitization directly stems from its experiences domestically. Securitization involves the conversion of SME loans into a purchasable investment vehicle for private investors; this is accomplished by pooling the various loans into a single financial entity and using the interest returns as payments to private investors. As early as the 1980s, KfW had promoted the securitization of domestic SME loans to sell to private investors, thereby raising additional capital and obviating the need for KfW to fund the SME loans itself (Harries 1998, 122). KfW's most formalized program, the Promise Program, was started in 2000 as a way for KfW to adopt the credit risk in portfolios of SME loans of German banks and free up capital for other uses. In 2002, KfW provided securitization cooperation with a credit-default swap program with the European Investment Fund (EIF 2002). However, even though KfW's portfolio of securitized SME loans performed relatively well during the 2008 financial crisis, following it there was little political appetite for complex financial instruments for SMEs.

Nevertheless, in the subsequent years KfW redoubled its efforts, particularly in the European markets. For one, KfW has held a series of workshops to enable other European development banks to engage in SME loan securitization, much in the way it has provided technical assistance to developing countries. KfW has also financially supported programs of other banks; in 2015, KfW jointly invested in a mezzanine tranche of a securitization fund sponsored by Italy's Cassa Depositi e Prestiti (CDP); it was the first time KfW had funded this investment abroad.[22] These programs have been subsequently expanded to Greece, Spain, and Portugal. Additionally, in conjunction with the EIF and other national promotional institutions, they have launched the "EIF-NPI Securitisation Initiative" (ENSI) in 2016, aimed at providing more funding to SMEs via the capital market. By September 2017, securitization transactions had been implemented in Portugal, the UK, Germany,

[22] "KfW Supports the European Securitisation Market," *KfW Press Release*, 4 December 2015.

and Italy, almost exclusively in conjunction with the European Investment Bank (EIB). As some scholars have argued, this has provided the basis for a European investment state (Mertens and Thiemann 2019).

These efforts have also complemented KfW's development strategies in middle-income countries as well. For instance, KfW cooperated with other international development agencies to help securitize SME funding. In 2006, KfW participated in the first on-shore securitization of a microloan portfolio of BRAC, a microfinance NGO in Bangladesh; the deal was designed to provide USD 180 million in capital over six years. KfW also lobbied the Bangladeshi authorities for the deal and supplied substantial technical advice to RSA Capital, the private arranger of the deal (Hartig 2011, 36). In this way, KfW not only provided financing, but also performed the tasks of a structuring investor and designed the deal. Later that year, KfW guaranteed the reinsurance of USD 100 million to support Kazakhstan's domestic securitization market and fund SMEs within the country. This project was jointly funded with the ADB (ADB 2006). In 2011, KfW cooperated with the EIF to jointly support true-sale securitization deals for SMEs in Bulgaria. This was designed to have the dual purpose of increasing private financing for SMEs and strengthening the development of the domestic Bulgarian financial sector. Incidentally, this securitization project was done in cooperation with ProCredit Bank Bulgaria, a bank in which KfW had not only provided technical assistance in the early 2000s, but also held an equity stake until the restructuring of ProCredit Holding. At the time, the EIF Chief Executive Richard Pelly applauded the deal, and said of the Bulgaria deal that the EIF hopes "that this will lead to further SME securitisation activity, providing necessary support for this vital part of the European economy."[23] Similar securitization programs were implemented in Serbia and Bangladesh, but given the reliance on a domestic financial sector, securitization promotion outside Europe has remained a relatively limited part of KfW's strategy.

KfW views securitization as an important strategy to bolster the domestic financial sector of developing countries and boost private investment. However, the utility of these financial instruments on behalf of developing countries has been relatively circumscribed. Neither has produced a new asset class, and neither has been able to replace the dominance of other instruments. Securitization is also less able to thrive in

[23]"EIF and KfW Sign Deal Helping to Develop the Bulgarian SME Securitisation Market," *KfW Press Release*, 29 June 2011.

the absence of financial markets, and development institutions have not devised a sustainable way to engage it in an effective manner. Nevertheless, KfW is constantly looking for new ways to apply commercial banking principles to the development context, and new options are routinely explored.

Conclusion

Within the past decade, KfW has continued to bolster its support for marketized development financial instruments. Following the successes of EFSE, KfW sought to replicate the structured fund model beyond Southeast Europe. KfW's establishment of numerous funds, and its participation in dozens of others, signifies the centrality they have assumed in development assistance, particularly to mobilize domestic finance, improve domestic financial sector capacity, and promote private entrepreneurship. The breadth of sectors—now including everything from ocean protection to green technology investments—and expansion of structured funds to other industries, like insurance, highlight the flexibility of the model. KfW's renewed interest in promotional banks has reinforced the financial sector as a priority. The facilitation of securitization programs and the potential framework for increased environmental funding follows a similar objective.

While financial instruments have become a widespread solution to promote development, the strategy continues to rely on donor government risk assumption. Both the structured funds and insurance funds are dependent on donor governments assuming the highest-risk, first-loss tranche to incentivize private investors. Moreover, donor government-backed development institutions provide the bulk of the mezzanine finance, which itself constitutes a majority of the funds' working capital. Even if the capital is raised on markets, credit-rating agencies still consider it backed by the government. Yet even this high level of risk mitigation has not generated enormous quantities of private capital, as some of these structured funds have less than 25% participation by private investors. Even the revival of DFCs is an extension of government risk assumption, as not only are the institutions themselves funded by the recipient government, but the credit lines offered to them are on a commercial basis from government-backed donor institutions. Nevertheless, development institutions—and KfW in particular—are confident that these marketized development financial instruments provide a fruitful avenue for the mobilization of private investment, and their future expansion into new sectors seems inevitable.

References

ActionAid. 2017. *The Wrong Model for Resilience: How G7-Backed Drought Insurance Failed Malawi, and What We Must Learn from It*. Johannesburg, South Africa: ActionAid.

ADB. 2006. ADB and KfW Promoting Cross-Border Securitization Market in Kazakhstan. *Asian Development Bank Press Release*.

ARC. 2017a. *African Risk Capacity Overview*. Johannesburg, South Africa: African Risk Capacity.

———. 2017b. *African Risk Capacity's Payouts: At Least 2.1 Million People Assisted*. Johannesburg, South Africa: ARC.

———. 2017c. *Lessons Learned: Implementation of a Sovereign Risk Management and Insurance Mechanism*. Johannesburg, South Africa: ARC.

Biallas, Margarete, and Mark Schwiete. 2006. Risk Perspectives of a Development Finance Institution. In *Microfinance Investment Funds: Leveraging Private Capital for Economic Growth and Poverty Reduction*, ed. Ingrid Matthäus-Maier and J.D. von Pischke. Berlin: Springer.

Blue Orchard. 2017. The 'InsuResilience Investment Fund.' *European Microfinance Platform Newsletter*.

CAF. 2016. Germany to Back CAF's Financing in Geothermal Projects and Urban Transportation for Latin America with €350 Million. *CAF Press Release*.

CISL. 2015. *Insurance Regulation for Sustainable Development: Protecting Human Rights Against Climate Risks and Natural Hazards*. Cambridge, UK: University of Cambridge Institute for Sustainability Leadership.

Climate Bonds Initiative. 2017. *German Green Bonds: Update and Opportunities*. Climate Bond Initiative.

EC. 2011. *Directive 2011/61/EU of the European Parliament and of the Council on Alternative Investment Fund Mangagers*. Brussels: European Commission.

Eco Business Fund. 2017a. *At a Glance*. Luxembourg: Eco Business Fund.

———. 2017b. *Eco Business Fund Development Facility at a Glance*. Luxembourg: Eco Business Fund.

EIF. 2002. EIF Participation in KfW's PROMISE Securitisation Programme. *European Investment Fund Press Release*.

European Commission. 2010. *EUROPE 2020 A Strategy for Smart, Sustainable and Inclusive Growth*. Brussels, Belgium: European Commission.

Ferrer, Jorge Núñez, and Federico Infelise. 2015. *Financial Instruments in Support of Territorial Development*. Brussels: Centre for European Policy Studies.

FINCA. 2016. *About FINCA Microfinance Holding Company LLC*. Washington, DC: FINCA Microfinance Holding Company.

———. 2017. *2016 FINCA International Annual Report*. Washington, DC: FINCA.

GGF. 2013. *Investing in Energy Efficiency and Renewable Energy*. Luxembourg: Green for Growth Fund.

———. 2016. *Annual Report 2016: Expanding Horizons*. Luxembourg: Green for Growth Fund.

Goodman, Patrick. 2006. Microfinance Investment Funds: Objectives, Players, Potential. In *Microfinance Investment Funds: Leveraging Private Capital for Economic Growth and Poverty Reduction*, ed. Ingrid Matthäus-Maier and J.D. von Pischke. Berlin: Springer.

———. 2008. Raising MFI Equity Through Microfinance Investment Funds. In *New Partnerships for Innovation in Microfinance*, ed. Ingrid Matthäus-Maier and J.D. von Pischke, 19–48. Berlin: Springer.

Griffith-Jones, Stephany, and José Antonio Ocampo (eds.). 2018. *The Future of National Development Banks*. Oxford: Oxford University Press.

Harries, Heinrich. 1998. *Wiederaufbau, Welt und Wende: Die KfW–Eine Bank mit öffentlichem Auftrag*. Frankfurt am Main: Knapp.

Hartig, Peter. 2011. The Role of Public and Private Investors for Structured Finance. In *Mobilising Capital for Emerging Markets*, ed. Ingrid Matthäus-Maier and J.D. von Pischke, 28–40. Berlin: Springer.

IDFC. 2015. *Development Banks Adopt Common Standards to Move Climate Finance Forward*. Frankfurt am Main: International Development Finance Club.

ISF. 2017. *Transforming Concepts into Products*. Frankfurt am Main: InsuResilience Solutions Fund.

KfW. 2005. *Promotion of Developing Countries*. Frankfurt am Main: KfW.

———. 2012. *Ex-Post Evaluation Brief TCX Subordinated Convertible Debt Facility*. Frankfurt am Main: KfW.

———. 2015. *2015 Annual Report*. Frankfurt am Main: KfW.

———. 2016a. *Current Topics: Insurance*. Frankfurt am Main: KfW.

———. 2016b. *Financial Report 2016*. Frankfurt am Main: KfW.

Maurer, Klaus. 2011. Mobilising Capital for the Poor–How Does Structured Finance Fit in Emerging Markets? In *Mobilising Capital for Emerging Markets*, ed. Ingrid Matthäus-Maier and J.D. von Pischke, 13–27. Berlin: Springer.

MEF. 2016. *2016 Annual Report*. Luxembourg: Microfinance Enhancement Facility.

———. 2017. *MEF Quarterly Factsheet—June*. Luxembourg: Microfinance Enhancement Facility.

Mertens, Daniel, and Matthias Thiemann. 2019. Building a Hidden Investment State? The European Investment Bank, National Development Banks and European Economic Governance. *Journal of European Public Policy* 26 (1): 23–43.

Moslener, Ulf, Matthias Thiemann, and Peter Volberding. 2018. National Development Banks as Active Financiers: The Case of KfW. In *The Future of National Development Banks*, ed. Stephany Griffith-Jones and José Antonio Ocampo, 63–85. Oxford, UK: Oxford University Press.

REGMIFA. 2015. *Annual Report 2015: Regional MSME Investment Fund for Sub-Saharan Africa S.A., SICAV-SIF*. Luxembourg: Regional MSME Investment Fund for Sub-Saharan Africa.

Sanad Fund. 2016. *Demonstrating Impact in the Middle East and North Africa Since 2011*. Luxembourg: Sanad Fund for MSME.

———. 2017a. *At a Glance, Q2 2017*. Luxembourg: Sanad Fund for MSME.

———. 2017b. *Sanad Technical Assistance Facility at a Glance, Q2 2017*. Luxembourg: Sanad Fund for MSME.

Stravens, Manon. 2017. The Currency Exchange Fund (TCX) Celebrates 10 Years of Achievement. *Development Finance*: 67–70.

Syroka, Joanna, and Richard Wilcox. 2006. Rethinking International Disaster Aid Finance. *Journal of International Affairs* 59 (2): 197–214.

TCX. 2013. *Local Currency Matters*. Amsterdam: TCX.

———. 2016. *Annual Report 2016*. Amsterdam: TCX.

Thiemann, Matthias, Daniel Mertens, and Peter Volberding. 2021. *The Reinvention of Development Banking in the European Union*. Oxford, UK: Oxford University Press.

Wälde, Helke. 2012. *An Overview of Innovative Financial Instruments Used to Raise Funds for International Development*. Frankfurt am Main: KfW.

CHAPTER 7

Toward the Future for Marketized Development Financial Instruments

Marketized development financial instruments have formed a cornerstone of development policy, and government and development practitioners alike have heralded them as a key to unlocking economic growth. Yet as this book has detailed, while these instruments enjoy widespread support, their emergence was neither straightforward nor inevitable. Donor governments, long skeptical of assuming the risks of private investment in developing countries, were often reluctant to take this burden themselves. Within developing countries, unstable macroeconomic environments, weak legal institutions, and low domestic savings rates hampered private investment. Among private investors, apprehension of investing in unknown markets with poor information reduced their appetite for investment opportunities. As few private investors were willing to invest in riskier projects within developing countries, the ambitions of a private investment-based development assistance regime disappointed.

Instead, development institutions spearheaded the creation, development, and expansion of marketized development financial instruments to attract private funds, and KfW was central in this evolution. While its early experiences closely mimicked the World Bank, by the early 1980s KfW experimented with new ways to align development policy with financial markets. Unlike the World Bank, KfW's flexibility permitted the institution extensive latitude with new financial instruments for the purposes of

P. Volberding, *Leveraging Financial Markets for Development*,
Executive Politics and Governance,
https://doi.org/10.1007/978-3-030-55008-0_7

development, and its own domestic experiences provided a solid foundation of knowledge. Moreover, the strong political backing from the German government following a series of crises gave KfW the mandate to pursue them. During these crises, KfW convinced the German government that some development assistance should be redirected to absorbing investment risk within financial instruments. In exchange, KfW directly created, owned, or operated the financial instruments and, to prevent moral hazards, distributed the financing at market rates. While KfW was not the only development institution to support marketized development financial instruments, it did play a pioneering role in microfinance banks and structured funds for development—a role that has been underappreciated by practitioners and scholars alike. Today, marketized development financial instruments have supplied billions of dollars for development projects and have become a critical pillar of development policy. Yet without KfW, and the German government more broadly, both the manifestation of marketized development financial instruments and the process by which they emerged would have certainly been different.

KfW Leads the Long Shift Toward Marketized Development Financial Instruments

From the early days of modern development policy in the 1950s, international development institutions like the World Bank endeavored to promote private investment. Funding was provided via grants and project loans, normally for large-scale industrial or infrastructure projects that were envisioned to relieve bottlenecks in the economy (cf. IBRD 1955, 1956). Policies were also designed to encourage domestic savings accumulation that could capitalize domestic banks and allow individuals and firms to borrow from the domestic financial sector, though in many developing countries, the financial sector remained underdeveloped for decades. In order to support smaller, private projects, the World Bank nurtured a global network of DFCs to solve two problems. First, the World Bank and other development institutions were prohibited from providing assistance without a recipient country guarantee; DFCs could be backed by the recipient government and could then guarantee the smaller loans itself. Second, DFCs could be used to provide funding directly to small businesses, a goal that dovetailed with the prioritization of private enterprise. DFCs themselves were supposed to be privately-owned, usually through a mix of industry association and domestic financial institutions. In this way, DFCs could also serve to mobilize domestic financial resources and deepen financial markets, making donor government funding catalytic (cf. DFC Department 1975; Diamond 1957).

Both encountered a litany of problems. Project assistance lacked evaluative measures until the late 1970s, meaning that development practitioners had little information regarding their impact. For DFCs, by the 1980s most were bankrupt and had failed to deliver any meaningful economic development. Poor economic incentives, unstable macroeconomic policies, and routine political interference neutered the ability of DFCs to provide sustainable investment (Diamond 1981, 1–4). Yet development institutions were consistent in their conviction that private investment was the key to unlocking economic development. By the beginning of the 1980s, development practitioners had honed in on the domestic financial sector as the missing ingredient. The landmark World Development Report (1989) solidified the financial sector as the main avenue for growth and established a template for supporting domestic financial sectors. The problem, as development practitioners had discovered, was finding the right tools to enable this shift.

Development institutions struggled to create market discipline. Critically, many institutions, the World Bank chief among them, were prohibited from creating new financial institutions in a recipient country. This restricted the ability to find effective recipient country financial partners; without the permission to create their own institutions, development institutions were forced to work with local banks, regardless of quality. Another way to improve management would have been to take a controlling stake and change the management, but development institutions were similarly limited as controlling stakes were impossible for even the most private-oriented institutions like the IFC. Finally, internal disagreements and the lack of political will for change further hampered the World Bank. Despite deepening capital markets and increased private interest in investing in the developing world, the growing interest in FDI did not translate into increased financing for developmental objectives.

While most development institutions were stymied by institutional inflexibility, KfW had advantages with marketized development financial instruments that enabled it to become a leading institution for the adoption of marketized development financial instruments. While in the beginning KfW's strategy in the 1960s and 1970s matched the World Bank's with an emphasis on project loans and DFCs, by the early 1980s,

KfW began to shift its policies toward utilizing financial instruments. Greater interest in promoting financial self-sufficiency was complemented by mounting German political pressure to have more cost effectiveness in development projects. A damaging 1981 report on the ineffectiveness of financing DFCs sparked a broader search to reform the policies (Nitsch et al. 1981).

While many institutions had experimented before with increasing the reliance on financial markets, KfW found more fruitful avenues for two reasons. First, the immense political economy problems facing the German government meant that political support was strong. In order to support German reunification, the collapse of the Soviet Union, and the reconstruction of the Balkans, the German government poured billions of Euros into grants and credit lines, mostly administered via KfW. Critically, KfW convinced lawmakers that the government should assume a portion of the investment risk in these new marketized development financial instruments. Microfinance banks and structured funds were not entirely novel concepts, but KfW's application of both to a commercial-oriented development policy context was, and German government risk assumption made this possible.

Second, the political support of the German government also enabled KfW to gain flexibility. In exchange for the risk guarantees of the government, KfW was able to exert greater control over these new instruments. Unlike the World Bank, KfW could invest in a recipient country without securing a government guarantee. In the case that there were no viable domestic financial institution partners, KfW was able to create the institution from scratch, providing an important tool in countries that were particularly underdeveloped. Finally, KfW could maintain a controlling stake for as long as necessary in order to build up internal capacity, meaning that KfW could ensure management preparedness. KfW continued to hold equity stakes in both microfinance institutions as well as in the international microfinance organizations like ProCredit. This ability was the primary means of eliminating moral hazards (Glaubitt et al. 2008, 353).

Ultimately, these factors allowed KfW to overcome the obstacle that had plagued development—how to encourage private investment when the macroeconomic environment and intermediary financial institutions were unsatisfactory. With the ability to create new institutions or control them long enough to enact managerial reforms, KfW could ensure that domestic partner institutions operated according to international best practices. The heavy reliance on both KfW's own market-raised capital and the German government's budget further meant that a donor government, rather than a recipient government, was ultimately responsible for the investment risk. In fact, this transfer of risk to the German government was key to the success of these marketized development financial instruments (Development Practitioner #27 2016). The German government absorbed the first-loss risk in all of the development structured funds and later the insurance funds, shielding private investors from risks. With the microfinance banks, the German government provided grants to form the base equity of the institution, or later, the working capital of the microfinance group. This transfer of risk made marketized development financial instruments not only possible, but essential to their operations. When complemented with KfW-supplied financing in mezzanine tranches and credit lines, the risk to private investors in the senior tranche was defrayed further.

Through meticulous documentation and analysis, this booked has argued that KfW—and Germany more broadly—led the transformation of development policy to deploy marketized development finance instruments. I contend that KfW, and not the World Bank, had the vision and the means to operationalize change within the development paradigm and align development policy with financial markets. That Germany has had a long shadow within the EU and abroad is not new—after all, everything from its ordoliberal ideology to an emphasis on the *Mittelstand* has impacted policy beyond its border. However, Germany's role within international development has often been relegated to a footnote, and its institutions viewed as passive executors. KfW's own actions have often been situated within those of the World Bank, if not entirely ignored. This book has therefore shed important light on this underappreciated contribution of both KfW and the German government, and highlighted how KfW played a transformational role to create and promote marketized development financial instruments.

While KfW was central to the emergence and development of marketized development financial instruments, a set of unique factors highlight the possible singularity of the event. Numerous interviewees noted that the 1990s and 2000s were a particularly innovative period in which an unprecedented open dynamic between KfW staff and the German government via BMZ developed (Development Practitioner #27 2016; Development Practitioner #34 2016; Development Practitioner #40 2016). The acute political pressures on the German government—with the quick succession of reunification, the collapse of the Soviet Union, and the Balkan crisis—were also particular in that it demanded immediate attention from a neighboring state. Subsequent crises such as the Syrian refugee crisis have not precipitated the same urgent political need to bolster the financial sector or maintain export markets (Development Practitioner #36 2016). Finally, new regulations by the EU enacted after the 2008 Global Financial Crisis severely circumscribed the innovative abilities of KfW. Under an agreement reached in 2013 with the European regulatory authorities, KfW fell under the regulatory jurisdiction of BaFin,[1] Germany's domestic banking supervisory authority. While the status of KfW has not changed, KfW has been pressured to abide by key aspects of the German Banking Act (Kreditwesengesetz, or KWG) such as risk reporting standards and solvency ratios.[2] This has limited KfW's ability to engage in more innovative financial instruments without the approval of BaFin, something that has dampened flexibility in the international development banking portion of KfW as well. It has also mitigated KfW's advantage of being able to establish new institutions (Development Practitioner #42 2016). Development bank practitioners fear that even if BaFin does not directly prohibit certain investments or instruments, apprehension surrounding potential regulatory action will circumscribe KfW's flexibility (Development Practitioner #40 2016; Development Practitioner #55 2017).

Marketized Development Financial Instruments as Development Policy—The Past and Future

The story of how KfW pushed for marketized development financial instruments is a microcosm within the broader shift of development. Throughout the process, there was a core conviction of private investment as the building block for sustained growth. However, KfW was unique because of its institutional flexibility and political support for risk assumption. More broadly, this enabled long-standing ideas of private capital mobilization to be implemented and proved to governments and

[1] Bundesanstalt für Finanzdienstleistungsaufsicht, or the Federal Financial Supervisory Authority.

[2] So far, BaFIN has not taken an active role in restricting KfW. For more details on the implementation "Regulation Concerning Application of the German Banking Act to KfW Enters into Force," *KfW Press Release*, 8 October 2013.

private investors alike that commercial-based financing for development was possible, provided that risk mitigation strategies were implemented. Today, development policy has embraced marketized development financial instruments.

Development Policy Expands Marketized Development Financial Instruments

Beginning in earnest with the Monterrey Consensus and Millennium Development Goals (MDGs), and concluding more recently with the Addis Ababa Action Agenda (AAAA) and the Sustainable Development Goals (SDGs) in 2015, the mobilization of private investment has preoccupied modern development policy. For instance, the AAAA clearly stated that mobilizing private investment would be the focus of future development policy via a dual strategy of increasing FDI and developing domestic capital markets. Complementing these normal propositions, the AAAA also argued for a wide range of finance-related measures, including enhanced global financial regulation, increased funding for technical assistance, greater programs for financial inclusion, and expanded education for financial literacy. Finance in all its forms is now seen as the linchpin for economic development.

The codification of finance and financial instruments has occurred across development policy and development institutions. The SDGs were an outgrowth of the 2030 Agenda for Sustainable Development, and they sought to eradicate poverty with an ambitious 17-point agenda. In order to achieve these goals, the SDGs aimed to align the interests of public and private actors such that it became a win-win proposition, noting that "the challenge for the private sector is to move towards inclusive and sustainable business models without undermining profitability" (UN 2016, 4). The World Bank has become a key supporter of new financial instruments, mainly for the use in infrastructure projects, and has expanded its support for guarantees through MIGA (Development Practitioner #31 2016). The G20 has similarly embraced marketized development financial instruments, and activities such as the SME Financing Forum were established to continue to augment the capacity of recipient country financial institutions via knowledge sharing (Development Practitioner #41 2016). In 2019, the World Bank announced its Maximizing Finance for Development (MFD) initiative, which has aimed to leverage private financial sources in a coordinated way. Combined, these initiatives highlight that donor institutions have solidified the approach for more innovative marketized development financial instruments.

Yet also reflecting the ways that KfW circumvented the problems of financing, all of these development policies hold government risk sharing is essential. For instance, the AAAA has numerous government risk-sharing schemes. The AAAA has argued that private investment mobilization will require numerous innovative ways of financing such as "development-oriented venture capital funds, potentially with public partners, blended finance, risk mitigation instruments, and innovative debt funding structures with appropriate risk management and regulatory frameworks" (UN 2015, 22). These government risk mitigation instruments include "insurance, investment guarantees, including through the Multilateral Investment Guarantee Agency [MIGA], and new financial instruments to incentivize foreign direct investment to developing countries," as well as special-purpose vehicles, non-recourse project financing, and pooled financing (UN 2015, 23–24). These instruments have together formed PPPs, which in recent years have found support from a wide range of international institutions. This has included the World Bank (2012), IFC (2016), and the ADB (2012), even though variations in definition and implementation remain underspecified (Thiemann and Volberding 2017). A popular but similarly undertheorized topic has been blended finance, which seeks to more effectively combine public and private funds for projects (WEF and OECD 2015).[3] Perhaps surprising given their historical difficulties, national promotional banks were reaffirmed by the AAAA as a key tool in development policy, a position that significantly revised a long-standing norm that was hesitant of state-owned financial institutions. Specifically, the AAAA stated that national promotional banks can be important "in financing sustainable development, particularly in credit market segments in which commercial banks are not fully engaged and where large financing gaps exist, based on sound lending frameworks and compliance with appropriate social and environmental safeguards" (UN 2015, 15–16). A worldwide resurgence, particularly after the 2008 Global Financial Crisis, has also heightened

[3] For a more thorough overview of blended finance, see Pereira (2017). For the IFC's experience, see IFC (2017). For setting standards for blended financial instruments and regulatory issues, see OECD (2015). For a critical take, see Development Initiatives (2016).

NDBs once more (Griffith-Jones and Ocampo 2018; Thiemann et al. 2021).

Outside of investments, development institutions are also likely to seek out additional sources of revenue. Bond and securitization arrangements have become the norm rather than the exception, and bonds have been issued in every major tradeable currency. There are also more creative uses being floated. For instance, Israel and India have successfully pioneered diaspora bonds, which are bonds sold to emigrants abroad. Proposals have also been made to tap institutional investors. These potential investors include private fund managers in OECD countries, pension funds, and sovereign wealth funds (SWFs), yet every proposed instrument requires coordination with and risk assumption by donor governments and public financial institutions (cf. Inderst and Stewart 2014). Both hold trillions of dollars in assets.

The Global Spread of Marketized Development Financial Instruments and Its Future Directions

For the first few decades, Western development financial institutions spearheaded this shift toward marketized development financial instruments. While KfW was certainly a leading institution because of its institutional flexibility and strong political backing to absorb investment risk, its partnering multilateral development financial institutions like the World Bank and the EBRD were of a similar mind-set in the promotion of financial instruments. Together, they agreed that market mechanisms provided the most efficient means of distributing capital and raising funds from private sources. Yet as financial markets have taken hold across the globe, other development institutions have adopted similar strategies to those pioneered by KfW. In many of these cases, KfW has actually provided important advice and technical assistance, further highlighting how KfW has shaped the global development paradigm.

Most notably, the China Development Bank (CDB) has shifted decisively toward financial markets, both to raise capital and to distribute funds. Despite its reputation of being a pass-through institution of the Chinese government, the CDB has increasingly relied on domestic and foreign capital markets to finance its growing list of activities. This is in part a consequence of the 1997 restructuring that commercialized the bank and sought international training programs from both state-owned banks and private banks alike, of which KfW played an important role. The CDB was given the mandate to support the objectives of the government, but to do so in a fiscally responsible manner (CDB 2013, 3–4). In 2016, the CDB raised more than 60% of its total funding via capital markets. The lion's share comes from the domestic RMB market—nearly RMB 6.5 billion outstanding in 2016—but with smaller amounts in foreign currencies and RMB issuances on foreign capital markets (CDB 2016, 15). The shift toward raising capital on financial markets has incentivized the CDB to abide by market principles and make investments in order to maintain its credit rating (Development Practitioner #17 2016). This reliance on capital markets and on foreign advisory services has also served to insulate the CDB from political influence (Development Practitioner #42 2016). And even to this day, KfW has provided training sessions and advisory services, and Hans Reich, a former executive of KfW, still maintains a seat on the CDB's advisory board.

The CDB has also embraced financial markets and its attendant financial instruments as a way of funding projects abroad. Within the Chinese government's ambitious "One Belt, One Road" initiative, financial instruments have become increasingly prevalent. Estimates for the required amount of project financing range from USD 4 to 8 trillion, meaning that the neither the CDB nor the Chinese government could directly finance such a large quantity. As such, the CDB has turned toward capital markets to compensate for the shortfall. For instance, the CDB has endeavored to become more attractive to international investors. In July 2017, the CDB underwrote CNY 1 billion for the first time in so-called Panda Bonds in cooperation with a Malaysian bank in order to gain access to foreign capital markets. The funding will be used to directly finance the projects in the One Belt, One Road program, all in recipient country currencies. The CDB has become an ardent supporter of green bonds for the purposes of refinancing. In November 2017, the CDB issued USD 500 billion in green bonds—its first in an international capital market—that will be used for renewable energy and energy efficiency projects as part of the government's One Belt, One Road initiative. In addition, the CDB is a co-sponsor of the Silk Road Fund, a Chinese state-backed investment fund created in 2014 with an initial pledge of USD 40 billion. So far, the Silk Road Fund has financed a smattering of infrastructure and energy projects in Central Asia and East Africa. Nevertheless, the Silk Road Fund does not combine a tranched risk design to encourage private investors, but rather consolidates financing into a single credit line (Development Practitioner #18 2016; Development Practitioner #20 2016; Development Practitioner #21 2016).

More visibly, China has also deployed new development institutions as a way to continue to expand its financing opportunities. The New Development Bank, originally entitled the BRICS Bank, and the Asian Infrastructure Investment Bank (AIIB) were designed to provide a mix of financing and technical assistance to projects across Asia and the developing world. Currently, these banks operate much like the World Bank and other multilateral development banks, as they use callable capital from donor countries to raise additional private investment on international capital markets. These then provide refinancing for domestic institutions for large-scale infrastructure projects or the development bank directly provides financing itself. So far, these have largely reflected the strategy of the World Bank and KfW until the 1990s as it directly funds specific projects and not a portfolio of investments, though some have found that Chinese development finance differs in its implications (Chin and Gallagher 2019). The CDB, NDB, and AIIB have not yet provided full-throated support for microfinance or SME finance,[4] nor have they supported the creation or capitalization of any of the global structured funds for development. Innovative financing mechanisms, such as the instrument that allowed local governments to use land as collateral for loans, have remained within the domestic market (Development Practitioner #28 2016).

Outside of China, development banks from BNDES in Brazil to DBSA in South Africa have endeavored to mimic the policies of KfW. For instance, BNDES has sponsored a financing program to increase the amount of funding for SMEs. The Korean Development Bank has copied the mixed financing schemes of KfW for international projects (Development Practitioner #32 2016). The Croatian development bank HBOR was intended to directly imitate KfW's institutional setup. Nevertheless, these efforts to increase market participation have so far been circumscribed to the promotion of investments within the country rather than as policy to encourage development abroad. Regardless, these trends toward the greater integration of state-backed institutions with private financial markets are a notable, and rapidly accelerating, trend.

[4] The CDB has implemented an SME financing program within China for the past decade. Incidentally, the first SME financing project in China was conducted in Shenzhen in a co-financed project with KfW (Development Practitioner #1 2015).

Challenges to Marketized Development Financial Instruments

Despite codification in development policy, marketized development financial instruments are not without their challenges. First, the entire process continues to heavily rely on public subsidy to function. Initially, KfW and other development banks hoped that their initial capitalization would eventually be supplemented with private injections of capital (Köhn and Jainzik 2005, 332–333). Donor government risk assumption was to simultaneously build domestic capacity while exposing international private actors to previously untapped markets. While private capital has certainly shown interest in the funds, public funding still provides a majority of financing. For instance, the structured funds for development are still largely capitalized with approximately one-third of grants from donor governments, and anywhere from one-quarter to one-third in mezzanine financing from development institutions, which themselves are financially backed by donor governments (Lepp 2017). Oftentimes, structured funds struggle to get institutional investors with more than USD 50 or 100 million in funding, leaving the structured fund to seek additional injections of donor government-sponsored capital.

Second, there is also widespread fear among development practitioners that these financial instruments will not be able to survive broader macroeconomic shifts in the global economy. In particular, low interest rates in the developed world and excess liquidity have made these financial instruments in development contexts attractive investments. However, an increase in global interest rates or higher returns on investment in the developing world could siphon off funds currently dedicated to developing countries. There is similar concern that a drop in institutional investor attention to so-called "impact investing" could diminish investment. Public pressure to have responsible investment could ultimately wane, a trend that development practitioners fear could also drastically reduce a key segment of financing in tools ranging from structured funds to microfinance banks (Development Practitioner #52 2017). A retrenchment of investment away from development countries that arises from an economic downturn might have a similar impact.

Third, there is a risk that the promises of sustainable economic development via private sector finance have been oversold (Development Practitioner #49 2017). The principle motivation for moving toward marketized development financial instruments was to compensate for the shortfall in investment. Limited public funds could be used to cover the risk premium for private investors or provide leverage, ultimately generating a virtuous cycle of investment, returns, and financial market creation. This perspective has formed the foundation for international development programs, embodied most directly in SDGs. However, as experience with these financial instruments has demonstrated, sustainable financing has not always materialized. The drive for financial multipliers does not mean funding for development (Development Practitioner #36 2016). Private financing has come largely through institutional investors and large private placements and, so far, has not generated a vibrant financial market for individual investors. Rates of return, although positive, often remain lower than other investment opportunities.

Fourth, while ambitious efforts to expand into previously unbankable segments, such as health funds or climate risk insurance funds, not every sector can be financed at market rates. Investments in education, for instance, oftentimes lack an underlying revenue stream, making them undesirable sectors for marketized development financial instruments (Development Practitioner #53 2017). Similar challenges have blocked the expansion of financial markets into areas of poverty reduction, water provision, vaccinations, and refugee assistance. Second, even in those sectors that are financially feasible, markets may already be saturated. As one expert familiar with microfinance investment stated, "[i]s it possible that there is USD 100 billion in good microfinance loans available per year? Probably not, there just aren't that many entrepreneurs in the world" (Development Practitioner #49 2017). In this way, the current market size for these financial instruments may be smaller than development practitioners envision. Without an underlying increase in the number of people willing to take microfinance loans, financial instruments will do little to expand this market.

Finally, even though these marketized development financial instruments are designed to avoid the problems that plagued earlier iterations of development assistance, they are still dependent on the broader macroeconomic environment to be effective. For one, a functioning financial and legal sector are prerequisites, as on-lending and refinancing is difficult without in-country partners. KfW compensated for this deficiency by creating new institutions with German government guarantees, but this is a difficult proposition for most donor governments—as well as recipient governments—to accept. Macroeconomic policies from currency exchange rates to domestic interest rates can also have grave impacts on even the best-designed policies. These policies are also still dependent on politics as well. For their part, national development banks are still susceptible to political interference and poor risk management, even with financial markets providing a disciplinary role. Politicians can also have more indirect effects. For instance, in India, a politician's promise for debt forgiveness for state-provided loans in the run-up to an election created a widespread belief that their microfinance loans would also be exempt; this was not the case, but non-performing loans skyrocketed to over 50% in some local microfinance institutions (Development Practitioner #47 2017). Together, these suggest that while marketized development financial instruments have mitigated the challenges of the previous development assistance regime from the 1950s through the 1990s, they have not solved the problems in their entirety.

The Impact and Limitations of KfW and Avenues for Future Research

This book has argued that KfW has played a critical role in the advent and diffusion of marketized development financial instruments. While I maintain that KfW has been at the forefront of this evolution, a few caveats are warranted. First, KfW cooperated with and took inspiration from other development institutions. For example, microfinance as a concept was established in the NGO community decades before KfW's own investments, and the World Bank had from an early stage saw microfinance as a promising pathway forward to encourage entrepreneurship (Robinson 2001, 19–22). The IFC was a co-investor of many of the microfinance banks in Eastern Europe, and played an important role in funding the initial EFSE structured fund. The EBRD was similarly a stable institutional partner for KfW, and even for the RSBF, had invited KfW to become an equity participant. Even FMO had experimented with creating proto-structured funds and issuing bonds on capital markets earmarked for development purposes in the early 1980s (Development Practitioner #33 2016). This suggests that there was a common conception of how development policy could proceed vis-à-vis financial markets. KfW was still instrumental because of its unique capacities to circumvent existing hurdles and create new instruments, but was not the only conceptual pioneer.

Second, it is possible that deepening financial markets could have created variations of these financial instruments, even without the leading role of KfW. The growth of financial markets, particularly within developing countries themselves, reflected the increasing importance of finance in all economic transactions. When coupled with a quickly liberalizing currency and investment regime, greater legal protections for private investors, as well as exploding interest on the part of private investors in developing countries, similar investment vehicles to those sponsored by KfW could have been eventually created by the private market. After all, KfW itself relied on financial markets to raise capital for these investments and on domestic financial institutions to serve as on-lending partners. Commercial instruments like investment funds and securitized portfolios were also touted as ways of mitigating investor risk in developing countries, though none had come to fruition by the time KfW had structured EFSE. While ultimately not identical to those created by KfW, the private sector nevertheless possessed both the potential to create similar financial instruments for developing countries.

Yet even though KfW was not always the primary instigator, I still contend that it had an indelible impact on the trajectory of these instruments. For instance, KfW was able to imprint its own values on the early structured funds. This likely skewed the initial investment portfolios to SMEs, microfinance, and environmental topics, areas in which KfW had been particularly active (Development Practitioner #54 2017; Private Investor #2 2017, 2). KfW also took much of its domestic experience using loans, technical assistance, and capital markets and applied them to the developing world context. The mixing of government grants with KfW-raised capital had occurred in its domestic SME financing for decades. This mixture was unique to KfW and could have been structured differently if administered by another institution (Development Practitioner #34 2016). Finally, the successes that KfW had also strongly signaled to other development institutions that government assistance leveraged as private risk mitigation was viable. Following the establishment of the ProCredit microfinance banks in Eastern Europe, other institutions like the IFC and the EBRD sought additional financing from their government backers for the provision of funds earmarked for technical assistance. The IFC also searched for exemptions from the limits on holding equity in financial intermediaries (Development Practitioner #9 2016). Both changes attempted to gain greater oversight over financial intermediaries and boost private investor confidence of good governance. As two private investors tersely remarked, while the growth of financial logic was inevitable in development practice, KfW nonetheless greatly impacted the timing and process by which this transition occurred, making it the most important development institution during the transition period to marketized instruments (Private Investor #1 2016; Private Investor #3 2017).

This book has also opened new opportunities for future scholars to push forward on additional research questions. First, and perhaps most importantly, this book has demonstrated how important actors other than the World Bank and the United States have been in development policy. Even though neither KfW nor the German government were the largest or most prominent actors within development, they were crucial in how the international development paradigm shifted to marketized development financial instruments. A mix of institutional flexibility and political resolve accentuated KfW's impact. Additional work would be welcome in further analyzing how Germany impacted global economic development. This might include digging deeper into KfW's own activities within Germany and in the EU, the interaction between the various German development aid agencies, as well as the relationship between German development institutions and the private sector. Recent work has recently emerged within national development banking and the EU (cf. Thiemann et al. 2021), but how Germany relates to countries further afield remains an area of potential research.

This book also highlights the need for scholars to continue to expand their analysis away from the United States and the World Bank and toward other actors within this space. Other large donor countries like France, the UK, and Japan have also made their own impacts on development, yet their contributions are similarly overlooked by scholars. Even institutions mentioned within this book—such as microfinance banks like Accion and ProCredit—have not received substantial scholarly attention, nor has the entire ecosystem that surrounds these marketized development financial instruments. Fund managers, for instance, are playing increasingly important roles in administering these development funds and serving as interlocutors between development institutions and private investors, yet little—if anything—has analyzed their operations. Looking to the future, important new actors like China could also have a profound shift on how development assistance is administered, and there is likely to be rich research opportunities on how newcomers impact the exist regime.

In addition, while this book has incorporated limited discussions on how marketized development financial instruments have differentially benefited and disadvantaged certain actors, there is still a large opportunity for future analysis. There are enduring questions about how effective market-oriented solutions to economic development are, who benefits from these instruments, and which countries are better suited to leveraging them for results. The shift to market-based mechanisms also warrants critiques on those who are left behind, and those investments that, despite improvements, are still left out of the process. As the SDGs continue to gain traction, this research will be welcome. Moreover, by understanding the pain points in how marketized development financial instruments are administered, future scholars might be able to identify how marketized development financial instruments may change in the future.

Finally, while the past few decades have seen a steady growth of marketized development financial instruments, the upward trajectory may not last forever. A slowdown in their creation by development institutions, a lack of interest on the part of private investors, a reduction in risk-bearing appetite on the part of donor countries, or a reluctance by recipients to continue to embrace them could all influence the course of development. Marketized development financial instruments are likely to be susceptible to global economic uncertainty, as liquidity contractions or a reduction in risk appetite would likely negatively impact demand. As these changes to marketized development financial instruments are realized, it will be imperative that researchers examine how the changes guide the future of these financial instruments.

The Road Ahead for Marketized Development Financial Instruments

The particular form of the future of development policy may be impossible to predict, but, if history is any guidance, the contours are clear. Given that development assistance has become increasingly intertwined with financial markets, it is likely that marketized development financial instruments will remain enduring fixtures of development policy. Codification within the AAAA, SDGs, and most recently with the MFD has provided the requisite political support to continue with further experimentation. Consequently, marketized development financial instruments are likely to continue their growth over the coming years. Structured funds have moved into more complex operations including currency swaps and SME loan securitization while simultaneously expanding into sectors previously thought unbankable. Insurance funds have also expanded in number and scope, and have moved beyond climate resilience and disaster insurance into fields such as public health. New sources of financing from green bonds to institutional investors will likely continue to increase the capital available to the ever-growing list of marketized development financial instruments.

However, as the rise and spread of marketized development financial instrument has highlighted, knowing how these financial instruments first emerged is crucial to understanding how they interact with the global political economy today. Development institutions, donor governments, recipient governments, and private investors all have vested stakes in how these instruments are initiated and implemented, and each has a different set of incentives and constraints that guide their engagement with them. Identifying these forces is crucial to dissecting the current set of marketized development financial instruments, their shortcomings, and their future potential. As global financial markets continue to deepen, and development institutions continue to seek private sources of funding, new financial instruments will inevitably emerge, with each new generation of instruments pushing the boundaries of what was thought to be possible. Yet how these new marketized development financial instruments are structured, which institutions will create them, and how governments will bear their risk, however, remains to be seen.

References

ADB. 2012. *Public-Private Partnership Operational Plan 2012–2020*. Manila, Philippines: Asian Development Bank.

CDB. 2013. *国家开发银行史: 1994–2012 (Guojia Kaifa Yinhang Shi, The History of the China Development Bank)*. Beijing: China Financial Publishing House.

———. 2016. *2016 Annual Report*. Beijing: China Development Bank.

Chin, Gregory T., and Kevin P. Gallagher. 2019. Coordinated Credit Spaces: The Globalization of Chinese Development Finance. *Development and Change* 50 (1): 245–274.

Development Initiatives. 2016. *Blended Finance: Understanding Its Potential for Agenda 2030*. Development Initiatives.

DFC Department. 1975. *DFC Policy Paper*. Washington, DC: World Bank.

Diamond, William. 1957. *Development Banks*. Baltimore, MD: The Economic Development Institute: International Bank for Reconstruction and Development.

———. 1981. *Reflections on the Performance of Development Banks and the Challenges Ahead*. National Bank of Egypt.

Glaubitt, Klaus, Hanns Martin Hagen, Johannes Feist, and Monika Beck. 2008. Reducing Barriers to Microfinance: The Role of Structured Finance. In *New Partnerships for Innovation in Microfinance*, ed. Ingrid Matthäus-Maier and J.D. von Pischke, 349–378. Berlin: Springer.

Griffith-Jones, Stephany, and José Antonio Ocampo (eds.). 2018. *The Future of National Development Banks*. Oxford: Oxford University Press.

IBRD. 1955. *Tenth Annual Report: 1954–1955*. Washington, DC: International Bank for Reconstruction and Development.

———. 1956. Some Concluding Remarks on the IBRD Development-Bank Operations.

IFC. 2016. *Blending Public and Private Finance: What Lessons Can Be Learned from IFC's Experience?* Washington, DC: International Finance Corporation.

———. 2017. *Blended Finance at IFC*. Washington, DC: International Finance Corporation.

Inderst, Georg, and Fiona Stewart. 2014. *Institutional Investment in Infrastructure in Developing Countries Introduction to Potential Models*. Washington, DC: World Bank.

Köhn, Doris, and Michael Jainzik. 2005. Microfinance Investment Funds—An Innovative Form of PPP to Foster the Commercialisation of Microfinance. In *EU Accession–Financial Sector Opportunities and Challenges for Southeast Europe*, ed. Ingrid Matthäus-Maier and J.D. von Pischke, 323–335. Berlin: Springer.

Lepp, Anja. 2017. Interview.

Nitsch, Manfred, Reinhardt Schmidt, and Claus-Peter Zeitinger. 1981. *Berichtsentwurf: Inspektion Der "Förderung von Entwicklungsbanken" in Lateinamerika*. Unpublished Manuscript.

OECD. 2015. *A How-To Guide for Blended Finance: A Practical Guide for Development Finance and Philanthropic Funders to Integrate Blended Finance Best Practices into Their Organizations*. Paris: OECD.

Pereira, Javier. 2017. *Blended Finance: What It Is, How It Works and How It Is Used*. Oxfam.

Robinson, Marguerite S. 2001. *The Microfinance Revolution: Sustainable Finance for the Poor*. Washington, DC: The World Bank.

Thiemann, Matthias, and Peter Volberding. 2017. *Financing Infrastructure in Developing Countries through Public-Private Partnerships*. Berlin: Bread for the World.

Thiemann, Matthias, Daniel Mertens, and Peter Volberding. 2021. *The Reinvention of Development Banking in the European Union*. Oxford, UK: Oxford University Press.

UN. 2015. *Addis Ababa Action Agenda of the Third International Conference on Financing for Development*. New York: United Nations.

———. 2016. *UNDP Support to the Implementation of the 2030 Agenda for Sustainable Development*. New York: United Nations Development Program.
WEF and OECD. 2015. *Blended Finance Vol. 1: A Primer for Development Finance and Philanthropic Funders*. Cologny, Switzerland: World Economic Forum.
World Bank. 1989. *World Development Report 1989: Financial Systems and Development*. Washington, DC: World Bank.
———. 2012. *World Bank Group Support to Public-Private Partnerships*. Washington, DC: World Bank.

Appendix

See Table A.1.

Table A.1 List of interviews

	Name	*Interview date*
1	Development Practitioner #1	7 July 2015
2	Miles Kellerman	8 October 2015
3	Armin Gruenbacher	9 October 2015
4	Development Practitioner #2	16 October 2015
5	Development Practitioner #3	13 November 2015
6	Development Practitioner #4	3 February 2016
7	Development Practitioner #5	12 February 2016
8	Willem Pieter De Groen	24 February 2016
9	Karel Lannoo	24 February 2016
10	Development Practitioner #6	25 February 2016
11	Government Official #1	26 February 2016
12	Government Official #2	26 February 2016
13	Hans-Helmut Kotz	9 March 2016

(continued)

P. Volberding, *Leveraging Financial Markets for Development*, Executive Politics and Governance,
https://doi.org/10.1007/978-3-030-55008-0

Table A.1 (continued)

	Name	*Interview date*
14	Development Practitioner #7	16 March 2016
15	Development Practitioner #8	16 March 2016
16	Development Practitioner #9	16 March 2016
17	Development Practitioner #10	16 March 2016
18	Development Practitioner #11	16 March 2016
19	Development Practitioner #12	16 March 2016
20	Development Practitioner #13	16 March 2016
21	Development Practitioner #14	7 April 2016
22	Xu Jiajun	8 April 2016
23	Development Practitioner #15	9 April 2016
24	Reporter #1	11 April 2016
25	Development Practitioner #16	11 April 2016
26	Development Practitioner #17	12 April 2016
27	Development Practitioner #18	13 April 2016
28	Development Practitioner #19	13 April 2016
29	Development Practitioner #20	13 April 2016
30	Development Practitioner #21	13 April 2016
31	Development Practitioner #22	13 April 2016
32	Reporter #2	13 April 2016
33	Development Practitioner #23	20 April 2016
34	Development Practitioner #24	20 April 2016
35	Development Practitioner #25	20 April 2016
36	Development Practitioner #26	21 April 2016

(continued)

Table A.1 (continued)

	Name	*Interview date*
37	Development Practitioner #27	22 April 2016
38	Development Practitioner #28	3 May 2016
39	Development Practitioner #29	16 May 2016
40	Development Practitioner #30	17 May 2016
41	Development Practitioner #31	23 May 2016
42	Development Practitioner #32	24 May 2016
43	Development Practitioner #33	27 May 2016
44	Development Practitioner #34	30 May 2016
45	Development Practitioner #35	30 May 2016
46	Reinhard Schmidt	31 May 2016
47	Development Practitioner #36	3 June 2016
48	Development Practitioner #37	22 June 2016
49	Malcolm Harper	11 July 2016
50	Jan Krahnen	21 July 2016
51	Development Practitioner #38	22 July 2016
52	Development Practitioner #39	23 July 2016
53	Development Practitioner #40	26 July 2016
54	Development Practitioner #41	6 September 2016
55	Development Practitioner #42	3 November 2016
56	Development Practitioner #43	4 November 2016
57	Development Practitioner #44	7 November 2016
58	Development Practitioner #45	9 November 2016
59	Development Practitioner #46	14 November 2016

(continued)

Table A.1 (continued)

	Name	*Interview date*
60	Development Practitioner #47	15 November 2016
61	Private Investor #1	15 December 2016
62	Private Investor #2	18 April 2017
63	Development Practitioner #48	22 April 2017
64	Private Investor #3	22 April 2017
65	Development Practitioner #49	22 April 2017
66	Development Practitioner #50	23 April 2017
67	Development Practitioner #51	27 April 2017
68	Development Practitioner #52	10 August 2017
69	Development Practitioner #53	16 August 2017
70	Development Practitioner #54	27 September 2017
71	Development Practitioner #55	28 September 2017
72	Development Practitioner #56	10 October 2017
73	Anja Lepp	24 October 2017
74	Development Practitioner #57	23 February 2018

References

ActionAid. 2017. *The Wrong Model for Resilience: How G7-Backed Drought Insurance Failed Malawi, and What We Must Learn from It*. Johannesburg, South Africa: ActionAid.
ADB. 2006. ADB and KfW Promoting Cross-Border Securitization Market in Kazakhstan. *Asian Development Bank Press Release*.
———. 2012. *Public–Private Partnership Operational Plan 2012–2020*. Manila, Philippines: Asian Development Bank.
Ahmed, Syed Aftab. 2004. Strengthening Financial Sectors in Transition Countries. In *The Development of the Financial Sector in Southeast Europe*, ed. Ingrid Matthäus-Maier and J.D. von Pischke, 71–77. Berlin: Springer.
Aitken, Rob. 2010. Ambiguous Incorporations: Microfinance and Global Governmentality. *Global Networks* 10 (2): 223–243.
Alacevich, Michele. 2009. *The Political Economy of the World Bank: The Early Years*. Stanford, CA: Stanford University Press.
ARC. 2017a. *African Risk Capacity Overview*. Johannesburg, South Africa: African Risk Capacity.
———. 2017b. *African Risk Capacity's Payouts: At Least 2.1 Million People Assisted*. Johannesburg, South Africa: ARC.
———. 2017c. *Lessons Learned: Implementation of a Sovereign Risk Management and Insurance Mechanism*. Johannesburg, South Africa: ARC.
Baechle, Jan. 2004. Equity Participation in Microfinance Banks in Southeast Europe and Georgia—A Strategic Option for a Large Private German Bank? In *The Development of the Financial Sector in Southeast Europe*, ed. Ingrid Matthäus-Maier and J.D. von Pischke, 135–139. Berlin: Springer.

P. Volberding, *Leveraging Financial Markets for Development*, Executive Politics and Governance,
https://doi.org/10.1007/978-3-030-55008-0

Bateman, Milford. 2010. *Why Doesn't Microfinance Work? The Destructive Rise of Local Neoliberalism*. London: Zed Books Ltd.

———. 2017. *From Panacea to "Anti-Development" Intervention: The Rise and Fall of Microcredit*. Rochester, NY: Social Science Research Network. SSRN Scholarly Paper (July 18, 2017).

Becker, William H. 2003. *The Market, the State, and the Export-Import Bank of the United States, 1934–2000*. Cambridge, UK: Cambridge University Press.

Biallas, Margarete, and Mark Schwiete. 2006. Risk Perspectives of a Development Finance Institution. In *Microfinance Investment Funds: Leveraging Private Capital for Economic Growth and Poverty Reduction*, ed. Ingrid Matthäus-Maier and J.D. von Pischke. Berlin: Springer.

Bladen, John. 1971. Disbursements to Development Finance Companies.

Blue Orchard. 2017. The 'InsuResilience Investment Fund.' *European Microfinance Platform Newsletter*.

BMZ. 1982. Finanzielle Zusammenarbeit Mit Nicaragua.

Bohnet, Michael. 2004. Foreword. In *The Development of the Financial Sector in Southeast Europe*, ed. Ingrid Matthäus-Maier and J.D. von Pischke, v–ix. Berlin: Springer.

Boskey, Shirley. 1959. *Problems and Practices of Development Banks*. Baltimore, MD: Johns Hopkins Press.

———. 1962. Industrial Credit Institutions. In *Methods of Industrial Development*, ed. Albert Winsemius and John Pincus. Paris: Organization for Economic Co-operation and Development (OECD).

Buckley, Graeme. 1997. Microfinance in Africa: Is It Either the Problem or the Solution? *World Development* 25 (7): 1081–1093.

CAF. 2016. Germany to Back CAF's Financing in Geothermal Projects and Urban Transportation for Latin America with €350 Million. *CAF Press Release*.

Caprio Jr, Gerard, and Asli Demirguc-Kunt. 1997. *The Role of Long Term Finance: Theory and Evidence*. Washington, DC: World Bank.

Carroll, Toby, and Darryl S.L. Jarvis. 2014. Introduction: Financialisation and Development in Asia Under Late Capitalism. *Asian Studies Review* 38 (4): 533–543.

———. 2015. The New Politics of Development: Citizens, Civil Society, and the Evolution of Neoliberal Development Policy. *Globalizations* 12 (3): 281–304.

Cassen, Robert, and Associates. 1986. *Does Aid Work? Report to an Intergovernmental Task Force*. Oxford: Oxford University Press.

CDB. 2013. *国家开发银行史: 1994-2012 (Guojia Kaifa Yinhang Shi, The History of the China Development Bank)*. Beijing: China Financial Publishing House.

———. 2016. *2016 Annual Report*. Beijing: China Development Bank.

Chin, Gregory T., and Kevin P. Gallagher. 2019. Coordinated Credit Spaces: The Globalization of Chinese Development Finance. *Development and Change* 50 (1): 245–274.

CISL. 2015. *Insurance Regulation for Sustainable Development: Protecting Human Rights Against Climate Risks and Natural Hazards*. Cambridge, UK: University of Cambridge Institute for Sustainability Leadership.

Climate Bonds Initiative. 2017. *German Green Bonds: Update and Opportunities*. Climate Bond Initiative.

David, Hulme, and Paul Mosley. 1996. *Finance Against Poverty Volume 1*, 1st ed. London: Routledge.

DBJ. 1988. *New Role of Policy Financing in the Federal Republic of Germany and in Japan: In Tokyo, October 24–28, 1988*. Tokyo: Development Bank of Japan.

———. 1992. *New Roles of Policy-Based Finance in Tackling Global Issues: In Tokyo, October 11–18, 1992*. Tokyo: Development Bank of Japan.

DBJ and KfW. 1987. *Aspects of Structural and Environmental Policy in Japan and in the Federal Republic of Germany: Working Papers, Materials, and Protocols of Discussions of a Workshop in Frankfurt am Main from October 12 to 19 1987*. Frankfurt am Main: Kreditanstalt für Wiederaufbau.

Demuth, R.H. 1958. Statement of R. H. Demuth, Director of Technical Assistance and Liaison, to Meeting of Executive Directors on June 12, 1958, Regarding Conference of Development Bank Representatives.

Development Finance Companies Department. 1969. Interest Rates Charged by Development Finance Companies and Terms of Government Loans to Such Companies.

Development Initiatives. 2016. *Blended Finance: Understanding Its Potential for Agenda 2030*. Development Initiatives.

DFC Department. 1975. *DFC Policy Paper*. Washington, DC: World Bank.

Diamond, William. 1957. *Development Banks*. Baltimore, MD: The Economic Development Institute: International Bank for Reconstruction and Development.

———. 1969. Office Memorandum with Mr. William Gaud.

———. 1970a. Letter from William Diamond to Dr. Willi Engel.

———. 1970b. Use of Borrowed Funds for Investments in Share Capital by Development Finance Companies.

———. 1971. Development Bank Policy Changes.

———. 1981. *Reflections on the Performance of Development Banks and the Challenges Ahead*. National Bank of Egypt.

———. 1984. Transcript of a Taped Statement by William Diamond, East Asia and Pacific Department, Industrial Development and Finance Division Retreat.

Diamond, William, and Ravi Gulhati. 1973. World Bank's Experience with Development Finance Companies. *Economic and Political Weekly* 8 (23): M47–56.
Diamond, William, and V.S. Raghavan (eds.). 1982. *Aspects of Development Bank Management*. Baltimore, MD: Johns Hopkins University Press.
Drezgić, Saša, Zoran Pavlović, and Dragoljub Stoyanov. 2011. Microfinance Saturation in Bosnia and Herzegovina: What Has Really Been Achieved for the Poor? In *Confronting Microfinance: Undermining Sustainable Development*, ed. Milford Bateman. Sterling, VA: Kumarian Press.
DSE. 1986. *Armutsbekämpfung Durch Selbsthilfe II*. Berlin: Deutsche Stiftung für Internationale Entwicklung.
Easterly, William. 2009. How the Millennium Development Goals Are Unfair to Africa. *World Development* 37 (1): 26–35.
EC. 2011. *Directive 2011/61/EU of the European Parliament and of the Council on Alternative Investment Fund Managers*. Brussels: European Commission.
Eco Business Fund. 2017a. *At a Glance*. Luxembourg: Eco Business Fund.
———. 2017b. *Eco Business Fund Development Facility at a Glance*. Luxembourg: Eco Business Fund.
EFSE. 2006. *Annual Report 2006: Building Bridges: Public-Private Partnership for Development Finance in Southeast Europe*. Frankfurt am Main: European Fund for Southeast Europe.
———. 2012. *Annual Report 2012: Strong Partners—Strong Impact*. Frankfurt am Main: European Fund for Southeast Europe.
———. 2016a. *Annual Report 2016: EFSE. Creating Opportunities*. Frankfurt am Main: European Fund for Southeast Europe.
———. 2016b. *At a Glance*. Luxembourg: European Fund for Southeast Europe.
———. 2017. *Q2 2017: Investment Portfolio and Funding Quarterly Fact Sheet*. Frankfurt am Main: European Fund for Southeast Europe.
EIB. 2017. *Mobilization of Private Finance by Multilateral Development Banks*. Luxembourg: European Investment Bank.
EIF. 2002. EIF Participation in KfW's PROMISE Securitisation Programme. *European Investment Fund Press Release*.
Engel, Willi. 1967. Credit Control by Development Banks. In *The Role of Development Banks in Economic and Social Development*. Berlin: German Foundation for Developing Countries.
European Commission. 2010. *Europe 2020: A Strategy for Smart, Sustainable and Inclusive Growth*. Brussels, Belgium: European Commission.
Ferrer, Jorge Núñez, and Federico Infelise. 2015. *Financial Instruments in Support of Territorial Development*. Brussels: Centre for European Policy Studies.

FINCA. 2016. *About FINCA Microfinance Holding Company LLC*. Washington, DC: FINCA Microfinance Holding Company.
———. 2017. *2016 FINCA International Annual Report*. Washington, DC: FINCA.
Franco, Marc. 2005. The Scenario for EU Accession by Southeast European Countries. In *EU Accession—Financial Sector Opportunities and Challenges for Southeast Europe*, ed. Ingrid Matthäus-Maier and J.D. von Pischke, 39–42. Berlin: Springer.
Führer, Helmut. 1996. *The Story of Official Development Assistance*. Paris: OECD.
G20. 2017a. Chair's Summary: G20 Finance and Central Bank Governors Meeting, Washington, DC, USA, 20–21 April 2017.
———. 2017b. *Joint MDB Statement of Ambitions for Crowding in Private Finance*.
Gaud, William S. 1970. IFC Investments in Development Finance Companies.
GCF. 2017. *Status of the Initial Resource Mobilization Process*. Incheon, South Korea: Green Climate Fund.
GGF. 2013. *Investing in Energy Efficiency and Renewable Energy*. Luxembourg: Green for Growth Fund.
———. 2016. *Annual Report 2016: Expanding Horizons*. Luxembourg: Green for Growth Fund.
Gibbon, Peter. 1993. The World Bank and the New Politics of Aid. *The European Journal of Development Research* 5 (1): 35–62.
Girishankar, Navin. 2009. *Innovating Development Finance—From Financing Sources to Financial Solutions*. Washington, DC: World Bank.
Glaubitt, Klaus, and Haje Schütte. 2004. Providing Long-Term Funds to Local Financial Institutions—The European Refinancing Funds in Southeast Europe. In *The Development of the Financial Sector in Southeast Europe*, ed. Ingrid Matthäus-Maier and J.D. von Pischke, 61–77. Berlin: Springer.
Glaubitt, Klaus, Hanns Martin Hagen, Johannes Feist, and Monika Beck. 2008. Reducing Barriers to Microfinance: The Role of Structured Finance. In *New Partnerships for Innovation in Microfinance*, ed. Ingrid Matthäus-Maier and J.D. von Pischke, 349–378. Berlin: Springer.
Glaubitt, Klaus, Hanns Martin Hagen, and Haje Schütte. 2006. Mainstreaming Microfinance—Quo Vadis Microfinance Investments. In *Microfinance Investment Funds: Leveraging Private Capital for Economic Growth and Poverty Reduction*, ed. Ingrid Matthäus-Maier and J.D. von Pischke. Berlin: Springer.
Goffin, P.C. 1969. Development Finance Companies—Comments on Mr. Diamond's Memorandum of September 12, 1969.
Gonzalez, Anabel, Christine Zhenwei Qiang, and Peter Kusek. 2018. Overview. In *Foreign Investor Perspectives and Policy Implications*. Washington, DC: World Bank.

Goodman, Patrick. 2006. Microfinance Investment Funds: Objectives, Players, Potential. In *Microfinance Investment Funds: Leveraging Private Capital for Economic Growth and Poverty Reduction*, ed. Ingrid Matthäus-Maier and J.D. von Pischke. Berlin: Springer.

———. 2008. Raising MFI Equity Through Microfinance Investment Funds. In *New Partnerships for Innovation in Microfinance*, ed. Ingrid Matthäus-Maier and J.D. von Pischke, 19–48. Berlin: Springer.

Gordon, David L. 1983. *Development Finance Companies, State and Privately Owned: A Review*. Washington, DC: The World Bank.

Gore, Charles. 2013. The New Development Cooperation Landscape: Actors, Approaches, Architecture. *Journal of International Development* 25 (6): 769–86.

Grasso, Patrick G., Sulaiman S. Wasty, and Rachel V. Weaving (eds.). 2003. *World Bank Operations Department: The First 30 Years*. Washington, DC: World Bank.

Griffith-Jones, Stephany, and José Antonio Ocampo (eds.). 2018. *The Future of National Development Banks*. Oxford University Press.

Grünbacher, Armin. 2001. The Early Years of a German Institution: The Kreditanstalt Für Wiederaufbau in the 1950s. *Business History* 43 (4): 68–86.

———. 2005. *Reconstruction and Cold War in Germany: The Kreditanstalt Für Wiederaufbau (1948–1961)*. Aldershot, UK: Ashgate Publishing.

GTZ. 1991. Development Aid Concerns Society as a Whole. *GTZ Gate*.

Gulhati, Ravi. 1970a. A Few Thoughts on Present Bank Policies Regarding Development Finance Companies.

———. 1970b. Appraisal Reports on Development Finance Companies.

———. 1970c. Economic Appraisal of DFC Projects.

———. 1970d. Economic Aspects of Development Finance Companies Project Appraisal—December 30.

———. 1970e. Questionnaire on DFC Sub-Projects.

———. 1971. A Few Thoughts for 1972.

Gustafson, Douglas. 1969a. Currency Repayment Provisions on Bank Loans to Development Finance Companies (DFCs).

———. 1969b. Four General Points on DFC Lending Policy.

Harper, Malcolm. 2016. Interview.

Harries, Heinrich. 1998. *Wiederaufbau, Welt und Wende: Die KfW—Eine Bank mit öffentlichem Auftrag*. Frankfurt am Main: Knapp.

Hartig, Peter. 2011. The Role of Public and Private Investors for Structured Finance. In *Mobilising Capital for Emerging Markets*, ed. Ingrid Matthäus-Maier and J.D. von Pischke, 28–40. Berlin: Springer.

Hasan, Zamir. 1969. Some Thoughts on Your Four General Points on DFC Lending.

Heber, Gabriele, Witold Teplitz, and Claus-Peter Zeitinger. 1982. *Nutzungsmöglichkeiten alternativer Kraftstoffe in Entwicklungsländern*. Eschborn.

Helms, Brigit. 2006. *Access for All: Building Inclusive Financial Systems*. Washington, DC: World Bank.

Hermes, Niels, and Robert Lensink. 2011. Microfinance: Its Impact, Outreach, and Sustainability. *World Development* 39 (6): 875–881.

Heussen, Hejo, Bernd Breuer, and Lore Wellmann (eds.). 1987. *Promotion of Self-Help by Savings Banks: A Dialogue Programme; St. Blasien, Bonn, 25.5. - 5.6.1987*. Berlin: ZWS.

Hu, Yao-Su. 1981. The World Bank and Development Finance Companies. *Journal of General Management* 7 (Autumn): 46–57.

Hüttenrauch, Harald, and Claudia Schneider. 2008. Securitisation: A Funding Alternative for Microfinance Institutions. In *New Partnerships for Innovation in Microfinance*, ed. Ingrid Matthäus-Maier and J.D. von Pischke, 299–347. Berlin: Springer.

IBRD. 1947. *Second Annual Report to the Board of Governors: 1946–1947*. Washington, DC: International Bank for Reconstruction and Development.

———. 1948. *Third Annual Report to the Board of Governors: 1947–1948*. Washington, DC: International Bank for Reconstruction and Development.

———. 1950a. *Fifth Annual Report to the Board of Governors: 1949–1950*. Washington, DC: International Bank for Reconstruction and Development.

———. 1950b. *Report and Recommendations of the President to the Executive Directors on the Industrial Development Bank of Turkey Loan Application Guaranteed by the Republic of Turkey*. Washington, DC: International Bank for Reconstruction and Development.

———. 1950c. *The Basis of a Development Program for Colombia*. Washington, DC: International Bank for Reconstruction and Development.

———. 1952. *Seventh Annual Report to the Board of Governors: 1951–1952*. Washington, DC: International Bank for Reconstruction and Development.

———. 1953. *Eighth Annual Report to the Board of Governors: 1952–1953*. Washington, DC: International Bank for Reconstruction and Development.

———. 1955. *Tenth Annual Report: 1954–1955*. Washington, DC: International Bank for Reconstruction and Development.

———. 1956a. *Eleventh Annual Report: 1955–1956*. Washington, DC: International Bank for Reconstruction and Development.

———. 1956b. Some Concluding Remarks on the IBRD Development-Bank Operations.

———. 1968. *The World Bank, IDA and IFC*. Washington, DC: International Bank for Reconstruction and Development.

———. 1972. Project Appraisals Reviewed by Development Finance Companies—Div. II.

———. 1975. DFC Policy Paper.

IBRD, IDA, and KfW. 1961. *Administration Agreement (Roseires Irrigation Project) Between the Republic of the Sudan and Kreditanstalt Für Wiederaufbau and International Development Association and International Bank for Reconstruction and Development, Dated as of June 14, 1961.* Washington, DC: International Bank for Reconstruction and Development.

IDFC. 2015. *Development Banks Adopt Common Standards to Move Climate Finance Forward*. Frankfurt am Main: International Development Finance Club.

IFC. 1957. *First Annual Report 1956–1957*. Washington, DC: International Finance Corporation.

———. 1958. *Second Annual Report 1957–1958*. Washington, DC: International Finance Corporation.

———. 1959. *Third Annual Report 1958–1959*. Washington, DC: International Finance Corporation.

———. 1961. *Fifth Annual Report: 1960–1961*. Washington, DC: International Finance Corporation.

———. 1962. *Sixth Annual Report: 1961–1962*. Washington, DC: International Finance Corporation.

———. 1963. *IFC Annual Report: 1962–1963*. Washington, DC: International Finance Corporation.

———. 1964. *IFC Annual Report: 1963–1964*. Washington, DC: International Finance Corporation.

———. 1965. *IFC Annual Report: 1964–1965*. Washington, DC: International Finance Corporation.

———. 1967. *IFC Annual Report 1967*. Washington, DC: International Finance Corporation.

———. 1969. *IFC Annual Report 1969*. Washington, DC: International Finance Corporation.

———. 1970. *IFC Annual Report 1970*. Washington, DC: International Finance Corporation.

———. 1971. *IFC Annual Report 1971*. Washington, DC: International Finance Corporation.

———. 2016. *Blending Public and Private Finance: What Lessons Can Be Learned from IFC's Experience?* Washington, DC: International Finance Corporation.

———. 2017. *Blended Finance at IFC*. Washington, DC: International Finance Corporation.

Inderst, Georg, and Fiona Stewart. 2014. *Institutional Investment in Infrastructure in Developing Countries Introduction to Potential Models*. Washington, DC: World Bank.

IPC. 1983. *Errichtung Der Städtischen Sparkasse Piura/Peru*. Frankfurt am Main: Interdisziplinäre Projekt Consult.

ISF. 2017. *Transforming Concepts into Products*. Frankfurt am Main: InsuResilience Solutions Fund.

Jones, Sam. 2012. Innovating Foreign Aid—Progress and Problems. *Journal of International Development* 24 (1): 1–16.

Kalmanoff, George. 1969. Bank Group Assistance to Development Finance Companies, Compared to Other New Resources Mobilized by the Companies.

Kamarck, Andrew. 1969. Paper for Board on Some Aspects of DFC Policy.

Kapur, Devesh, John Prior Lewis, and Richard Charles Webb. 1997. *The World Bank: Its First Half Century*. Washington, DC: Brookings Institution Press.

Ketkar, Suhas, and Dilip Ratha (eds.). 2009. *Innovative Financing for Development*. Washington, DC: World Bank.

KfW. 1957. *Ninth Annual Report Covering the Year 1957*. Frankfurt am Main: Kreditanstalt für Wiederaufbau.

———. 1960. *Twelfth Annual Report Covering the Year 1960*. Frankfurt am Main: Kreditanstalt für Wiederaufbau.

———. 1967a. *Annual Report for the Year 1967*. Frankfurt am Main: Kreditanstalt für Wiederaufbau.

———. 1967b. Kreditanstalt as Development Bank.

———. 1969. *Annual Report for the Year 1969*. Frankfurt am Main: Kreditanstalt für Wiederaufbau.

———. 1970. *Annual Report for the Year 1970*. Frankfurt am Main: Kreditanstalt für Wiederaufbau.

———. 1971a. *Annual Report for the Year 1971*. Frankfurt am Main: Kreditanstalt für Wiederaufbau.

———. 1971b. Länderdirektorium, 8. Sitzung Am 15. Mai 1971.

———. 1972. Länderdirektorium, 29. Sitzung Am 17. April 1972.

———. 1973a. Arbeitsgruppe Zur Besprechung von Grundsatzfragen Im Rahmen Der Kapitalhilfe.

———. 1973b. Ergebnisvermerk Über Die Diskussionsveranstaltung 'Entwicklungsbankenfinanzierung'.

———. 1973c. Gemeinschaftsfinanzierung Mit Der Weltbank Oder Anderen Internationalen Finanzierungsinstitutionen.

———. 1973d. Vermerk: Gemeinschaftsfinanzierung Mit Der Weltbank Oder Anderen Internationalen Finanzierungsinstitutionen.

———. 1974. *Annual Report for the Year 1974*. Frankfurt am Main: Kreditanstalt für Wiederaufbau.

———. 1975a. *Annual Report for the Year 1975*. Frankfurt am Main: Kreditanstalt für Wiederaufbau.

———. 1975b. Arbeitsgruppe Zur Besprechung von Grundsatzfragen Im Rahmen Der Kapitalhilfe.
———. 1976a. *Annual Report for the Year 1976*. Frankfurt am Main: Kreditanstalt für Wiederaufbau.
———. 1976b. Entwicklungsbanken - Berichtssystem Der Weltbank.
———. 1977. Prüfungsleitfaden Entwicklungsbanken.
———. 1980a. *Annual Report for the Year 1980*. Frankfurt am Main: Kreditanstalt für Wiederaufbau.
———. 1980b. Ergebnisvermerk Der Sonderarbeitsgruppe Über 'Arbeitsweise Der KfW Bei Der Abwicklung von Entwicklungsbankendarlehen'.
———. 1980c. Grundsätze Für Gemeinsame Finanzierungen Mit Anderen Bi- Oder Multilateralen Geberinstitutionen.
———. 1982. *Projektfinanzierung in Entwicklundsländern*. Frankfurt am Main: Kreditanstalt für Wiederaufbau.
———. 1983. Länderdirektorium, 168. Sitzung Am 24. März 1983.
———. 1984. *Annual Report for the Year 1984*. Frankfurt am Main: Kreditanstalt für Wiederaufbau.
———. 1985a. *Annual Report for the Year 1985*. Frankfurt am Main: Kreditanstalt für Wiederaufbau.
———. 1985b. Gliederung Und Inhalt Der KfW-Berichte Über Die Prüfung von Entwicklungsbanken.
———. 1988. *Annual Report for the Year 1988*. Frankfurt am Main: Kreditanstalt für Wiederaufbau.
———. 1989. *Annual Report for the Year 1989*. Frankfurt am Main: Kreditanstalt für Wiederaufbau.
———. 1990. *Annual Report for the Year 1990*. Frankfurt am Main: Kreditanstalt für Wiederaufbau.
———. 1991. *Ergebnisse Der Projektarbeit: Aus Der Praxis Der Finanziellen Zusammenarbeit Mit Entwicklungslädern*. Frankfurt am Main: Kreditanstalt für Wiederaufbau.
———. 1992. *Annual Report for the Year 1992*. Frankfurt am Main: Kreditanstalt für Wiederaufbau.
———. 1993. *Annual Report for the Year 1993*. Frankfurt am Main: Kreditanstalt für Wiederaufbau.
———. 1994a. *Annual Report for the Year 1994*. Frankfurt am Main: Kreditanstalt für Wiederaufbau.
———. 1994b. *Results of Financial Cooperation with Developing Countries: Second Evaluation Report 1994*. Frankfurt am Main: KfW.
———. 1996a. *Annual Report for the Year 1996*. Frankfurt am Main: Kreditanstalt für Wiederaufbau.
———. 1996b. KfW Organisiert Treffen von Förderbanken Aus Mittel- Und Osteuropa Sowie Der Europäischen Union. *KfW Aktuell*.

———. 1997. *Annual Report for the Year 1997*. Frankfurt am Main: Kreditanstalt für Wiederaufbau.
———. 1998. *Annual Report for the Year 1998*. Frankfurt am Main: Kreditanstalt für Wiederaufbau.
———. 2001. *Albanien: Förderung von KMU Über Die Stiftungsbank FEFAD*. Frankfurt am Main: KfW.
———. 2003. *Kosovo: Förderung Des Kleinkreditprograms Der Kosovarischen MEB*. Frankfurt am Main: KfW.
———. 2005. *Promotion of Developing Countries*. Frankfurt am Main: KfW.
———. 2012. *Ex-Post Evaluation Brief TCX Subordinated Convertible Debt Facility*. Frankfurt am Main: KfW.
———. 2013. *Bosnia and Herzegovina: Credit Guarantee Fund for the Promotion of SMEs and Business Start-Ups*. Frankfurt am Main: KfW.
———. 2015. *2015 Annual Report*. Frankfurt am Main: KfW.
———. 2016. *Current Topics: Insurance*. Frankfurt am Main: KfW.
———. 2019. *Financial Report 2018*. Frankfurt am Main: KfW.
Kloppenburg, Norbert. 2006. Microfinance Investment Funds: Where Wealth Creation Meets Poverty Reduction. In *Microfinance Investment Funds: Leveraging Private Capital for Economic Growth and Poverty Reduction*, ed. Ingrid Matthäus-Maier and J.D. von Pischke, 1–6. Berlin: Springer.
Köhn, Doris, and Wolfram Erhardt. 2004. Competition and Complementarity: KfW's Approach to Financial Sector Development in Southeast Europe. In *The Development of the Financial Sector in Southeast Europe*, ed. Ingrid Matthäus-Maier and J.D. von Pischke, 51–59. Berlin: Springer.
Köhn, Doris, and Michael Jainzik. 2005. Microfinance Investment Funds—An Innovative Form of PPP to Foster the Commercialisation of Microfinance. In *EU Accession—Financial Sector Opportunities and Challenges for Southeast Europe*, ed. Ingrid Matthäus-Maier and J.D. von Pischke, 323–335. Berlin: Springer.
Kpognon, Stanislas. 1971. Ethiopia: AIDB Lending Program.
Krahnen, Jan Pieter. 2016. Interview.
Krahnen, Jan Pieter, and Manfred Nitsch. 1987. *Studie Der Interdisziplinären Projekt Consult GmbH Im Rahmen Des Projekts "Förderung Des Aufbaus von Kommunalen Sparkassen (Cajas Municipales de Ahorro y Crédito) in Peru*. Frankfurt am Main: GTZ.
Lamby, Werner. 1967. The Role of Regional Development Banks. In *The Role of Development Banks in Economic and Social Development*. Berlin: German Foundation for Developing Countries.
Lepp, Anja. 2017. Interview.
———. *30 Years of IPC and PCH Development*. Frankfurt am Main: ProCredit.
Lessard, Donald R. 1986. *International Financing for Developing Countries: The Unfulfilled Promise*. Washington, DC: World Bank.

Ligeti, Sàndor. 1985. Development Banks in the Developing Countries/Les Banques De Dèveloppement. *Savings and Development* 9 (3): 297–323.
Loganathan, C. 1971. The DFC Department of the Bank and Its Role in Small Developing Member Countries.
Mader, Philip. 2014. Financialisation Through Microfinance: Civil Society and Market-Building in India. *Asian Studies Review* 38 (4): 601–619.
———. 2015. *The Political Economy of Microfinance: Financializing Poverty*, 1st ed. New York, NY: Palgrave Macmillan.
Mason, Edward S., and Robert E. Asher. 1973. *The World Bank Since Bretton Woods: The Origins, Policies, Operations, and Impact of the International Bank for Reconstruction and Development and the Other Members of the World Bank Group: The International Finance Corporation, the International Development Association [and] the International Centre for Settlement of Investment Disputes*. Washington, DC: Brookings Institution.
Matecki, Bronisław. 1957. *Establishment of the International Finance Corporation and United States Policy*. New York: FA Praeger.
Mathew, P.M. 1970a. Changes in Policies and Practices.
———. 1970b. Development Finance Companies in Which IFC Has Participated, That Can Make Equity Investment in Majority Government-Owned Enterprise.
Mathéy, Kosta. 1982. *Literaturübersicht: Selbsthilfe als Instrument zur Bewältigung der Wohnungsnot in Entwicklungsländern: Tagungsbeitrag am DSE Wissenschaftsbörse Bonn am 7.,8. Dezember 1982*. Darmstadt: Technische Hochschule Darmstadt Fachgebiet Planen und Bauen in Entwicklungsländern.
Matthäus-Maier, Ingrid. 2005. Opportunities and Challenges Facing Financial Sectors Moving Towards EU Accession. In *EU Accession—Financial Sector Opportunities and Challenges for Southeast Europe*, ed. Ingrid Matthäus-Maier and J.D. von Pischke, IX–XII. Berlin: Springer.
Matthäus-Maier, Ingrid, and J.D. von Pischke. 2004a. Introduction. In *The Development of the Financial Sector in Southeast Europe*, ed. Ingrid Matthäus-Maier and J.D. von Pischke, 1–6. Berlin: Springer.
———. 2004b. Summary and Conclusion. In *The Development of the Financial Sector in Southeast Europe*, ed. Ingrid Matthäus-Maier and J.D. von Pischke, 225–234. Berlin: Springer.
———. 2005. Foreword. In *EU Accession—Financial Sector Opportunities and Challenges for Southeast Europe*, ed. Ingrid Matthäus-Maier and J.D. von Pischke, V–VIII. Berlin: Springer.
Maurer, Klaus. 2011. Mobilising Capital for the Poor—How Does Structured Finance Fit in Emerging Markets? In *Mobilising Capital for Emerging Markets*, ed. Ingrid Matthäus-Maier and J.D. von Pischke, 13–27. Berlin: Springer.
Mawdsley, Emma. 2016. Development Geography II: Financialization. *Progress in Human Geography*, 1–11.

Mayer, Colin. 1989. *Myths of the West: Lessons from Developed Countries for Development Finance*. Washington, DC: World Bank.
McCarthy, Stephen. 1978. The Administration of Capital Aid. *Development Dialogue* 1.
MEF. 2016. *2016 Annual Report*. Luxembourg: Microfinance Enhancement Facility.
———. 2017. *MEF Quarterly Factsheet—June*. Luxembourg: Microfinance Enhancement Facility.
Mertens, Daniel, and Matthias Thiemann. 2019. Building a Hidden Investment State? The European Investment Bank, National Development Banks and European Economic Governance. *Journal of European Public Policy* 26 (1): 23–43.
Mirabile, Mariana, Julia Benn, and Cécile Sangaré. 2013. *Guarantees for Development*. Paris: OECD.
Mirabile, Mariana, Cécile Sangaré, and Claudia Schmerler. 2014. Using Financial Instruments to Mobilise Private Investment for Development. In *Development Co-Operation Report 2014: Mobilising Resources for Sustainable Development*. Paris: OECD.
Miraki, J.Z. 1969. Comments on Mr. Gustafson's Memorandum of May 12, 1969 on Currency Repayment Provisions in the Bank's Loans to DFCs.
Morduch, Jonathan. 1999. The Microfinance Promise. *Journal of Economic Literature* 37 (4): 1569–1614.
———. 2000. The Microfinance Schism. *World Development* 28 (4): 617–629.
Moslener, Ulf, Matthias Thiemann, and Peter Volberding. 2018. National Development Banks as Active Financiers: The Case of KfW. In *The Future of National Development Banks*, ed. Stephany Griffith-Jones and José Antonio Ocampo, 63–85. Oxford, UK: Oxford University Press.
Neuschütz, Volker. 2004. Institutional Development and Commercialisation—Optimal Exit for Equity Financiers. In *The Development of the Financial Sector in Southeast Europe*, ed. Ingrid Matthäus-Maier and J.D. von Pischke, 101–111. Berlin: Springer.
Nevin, Michael. 1985. Dilemmas in Development Banking. *Savings and Development* 9 (4): 421–440.
———. 1994. The European Investment Bank and African Development Finance Companies. In *The European Economy in Perspective: Essays in Honour of Edward Nevin*, ed. Jeffery Round. Cardiff: University of Wales Press.
Nitsch, Manfred. 1970. *Entwicklungsfinanzierung in Lateinamerika-Dargestellt Am Beispiel Columbiens*. Stuttgart: Ernst Klett Verlag.
———. 1973. *Ergebnisvermerk Über Die Diskussionsveranstaltung "Entwicklungsbankenfinanzierung" Am 22. Und 23. Januar 1973 in Der Kreditanstalt Für Wiederaufbau*. Frankfurt am Main: KfW.

———. 2002. Die Neuen Mikrofinanzinstitutionen in Osteuropa. In *Glaspaläste Und Mikrofinanz: Beiträge Zur Entwicklungsfinanzierung*, 203–209. Frankfurt am Main: Peter Lang Verlag.
Nitsch, Manfred, Reinhardt Schmidt, and Claus-Peter Zeitinger. 1981a. *Berichtsentwurf: Inspektion Der "Förderung von Entwicklungsbanken" in Lateinamerika*. Unpublished manuscript.
———. 1981b. *Sozio-Ökonomische Auswirkungen Der Bisherigen Deutschen Entwicklungsbankenförderung in Ekuador Und Kolumbien*. Berlin: BMZ.
Nougaim, Khalil. 1971. Assistance to DFC Clients Through Management Consulting Firms.
OECD. 1964. *Intermediate Financial Institutions*. Paris: OECD.
———. 1981. *Compendium of Aid Procedures*. Paris: OECD.
———. 1998. *Development Co-Operation Reviews: Germany 1998*. Paris: OECD.
———. 2008. *Is It ODA?* Paris: OECD.
———. 2011. *Measuring Aid: 50 Years of DAC Statistics—1961–2011*. Paris: OECD.
———. 2015. *A How-To Guide for Blended Finance: A Practical Guide for Development Finance and Philanthropic Funders to Integrate Blended Finance Best Practices into Their Organizations*. Paris: OECD.
Oxfam. 2017. *Private-Finance Blending for Development: Risks and Opportunities*. Oxfam.
Pearson, Lester B. 1969. *Partners in Development: Report of the Commission on International Development*. New York, NY: Praeger Publishers.
Pereira, Javier. 2017. *Blended Finance: What It Is, How It Works and How It Is Used*. Oxfam.
Picciotto, R. 1969. DFC—Government Financing and Return on Capital.
Pollan, Hans. 1971. Financing of State Controlled Enterprises by DFCs.
Private Investor #1. 2016. Anonymous Interview.
Private Investor #2. 2017. Anonymous Interview.
Private Investor #3. 2017. Anonymous Interview.
Rao, Badri. 1958. Proceedings of the Meeting on Development Banks Held at the Economic Development Institute from May 5, to May 9, 1958.
REGMIFA. 2015. *Annual Report 2015: Regional MSME Investment Fund for Sub-Saharan Africa S.A., SICAV-SIF*. Luxembourg: Regional MSME Investment Fund for Sub-Saharan Africa.
Robinson, Marguerite S. 2001. *The Microfinance Revolution: Sustainable Finance for the Poor*. Washington, DC: World Bank.
Roy, Ananya. 2010. *Poverty Capital: Microfinance and the Making of Development*. New York: Routledge.
Rüland, Jürgen, and Nikolaus Werz. 2002. Germany's Hesitant Role in Promoting Democracy. In *Exporting Democracy: Rhetoric vs. Reality*, ed. Peter J. Schraeder. Boulder, CO: Lynne Rienner Publishers.

Sachs, Jeffrey D., and John W. McArthur. 2005. The Millennium Project: A Plan for Meeting the Millennium Development Goals. *The Lancet* 365: 347–353.
Saini, Krishnan. 1986. *Capital Market Innovations and Financial Flows to Developing Countries*. Washington, DC: World Bank.
Saith, Ashwani. 2006. From Universal Values to Millennium Development Goals: Lost in Translation. *Development and change* 37 (6): 1167–1199.
Sanad Fund. 2016. *Demonstrating Impact in the Middle East and North Africa Since 2011*. Luxembourg: Sanad Fund for MSME.
———. 2017a. *At a Glance, Q2 2017*. Luxembourg: Sanad Fund for MSME.
———. 2017b. *Sanad Technical Assistance Facility at a Glance, Q2 2017*. Luxembourg: Sanad Fund for MSME.
Sanchez-Marco, Carlos. 1970. Economic Appraisal of DFC Projects.
Schmidt, Reinhardt. 2004. *The Perspective of the Participant Observers: A Brief Account of the History of IPC and IMI from an Institutional Economics Perspective*. Frankfurt am Main: Unpublished manuscript.
———. 2016. Interview.
Shin, B.H. 1968. Sources of Finance of Development Finance Companies as of December 31, 1967.
———. 1969. On the Flow of Funds in Industrial Sector in Selected Countries.
Stravens, Manon. 2017. The Currency Exchange Fund (TCX) Celebrates 10 Years of Achievement. *Development Finance*, 67–70.
Syroka, Joanna, and Richard Wilcox. 2006. Rethinking International Disaster Aid Finance. *Journal of International Affairs* 59 (2): 197–214.
TCX. 2013. *Local Currency Matters*. Amsterdam: TCX.
———. 2016. *Annual Report 2016*. Amsterdam: TCX.
Thiebach, G. 1970. Activities of Kreditanstalt Fuer Wiederaufbau (KFW), Germany, in Chile, Paraguay and Uruguay.
Thiemann, Matthias, and Peter Volberding. 2017. *Financing Infrastructure in Developing Countries through Public-Private Partnerships*. Berlin: Bread for the World.
Thiemann, Matthias, Daniel Mertens, and Peter Volberding. 2021. *The Reinvention of Development Banking in the European Union*. Oxford, UK: Oxford University Press.
Thomas, Landon. 2018. The World Bank Is Remaking Itself as a Creature of Wall Street. *The New York Times* (February 6, 2018).
Uecker, Roland. 1967. Forms of Organization in the Development Bank Field. In *The Role of Development Banks in Economic and Social Development*. Berlin: German Foundation for Developing Countries.
Ullrich, Gabriele J., and DSE (eds.). 1982. *Report/DSE FAO Seminar on Promotion of Self-Help Organizations of the Rural Poor in Africa: Problems of Implementation, Monitoring and Evaluation: Berlin, West, 8 to 13 November 1982*. Feldafing.

UN. 1995. *General Framework for Peace in Bosnia and Herzegovina*. New York: United Nations.
———. 2002. *Implementation of the United Nations Millennium Declaration: Report of the Secretary-General*. New York: United Nations.
———. 2003. *Monterrey Consensus of the International Conference on Financing for Development*. New York: United Nations.
———. 2014. *Report of the Intergovernmental Committee of Experts on Sustainable Development Financing*. New York: United Nations.
———. 2015a. *Addis Ababa Action Agenda of the Third International Conference on Financing for Development*. New York: United Nations.
———. 2015b. *Consensus Reached on New Sustainable Development Agenda to Be Adopted by World Leaders in September*. New York: United Nations.
———. 2015c. *Transforming Our World: The 2030 Agenda for Sustainable Development*. New York: United Nations.
———. 2016. *UNDP Support to the Implementation of the 2030 Agenda for Sustainable Development*. New York: United Nations Development Program.
———. 2017a. *Implementing the Addis Ababa Action Agenda: The 2017 ECOSOC Forum on Financing for Development Follow-Up*. New York: United Nations.
———. 2017b. *Opening Remarks of H.E. Peter Thomson, President of the UN General Assembly at High Level SDG Action Event "SDG Financing Lab."* New York: United Nations.
UNCTAD. 1991. *World Investment Report 1991: The Triad in Foreign Direct Investment*. New York: UN Conference on Trade and Development.
UNIDO. 1979. *Development Banking in the 1980s: Selections from the Proceedings of the UNIDO/World Bank Symposium, Zurich, June 1979*. Vienna: United Nations Industrial Development Organization.
US Treasury. 1944. *Articles of Agreement: International Monetary Fund and International Bank for Reconstruction and Development*. Washington, DC: US Treasury.
Vibert, Frank. 1973. 'The World Bank and Development Finance Companies' Minutes of Staff Review.
Voigt, Heinz. 1967. Quantitative Measures and Criteria in Development Finance. In *The Role of Development Banks in Economic and Social Development*. Berlin: German Foundation for Developing Countries.
von Pischke, J.D. 2003. *Microfinance Institution Building: The IPC Story*. Unpublished book manuscript.
Wabnitz, Wolfdieter. 1967. Appraisal and Promotion of Industrial Projects by Development Finance Institutions. In *The Role of Development Banks in Economic and Social Development*. Berlin: German Foundation for Developing Countries.

Wälde, Helke. 2012. *An Overview of Innovative Financial Instruments Used to Raise Funds for International Development*. Frankfurt am Main: KfW.
WEF, and OECD. 2015a. *Blended Finance Vol. 1: A Primer for Development Finance and Philanthropic Funders*. Cologny, Switzerland: World Economic Forum.
———. 2015b. *Blending Capital, Catalyzing Change*. Cologny, Switzerland: World Economic Forum.
———. 2016. *Insights from Blended Finance Investment Vehicles & Facilities*. Cologny, Switzerland: World Economic Forum.
Winkler, Adalbert. 1999. Promotional Banks as an Instrument for Improving the Financing Situation of Small and Medium-Sized Enterprises in the Transition Economies of Central and Eastern Europe: Some Observations Based on the Development of the German Financial System. *Würzburg Economic Papers, No. 2e*.
Wolfensohn, James. 1997. *Address to the Closing Plenary Session of the Microcredit Summit*. Washington, DC: World Bank.
World Bank. 1964. *World Bank and IDA Annual Report 1963–1964*. Washington, DC: World Bank.
———. 1968. *World Bank Annual Report 1968*. Washington, DC: World Bank.
———. 1969. Draft Paper on Pearson Commission Recommendations Regarding Development Finance Companies.
———. 1973a. Annex—Conclusions of the DFC Case Studies.
———. 1973b. The World Bank and Development Finance Companies.
———. 1974. DFC Special Studies: Principal Findings.
———. 1976. *Development Finance Companies: Sector Policy Paper*. Washington, DC: World Bank.
———. 1979. *Operations Evaluation: World Bank Standards and Procedures*. Washington, DC: World Bank.
———. 1980. *World Bank Annual Report 1980*. Washington, DC: World Bank.
———. 1989. *World Development Report 1989: Financial Systems and Development*. Washington, DC: World Bank.
———. 1996. *Worldwide Inventory of Microfinance Institutions*. Washington, DC: World Bank.
———. 1997. *Global Development Finance*. Washington, DC: World Bank.
———. 2000. *Implementation Completion Report on an IDA Credit in the Amount of SDR4.9 Million to Bosnia and Herzegovina for the Local Initiatives Project*. Washington, DC: World Bank.
———. 2012. *World Bank Group Support to Public-Private Partnerships*. Washington, DC: World Bank.
———. 2015a. *2015 Development Finance Forum*. Washington, DC: World Bank.
———. 2015b. *Does Microfinance Still Hold Promise for Reaching the Poor?* Washington, DC: World Bank.

———. 2017. *Mobilization of Private Finance by Multilateral Development Banks: 2016 Joint Report*. Washington, DC: World Bank.

Yazici, Bulent. 1962. The Industrial Development Bank of Turkey. In *Methods of Industrial Development*, ed. Albert Winsemius and John Pincus. Paris: Organization for Economic Co-operation and Development (OECD).

Zeitinger, Claus-Peter. 2004. Sustainable Microfinance Banks—Problems and Perspectives. In *The Development of the Financial Sector in Southeast Europe*, ed. Ingrid Matthäus-Maier and J.D. von Pischke, 125–134. Berlin: Springer.

Zeitinger, Claus-Peter, Eberhardt R. Biermann, and Gerhard Zieroth. 1982. *The Utilization of Renewable Energy Resources: A Programme of the Federal Republic of Germany for the Third World; Analysis of the Planning Phase of the Special Energy Programme (SEP).* Eschborn, Germany: Deutsche Gesellschaft für Technische Zusammenarbeit (GTZ).

Zeitinger, Claus-Peter, and Reinhardt Schmidt. 1984. *Kreditgarantiefonds - Einige Überlegungen Zu Diesem Kreditfinanzierungsinstrument*. Frankfurt am Main: IPC Working Paper.

Ziller, Dominik. 2006. The European Fund for Southeast Europe: An Innovative Instrument for Political and Economic Stabilisation. In *Microfinance Investment Funds: Leveraging Private Capital for Economic Growth and Poverty Reduction*, ed. Ingrid Matthäus-Maier and J.D. von Pischke, 193–212. Berlin: Springer.

Index

P. Volberding, *Leveraging Financial Markets for Development*, Executive Politics and Governance,
https://doi.org/10.1007/978-3-030-55008-0

The manufacturer's authorised representative in the EU is Springer Nature Customer Service Centre GmbH, Europaplatz 3, 69115 Heidelberg, Germany. If you have any concerns regarding our products, please contact ProductSafety@springernature.com

Printed and bound by CPI Group (UK) Ltd, Croydon, CR0 4YY
30/09/2026
02225502-0010